The Grand Forbidden City

大紫禁城

王者的軸線

The enormity of this complex of
The Forbidden City is unsurpassed in the World

The Purple Forbidden Enclosure in the middle
of the sky symbolises the emperor

Public access was strictly forbidden

Its size is similar to that of
a small city

— The Imperial Axis

Book Title :	The Grand Forbidden City — The Imperial Axis
Author :	Chiu Kwong Chiu
Translator :	Paul K. Lee
Editor :	Jiang Ying, Zhang Nan
Designed by :	AllRightsReserved Ltd.
Publisher :	The Palace Museum Publisher
	4 Jing Shan Qian Jie, Dong Cheng Qu, Beijing, Postcode 100009
Printer :	Vision & Mission Company Limited
	3/F., 334 - 336 Kwun Tong Road, Ngau Tau Kok, Kowloon, Hong Kong

图书在版编目（CIP）数据

大紫禁城——王者的轴线＝ The Grand Forbidden City—
The Imperial Axis: 英文 / 赵广超著. —北京: 紫禁
城出版社, 2008.4
ISBN 978-7-80047-688-4

Ⅰ.大… Ⅱ.赵… Ⅲ.故宫-简介-英文 Ⅳ. K928.74
中国版本图书馆CIP数据核字 (2008) 第035361号
©2008 The Palace Museum Publisher
Published in Hong Kong

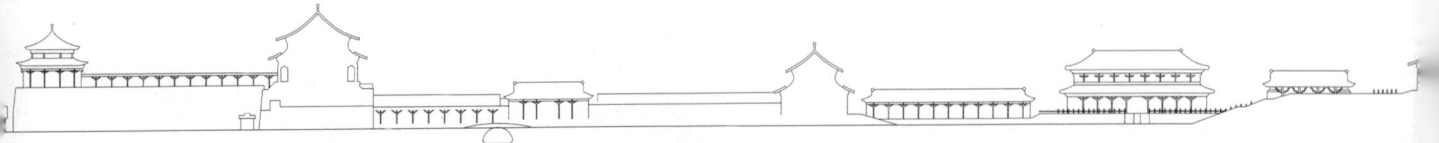

The Grand Forbidden City
By Chiu Kwong Chiu

Published by The Palace Museum Publisher

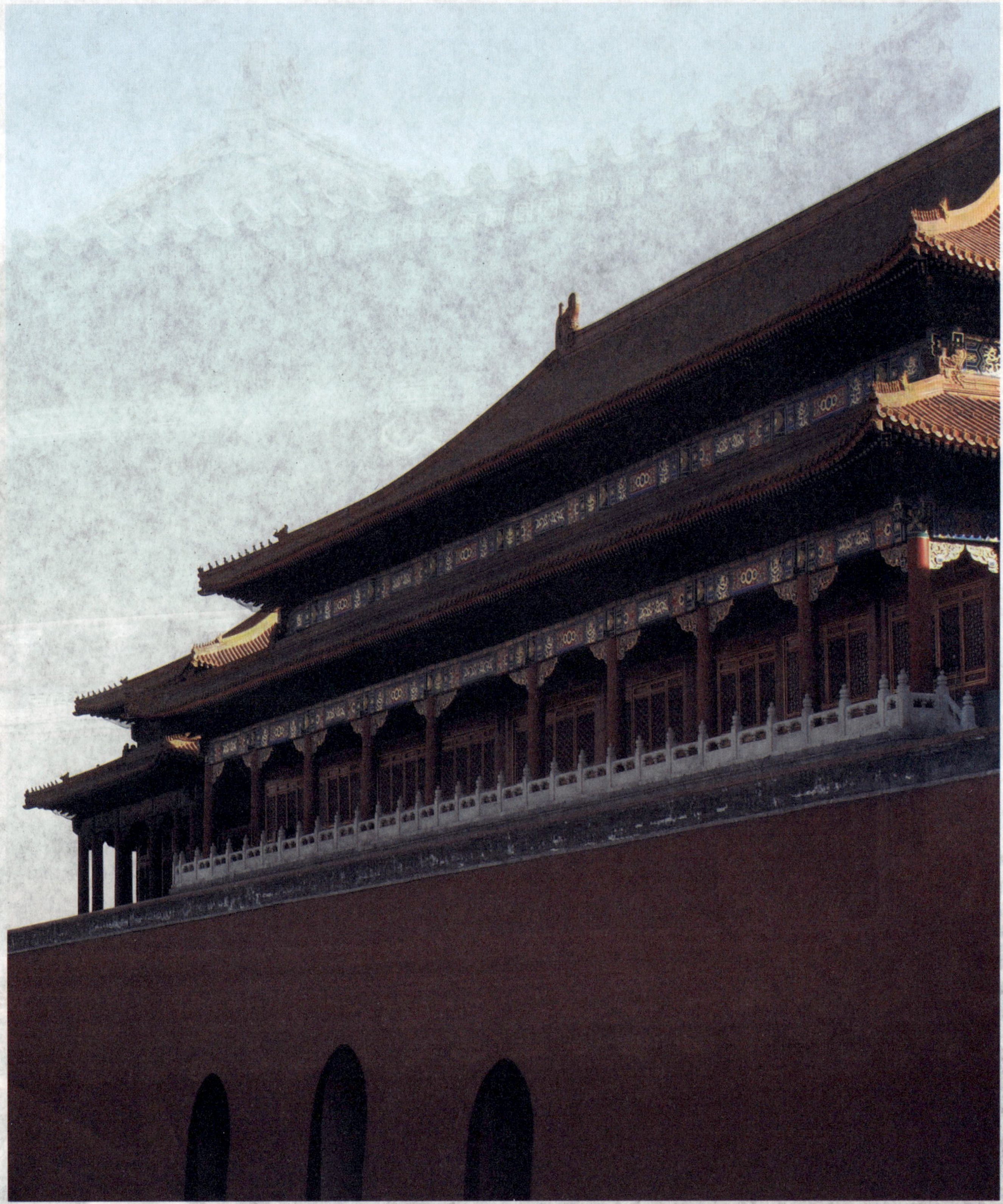

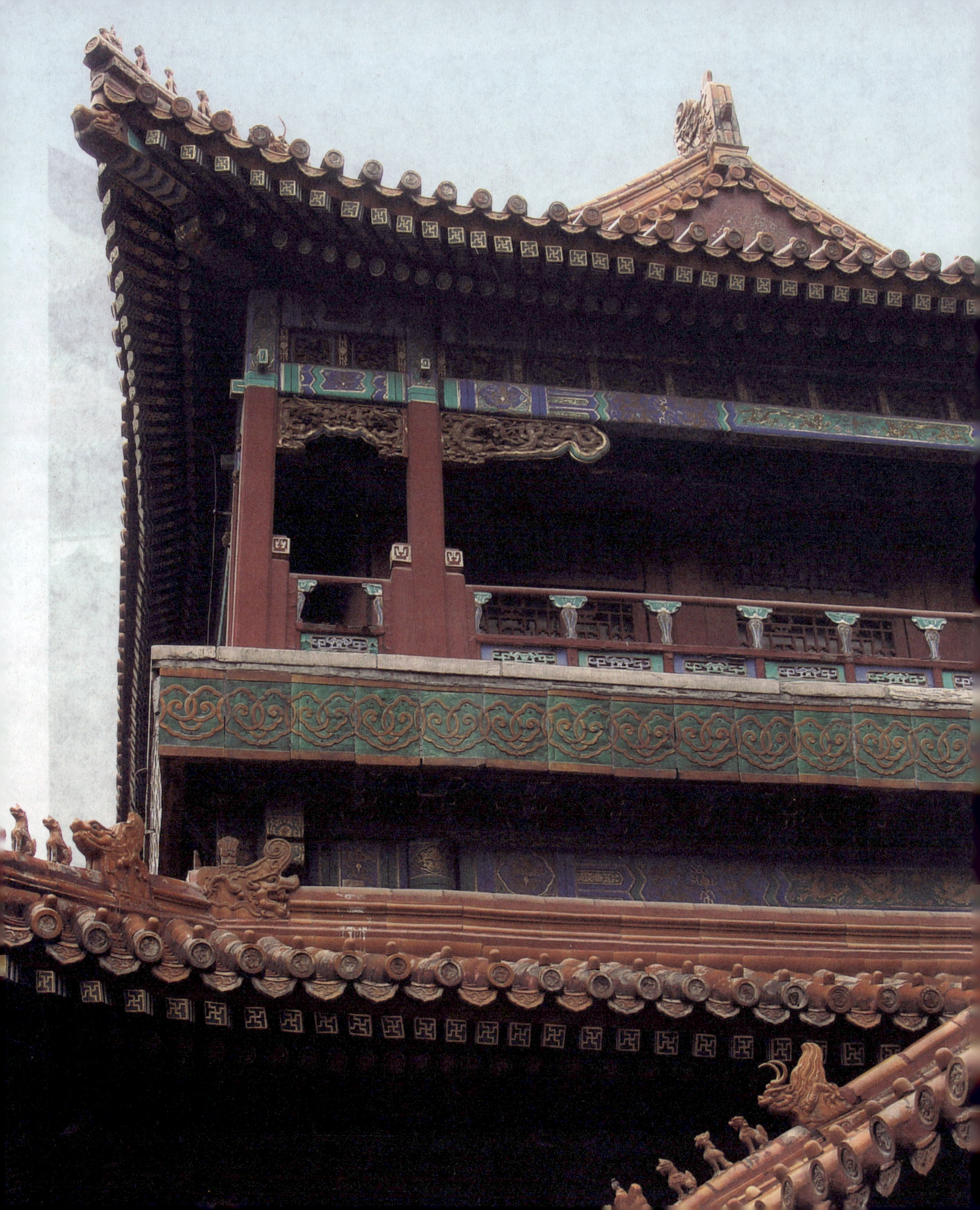

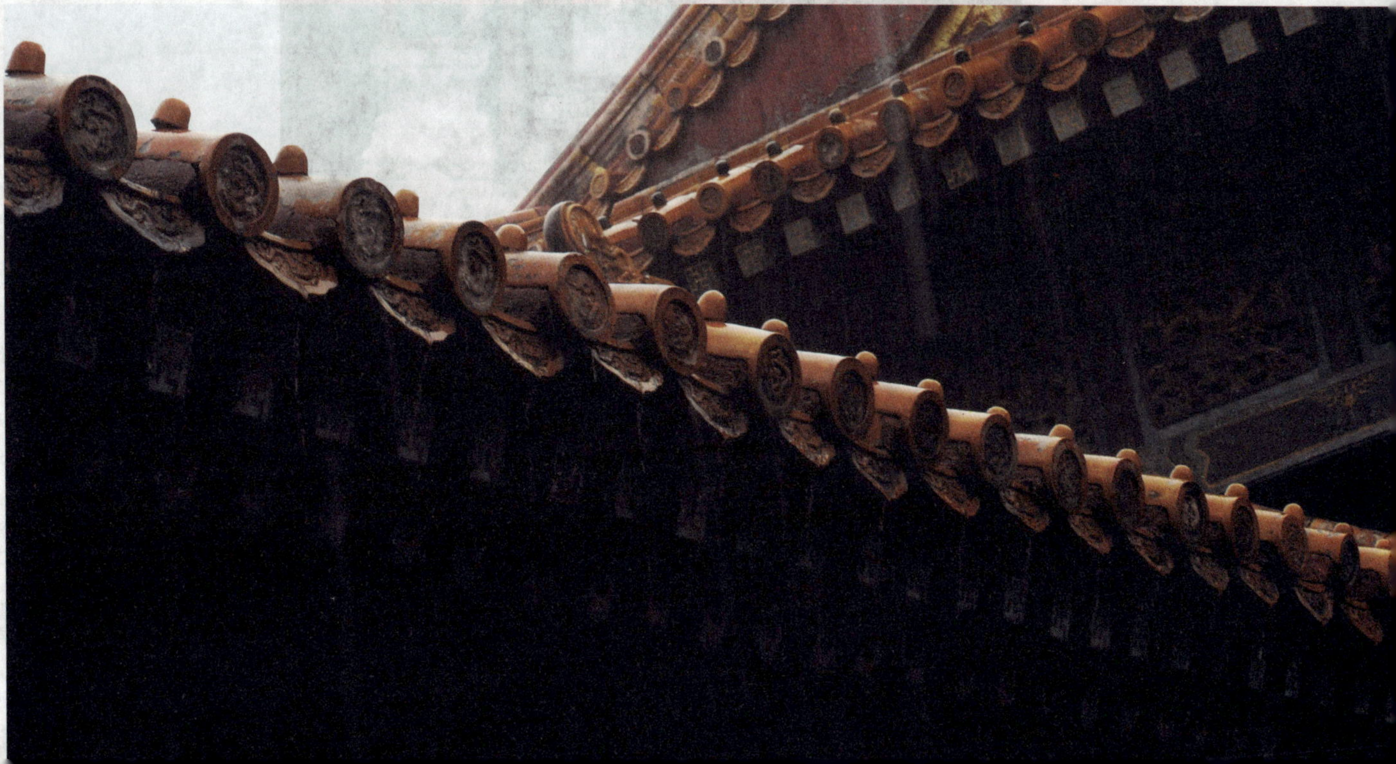

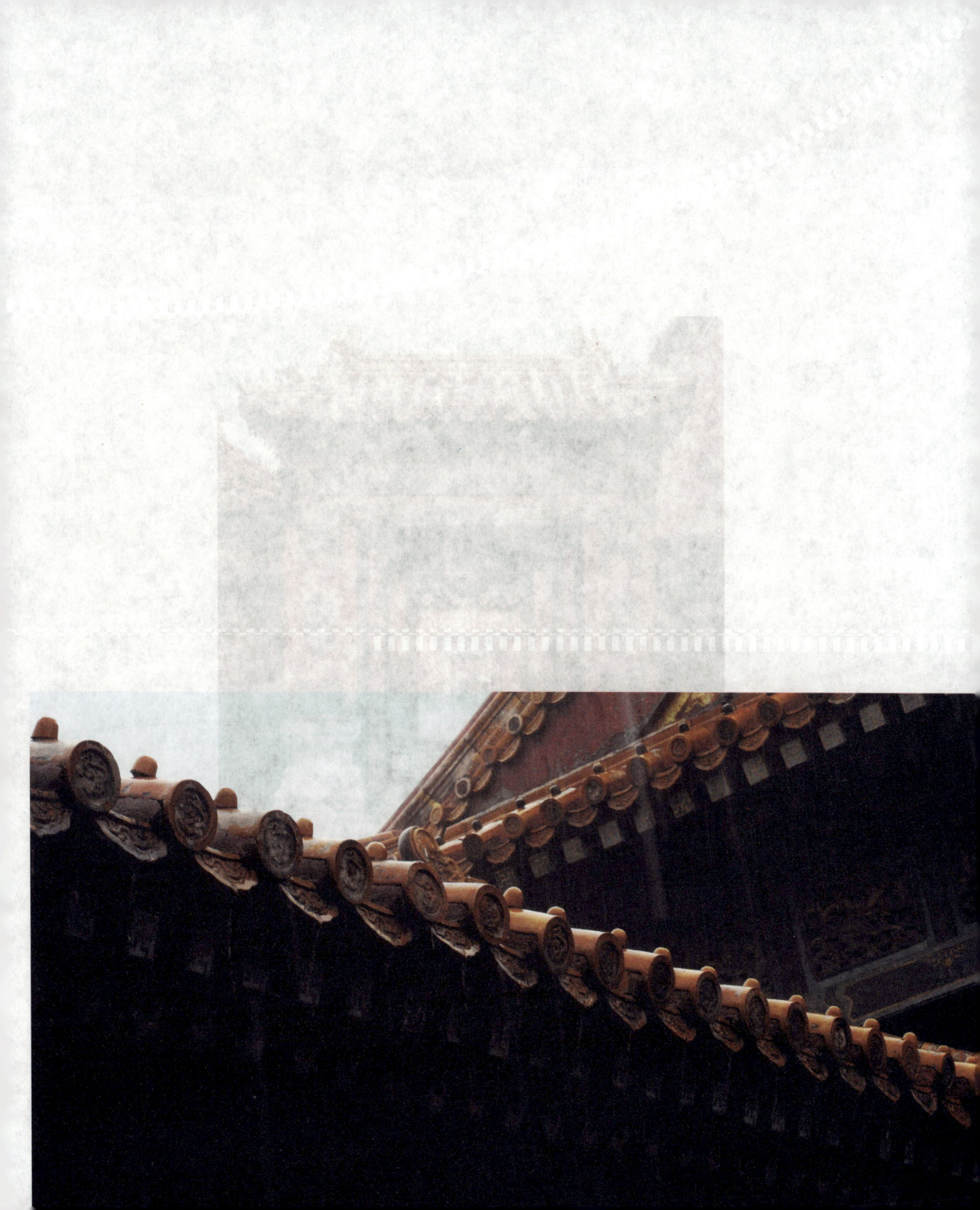

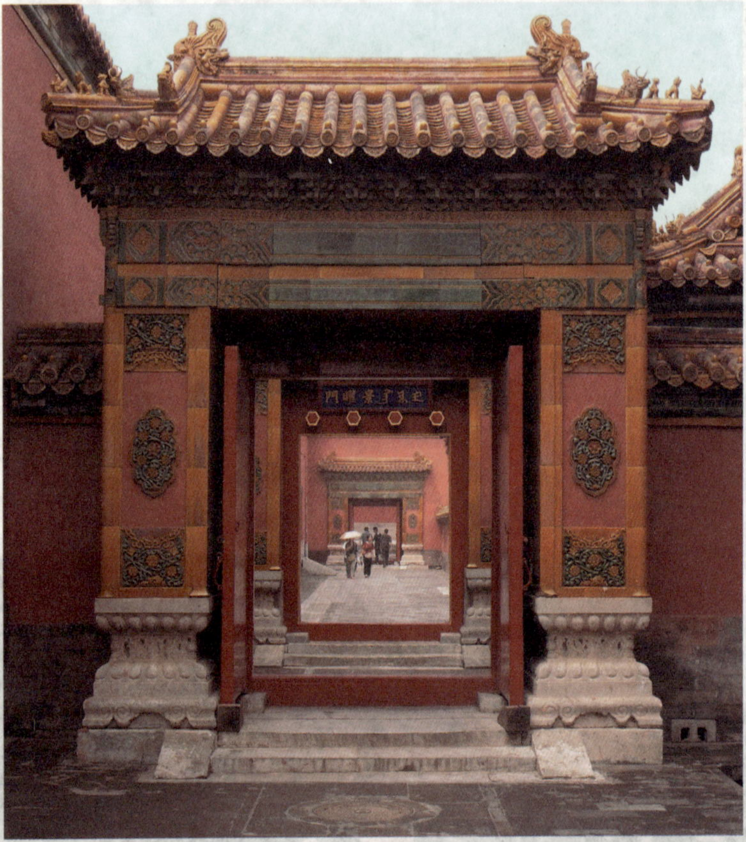

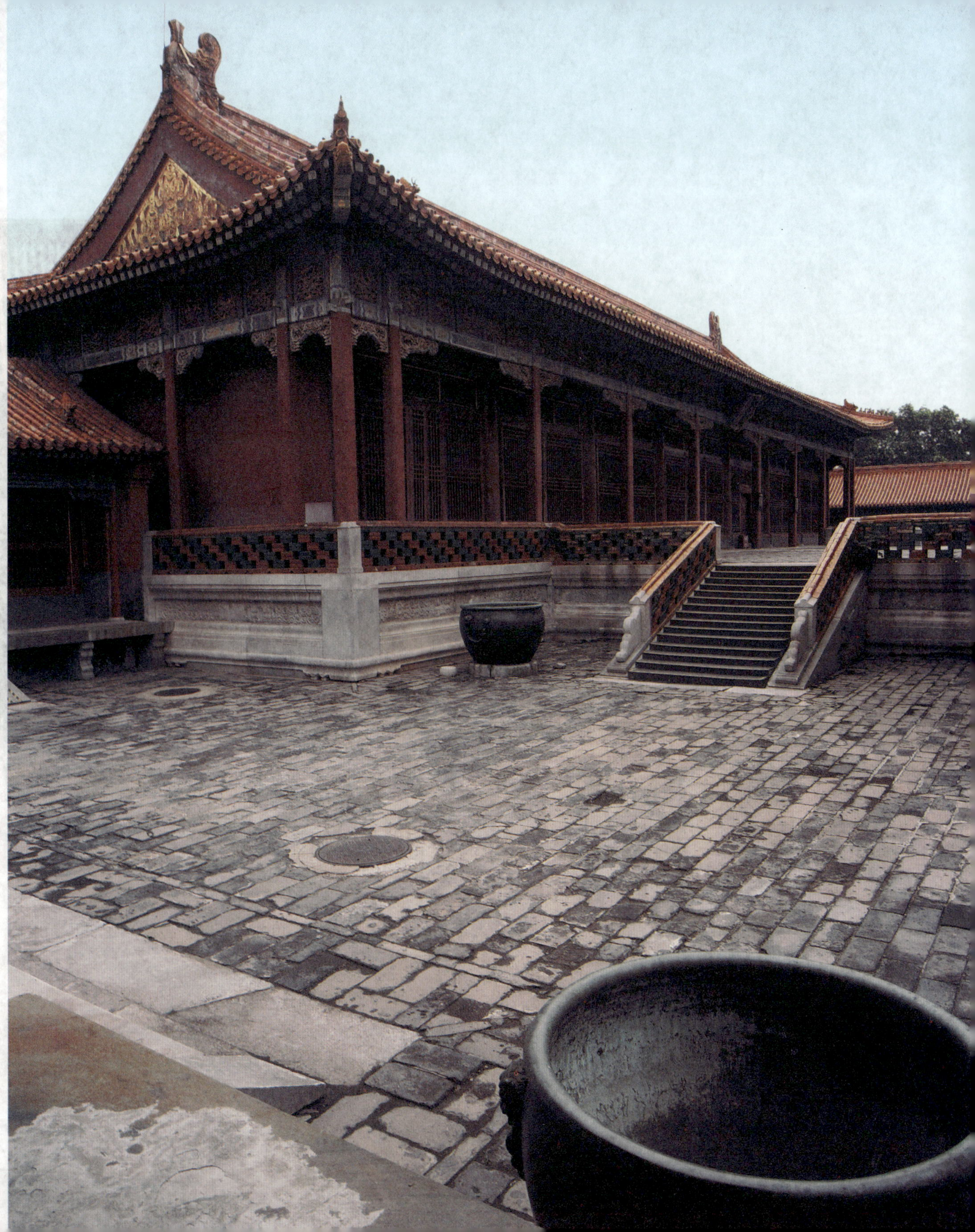

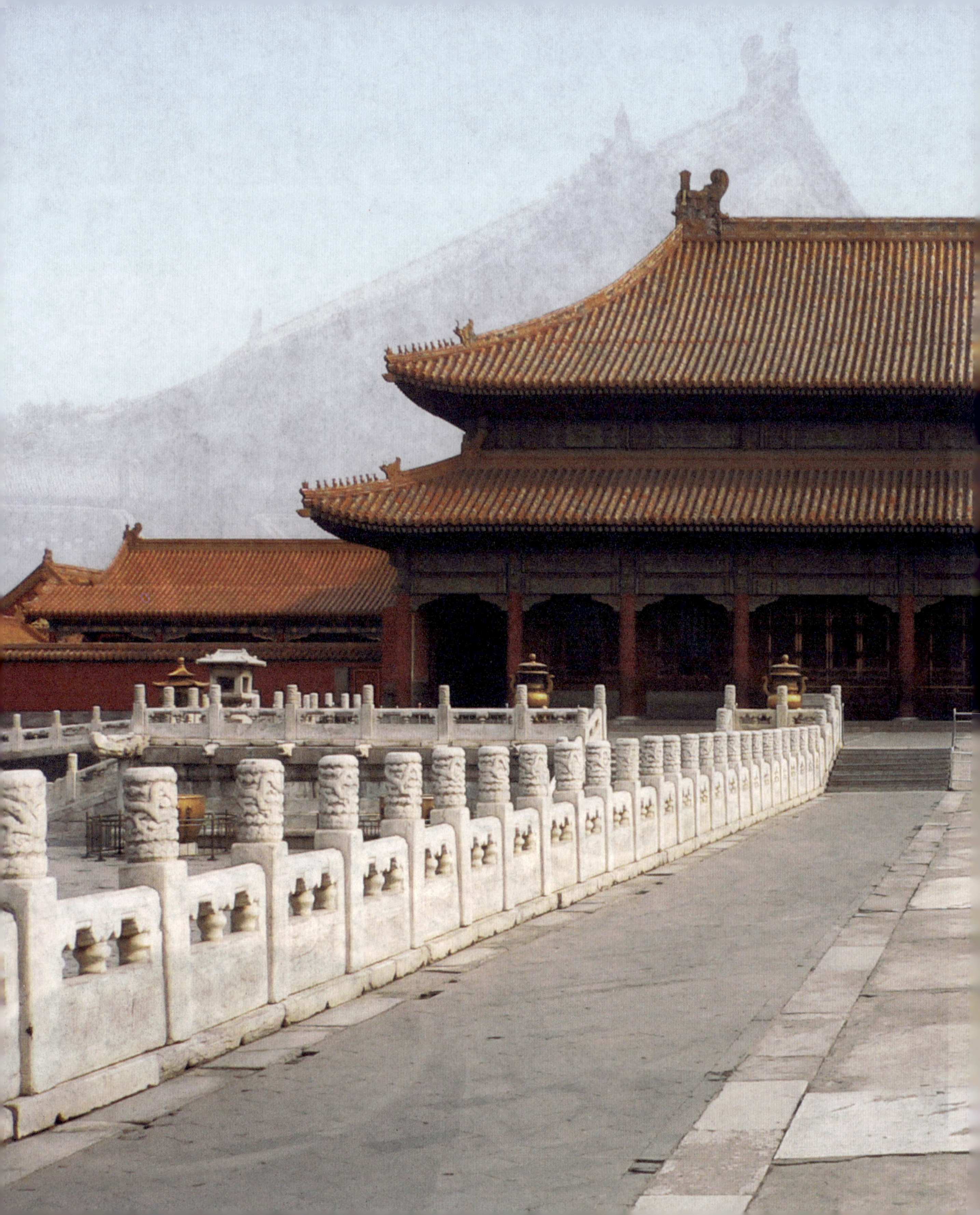

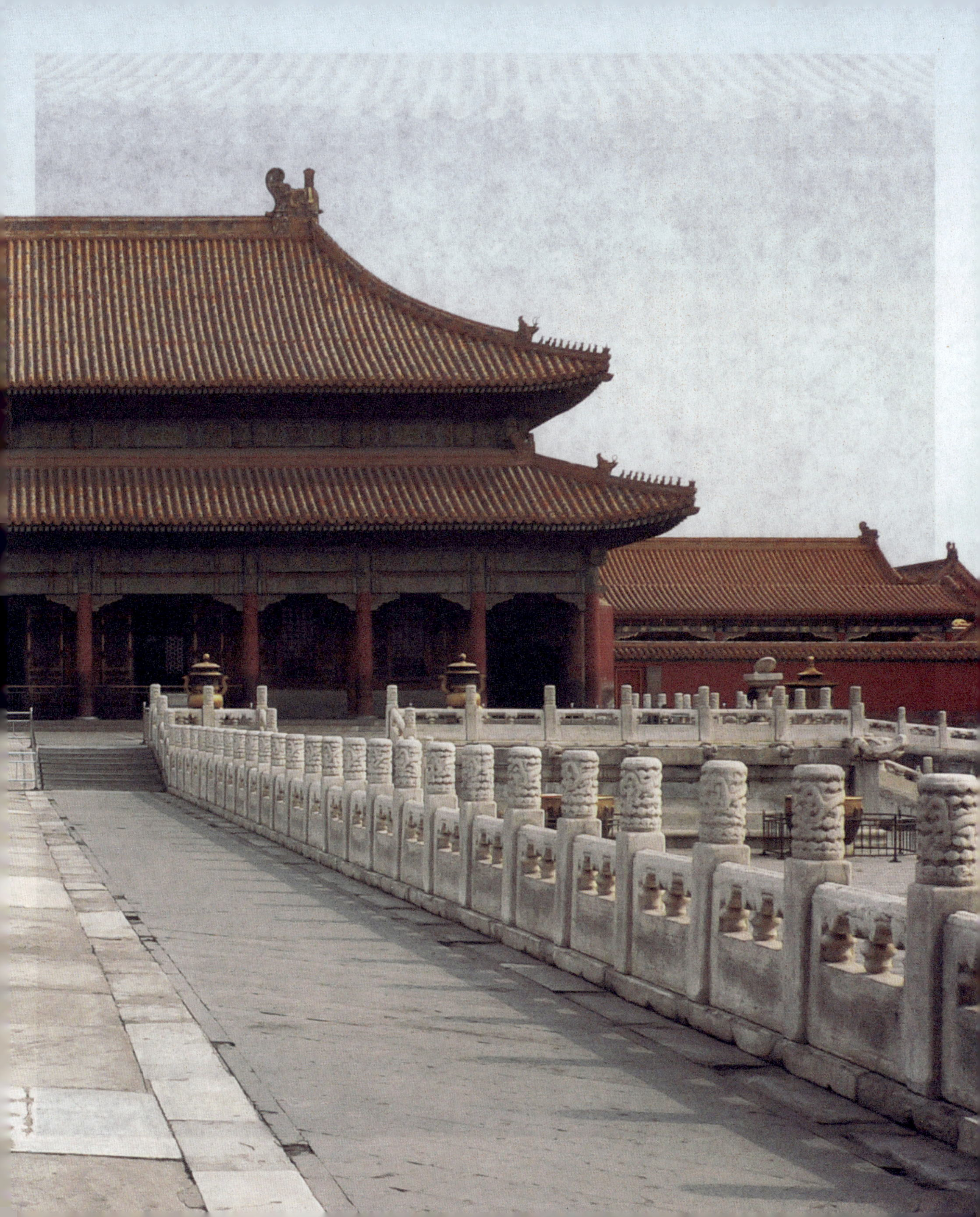

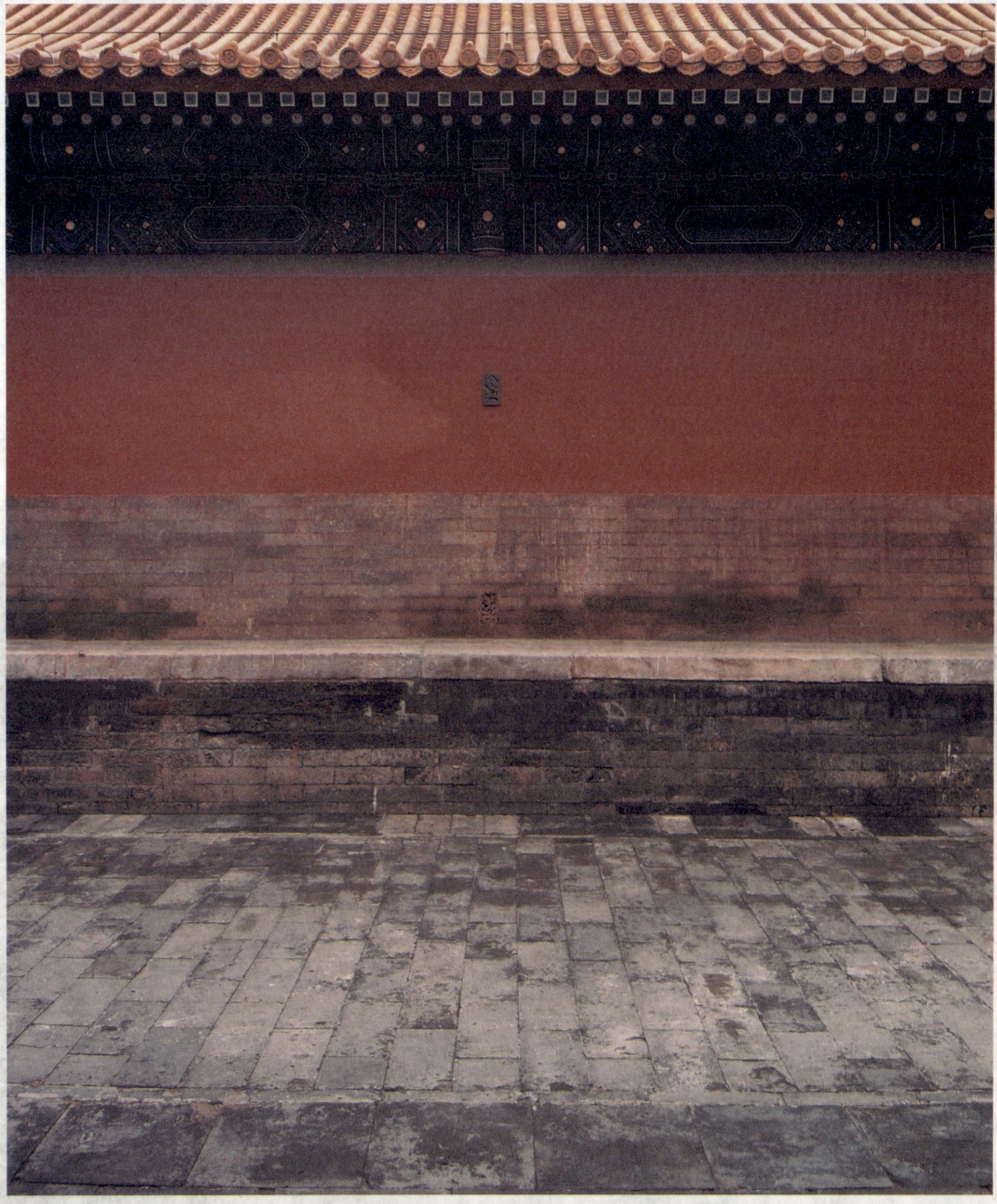

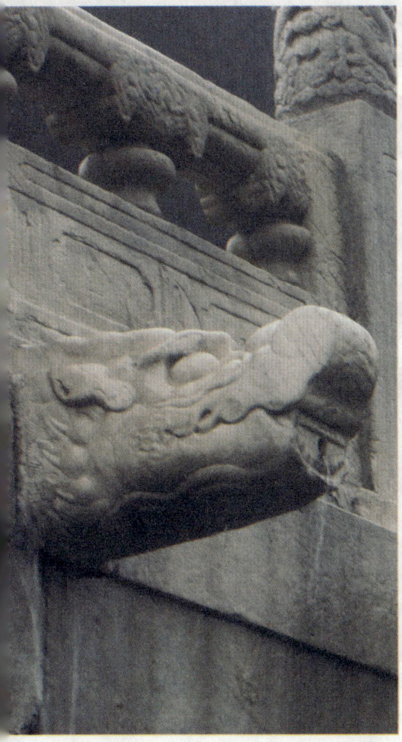

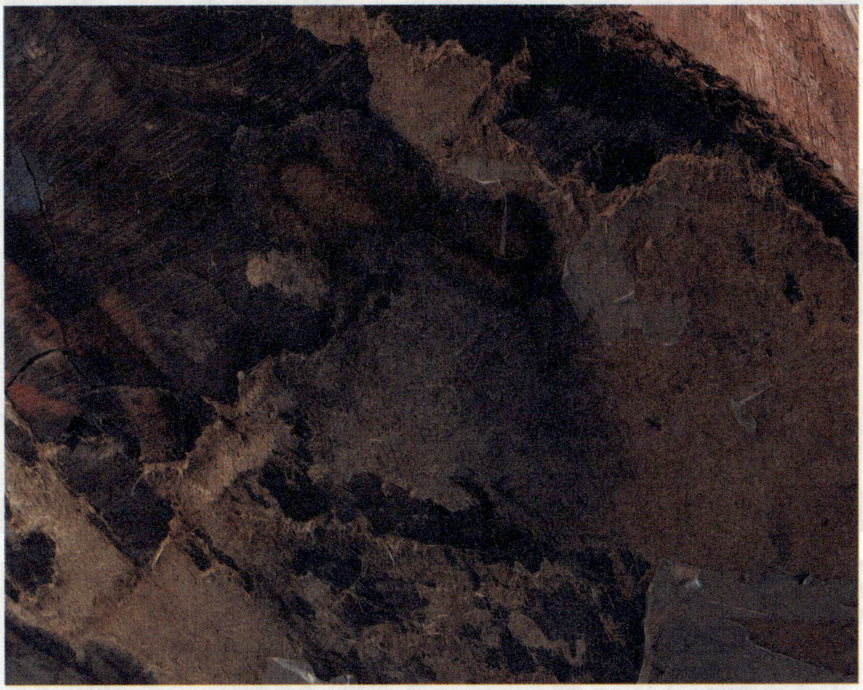

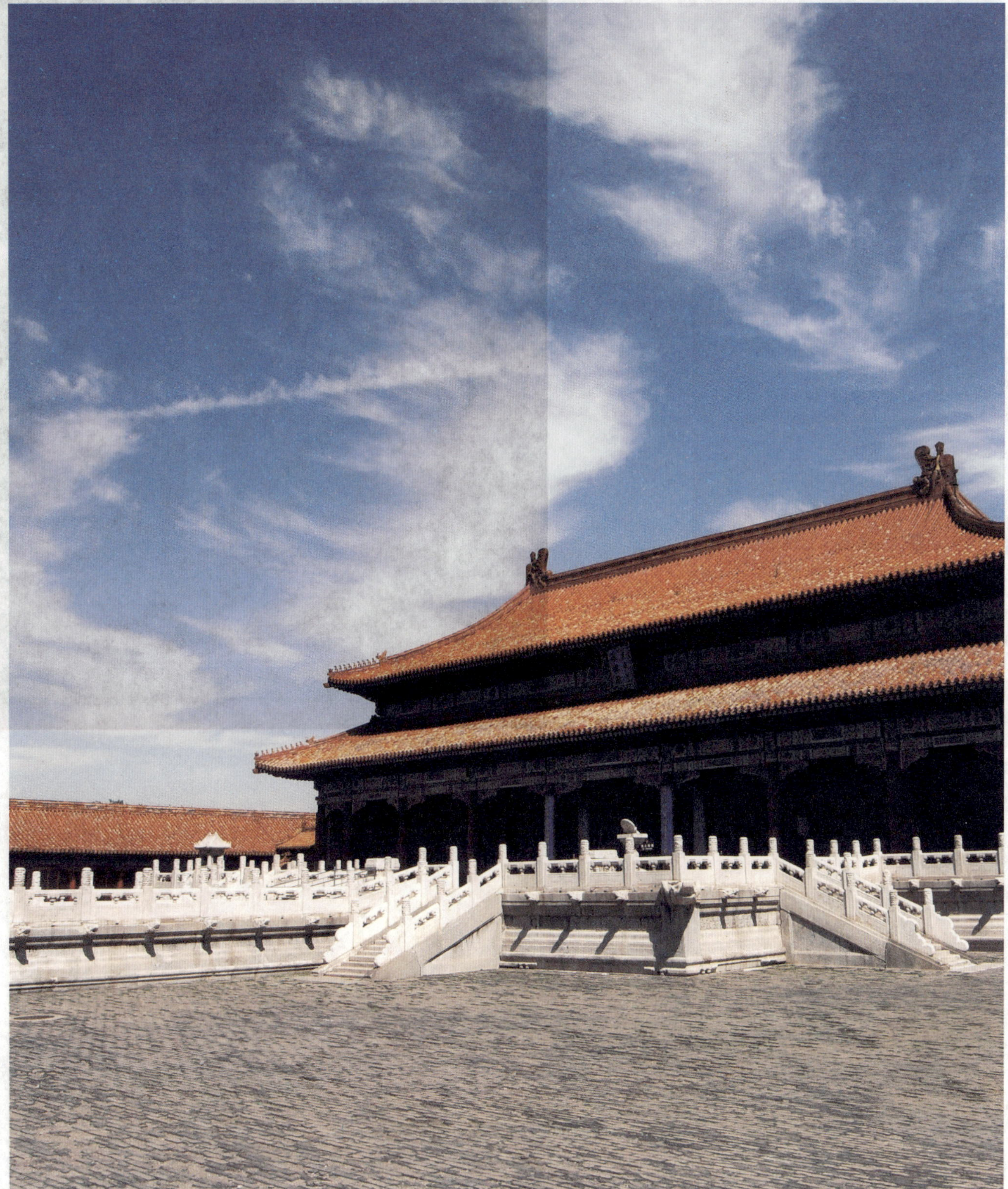

養心殿

中正仁和

齋

慶

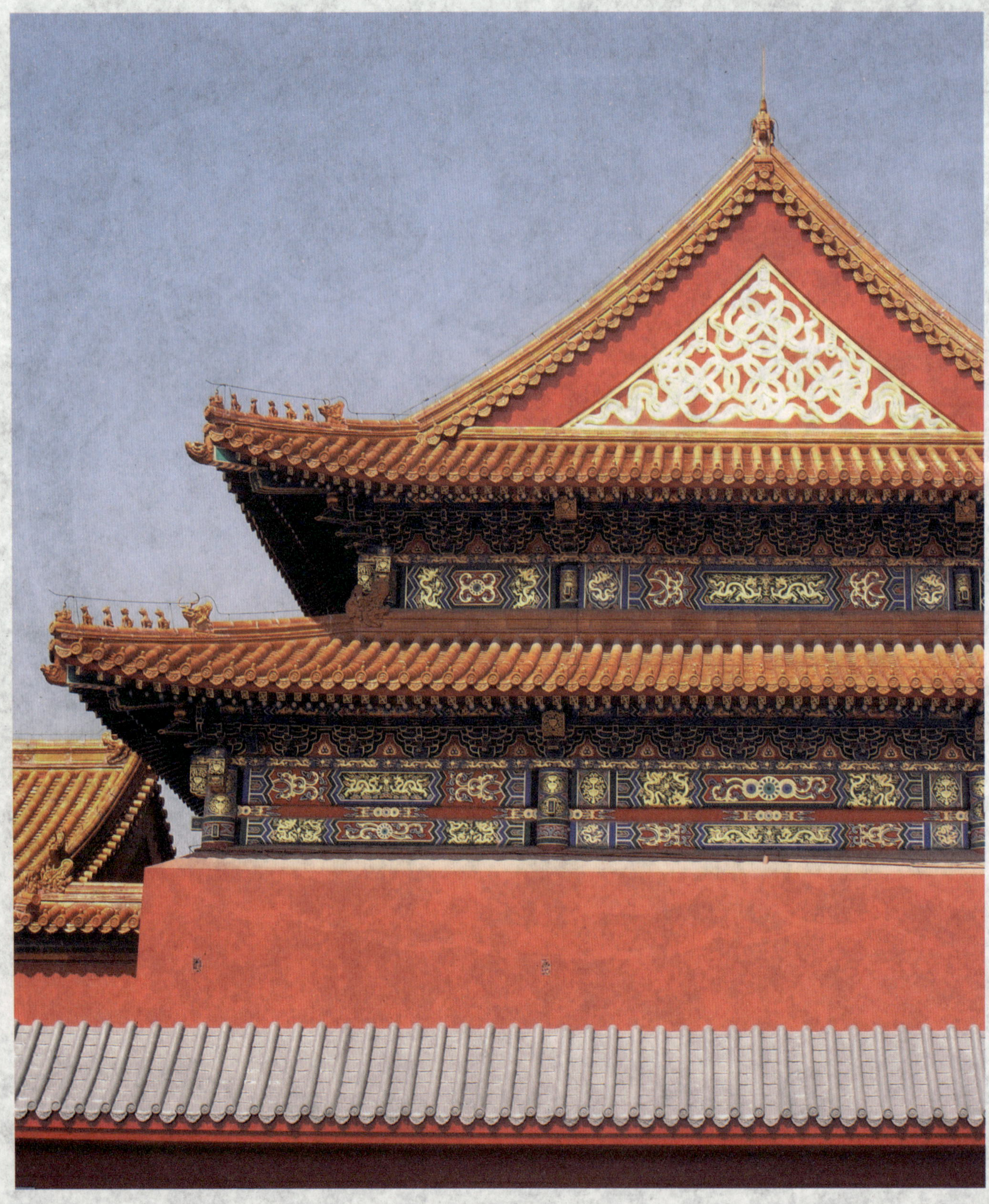

The Imperial Axis

The Forbidden City stretches 753 meters from east to west, and 961 meters from north to south, in the shape of a rectangle. However, a birdseye view from whichever commanding point (The Meridian Gate [Wumen] or The Prospect Hill [Jingshan]) will always give you a square-shaped palatial city.

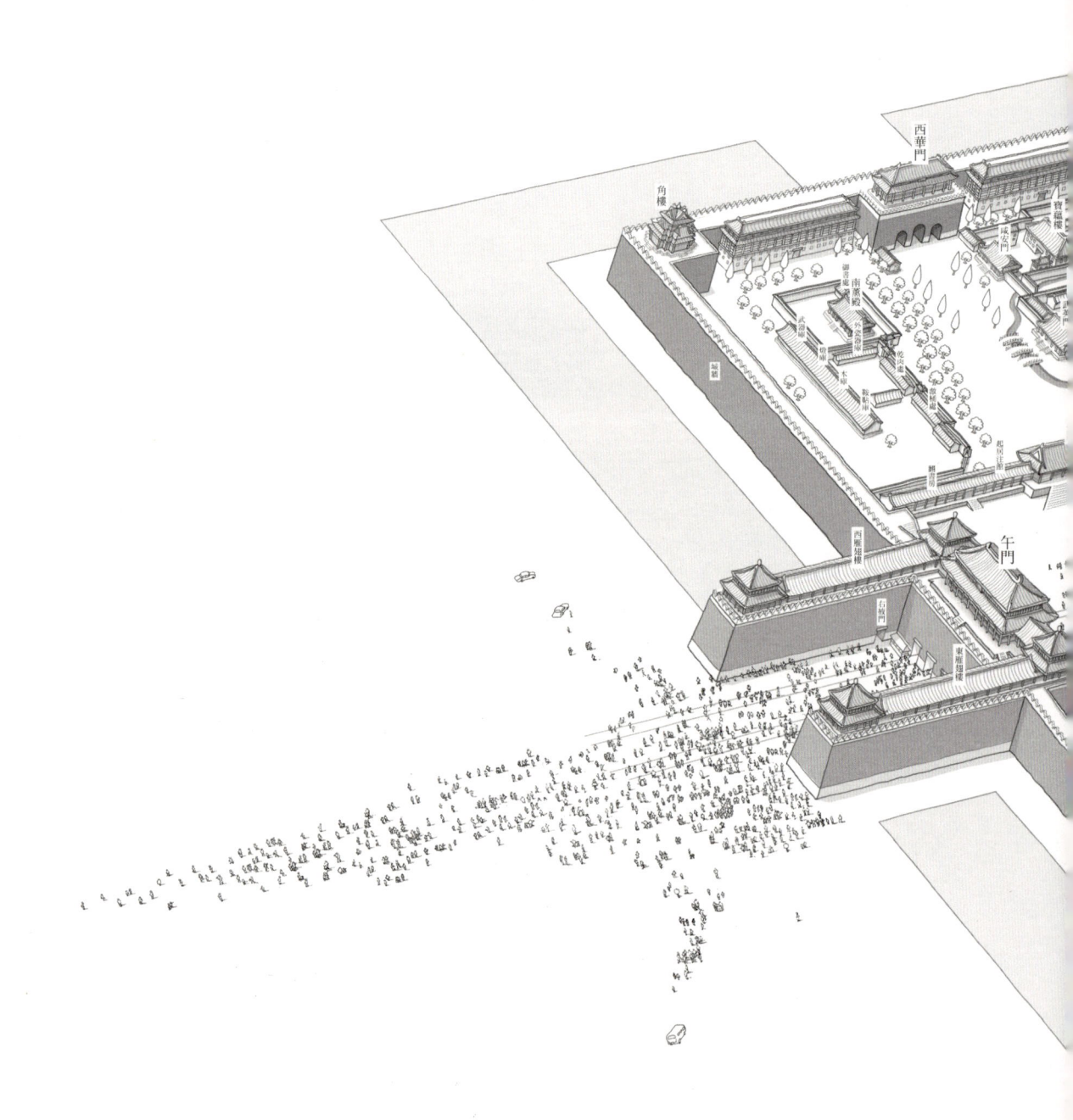

Today, it is in itself a museum with the most significant exhibits, attracting visitors from all over the world.

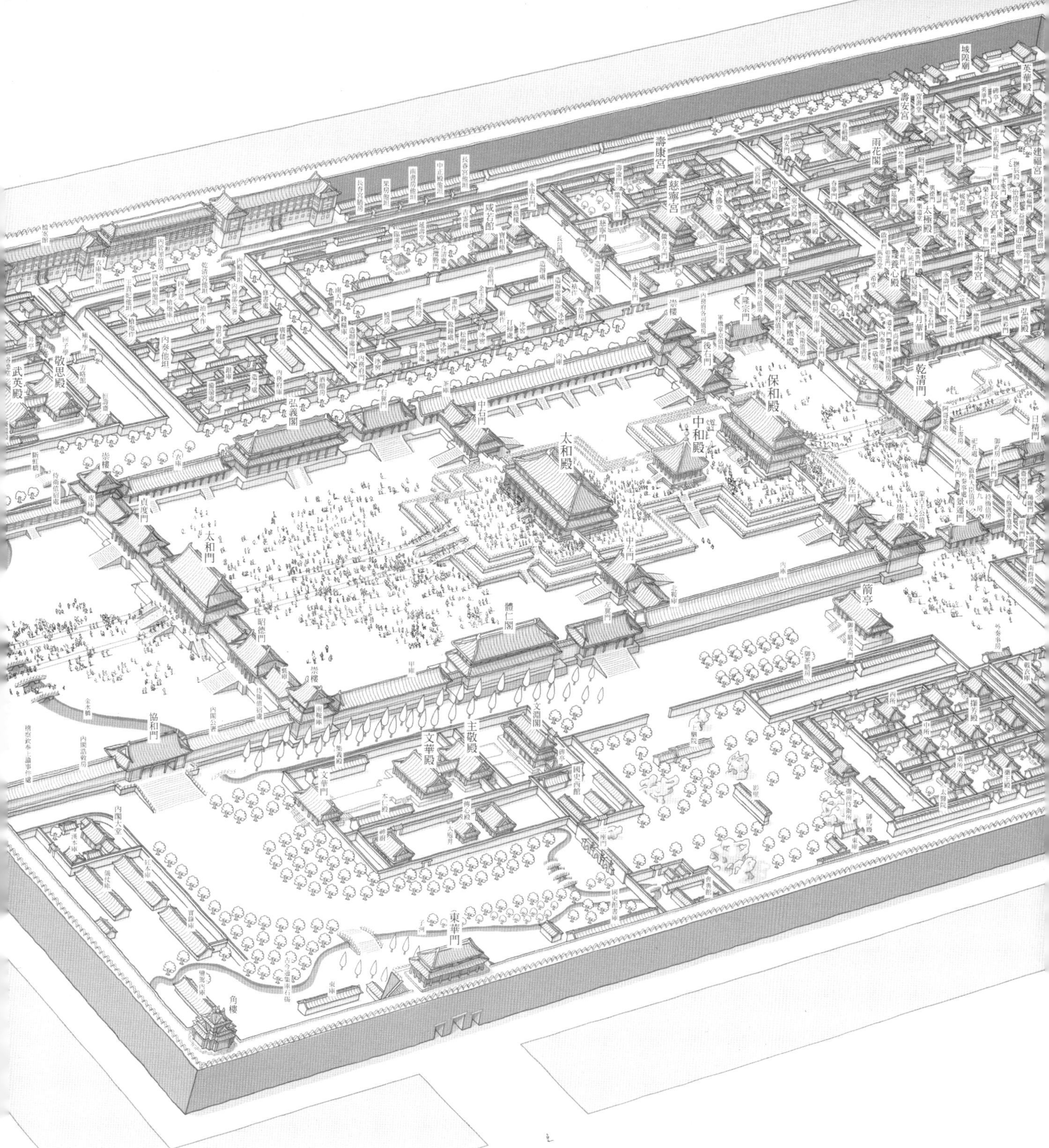
城隍廟
英華殿
壽安宮
雨花閣
建福宮
壽康宮
慈寧宮
咸若館
長春宮
太極殿
永壽宮
養心殿
弘德殿
隆宗門
軍機處
乾清門
月華門
日精門
保和殿
中和殿
太和殿
崇樓
後右門
後左門
弘義閣
中右門
中左門
武英殿
敬思殿
內奏他坦
貞度門
太和門
昭德門
協和門
體仁閣
景運門
箭亭
文淵閣
主敬殿
文華殿
文華門
擷芳殿
東華門
角樓
內閣大堂

In the old days, it was the heavily guarded Forbidden City of The Imperial Palace.

Though the main hall inside The Forbidden City is only a little over 30 meters high, it was once the tallest building in the ancient City of Beijing. The only hill in the capital city was man-made especially to act as a backdrop for the Imperial City. In front of the hall, the area of the Imperial Terrace (Danbi) and the Square is 36,000 square meters. Every year there were a few rare assemblies of thousands of envoys, military leaders and the privileged classes.

In the 500 years following the completion of the palace in January 1420, only two hereditary families sharing a single-character last name lived there, and which had adult males as the official heirs (the emperors). During the most glorious days in the Ming Dynasty, there were more than 100,000 servants and eunuchs in The Inner Court [Neichao] and 9,000 maids. It was the largest centre of power in the ancient world. It was also the largest bedrock for rites (li) and prohibitory regulations (fa).

The names of palaces mentioned in this book are based on those used in the Qing Dynasty. (Those used in the Ming Dynasty or in individual cases are shown in brackets).

The Palace Museum Publisher

/ Preface

The Forbidden City (Zijincheng) stands proud to welcome the morning sun and The Hall of Supreme Harmony (Taihedian) bathes in the light of dawn.

The Imperial Palace (Gugong) in The Forbidden City in Beijing is well preserved. It is the largest architectural complex of imperial palaces, not only in China, but in the world.

It is situated in the middle of the 7.8-kilometer axis passing through Beijing, a world famous old capital, renowned for its revered status in history, art and science. Hence, it has long been listed in the first group of State Cultural Relics Preservation Units and the List of the First Group of World Cultural Heritage of China.

Numerous books and articles with different viewpoints have been written about The Imperial Palace. However, *The Grand Forbidden City — The Imperial Axis* is the only book written with a focus on history, culture and architecture, and in a language complemented by architectural diagrams. A piece of research that reads well and makes use of diagrams and pictures to portray the history, culture and architectural art of The Imperial Palace in The Forbidden City is a rare find and this book is a delightful creation.

Using exciting illustrations and clear language to depict a study of architecture is a very important technique in presentation. Personally, I particularly admire this style.

65 years ago when I was first admitted to The Construction School of China, I benefited a lot through reading the illustrated *Standards and Rules of The Qing Style of Construction* [in Chinese], written by my amazing teachers, Liang Ssu Cheng and Lin Hui Yin. During that time, Mr. Liang edited the book *A Pictorial History of Chinese Architecture* [in English]. It was well received by experts, scholars and wide spectrum of readers.

Mr. Chiu Kwong Chiu has excelled himself once again producing *The Grand Forbidden City — The Imperial Axis* [in Chinese] after publishing his other works. *Beyond Chinese Wooden Architecture* [in Chinese] and *Running Notes on Qingming Shanghe Tu* [in Chinese], both demonstrate the unique writing style of Mr. Chiu. His tremendous contribution to the research and promotion of The Imperial Palace of The Forbidden City is undeniable. Also, his insight into the topic has acted as a catalyst in discussions and promotions regarding other historic building relics. It was a great pleasure to read Mr. Chiu's book and it was an honour to be asked to write the preface for it. Many congratulations on the publication of this sensational title!

LUO ZHEWEN
Senior Engineer (Professorial Grade)
Chief of the Experts Group on Historical Buildings
State Cultural Relics Bureau

A Chronology of the Emperors in the Ming Dynasty

Name	Reign Title	Posthumous Title	Years on the Throne
Zhu Yuanzhang	Ming Taizu	Emperor Hongwu	31 (1368-1398)
Zhu Biau	—	—	—
Zhu Yunwen	Ming Huidi	Emperor Jianwen	4 (1399-1402)
Zhu Di	Ming Chengzu	Emperor Yongle	22 (1403-1424)
Zhu Gaochi	Ming Renzong	Emperor Hongxi	8 months (1425)
Zhu Zhanji	Ming Xuanzong	Emperor Xuande	10 (1426-1435)
Zhu Qizhen*	Ming Yingzong	Emperor Zhengtong	14 (1436-1449)
Zhu Qiyu	Ming Daizong	Emperor Jingtai	7 (1450-1456)
Zhu Qizhen*	Ming Yingzong	Emperor Tianshun	8 (1457-1464)
Zhu Jianshen	Ming Xianzong	Emperor Chenghua	23 (1465-1487)
Zhu Youtang	Ming Xiaozong	Emperor Hongzhi	18 (1488-1505)
Zhu Houzhao	Ming Wuzong	Emperor Zhengde	16 (1506-1521)
Zhu Houcong	Ming Shizong	Emperor Jiajing	45 (1522-1566)
Zhu Zhaihou	Ming Muzong	Emperor Longqing	6 (1567-1572)
Zhu Yijun	Ming Shenzong	Emperor Wanli	48 (1573-1620)
Zhu Changlou	Ming Guangzong	Emperor Taichang	1 month (1620)
Zhu Youjiao	Ming Xizong	Emperor Tianqi	7 (1621-1627)
Zhu Youjian	Ming Sizong	Emperor Chongzhen	17 (1628-1644)

Zhu Qizhen was captured when he personally led the army to battle with Mongolia. He was reinstated eight years later. He had two stints in being an Emperor.

There were 17 emperors on the throne for a total of 276 years.

A Chronology of the Emperors in the Qing Dynasty

Name	Reign Title	Posthumous Title	Years on the Throne
Nurhachi	Qing Taizu	Tianming Han	11 (1616-1626)
Huangtaiji	Qing Taizong	Tiancong Han	9 (1627-1635)
	Qing Taizong	Emperor Chongde	8 (1636-1643)
Fulin	Qing Shizu	Emperor Shunzhi	18 (1644-1661)
Xuanye	Qing Shengzu	Emperor Kangxi	61 (1662-1722)
Yinzhen	Qing Shizong	Emperor Yongzhen	13 (1723-1735)
Hongli	Qing Gaozong	Emperor Qianlong	60 (1736-1795)
Yongyan	Qing Renzong	Emperor Jiaqing	25 (1796-1820)
Minning	Qing Xuanzong	Emperor Daoguang	30 (1821-1850)
Yizhu	Qing Wenzong	Emperor Xianfeng	11 (1851-1861)
Zaichun	Qing Muzong	Emperor Tongzhi	13 (1862-1874)
Zaitian	Qing Dezong	Emperor Guangxu	34 (1875-1908)
Puyi	—	Emperor Xuantong	3 (1909-1911)

There were 12 emperors who took their turns on the throne for a total of 295 years (267 if counted from the day of the initial entry into China through one of the passes of The Great Wall). The 10 Emperors from Emperor Shunzhi onward all resided in The Forbidden City.

/ Table of Contents

P. 31   Prologue

P. 37   Background

P. 41   Materials

P. 47   The Sacred Axis

P. 53   Five Gates and Three Courts for the Son of Heaven

P. 59   The Meridian Gate *(Wumen)*

P. 67   The Corner Tower *(Jiaolou)*

P. 73   The Gate of Surpreme Harmony Square
          (Taihemen Guangchang)

P. 89   The Hall of Supreme Harmony Square
          (Taihedian Guangchang)

P. 101 A Glimpse of Palatial Decorations within
          The Hall of Supreme Harmony *(Taihedian)*

P. 113 Accompaniment for Ceremonies

P. 123 The Three Large Halls under the Sky

P. 131 The Hall of Supreme Harmony *(Taihedian)*

P. 139 Colors

P. 147 The Roofs

P. 153 Between The Outer Court *(Waichao)* and
          The Inner Court *(Neichao)*

P. 169 Office of The Grand Council of State *(Junjichu)*

P. 177 The Hall of Mental Cultivation *(Yangxindian)*

P. 187 The Three Palaces of The Inner Court *(Neichao)*

P. 197 The Six Eastern and Western Palaces *(Dongxiliugong)* and The Imperial Garden *(Yuhuayuan)*

P. 211 The Imperial Garden *(Yuhuayuan)*

P. 226 Epilogue

P. 228 Acknowledgement

P. 229 References

/ Prologue

The Largest Palace The Longest Memory

In the past, the ordinary people were denied entry to the palace. Even the memories seemed to belong to the emperors alone. Nowadays, however, we can find the living history here unperturbed.

Zhu Yuanzhang, the first Emperor of the Ming Dynasty (on the throne between 1368 and 1398) once attempted to build a capital (Central Capital) in his hometown, the City of Fengyang in Anhui Province. He demanded every county in China to contribute 100 catties or jins [1 jin=1/2 kilogram] of quality soil for construction purposes. The construction work of the Central Capital was later deserted (the first capital of the Ming Dynasty was finally established in Nanjing). Zhu Yuanzhang's dream of returning to his hometown in glory was shattered. Otherwise, the emperor would have resided at a palace built with "superior earth" collected from all over the country. He would have been able to survey his kingdom symbolically by simple pacing up and down within his own palace.

Building a palace is the ultimate great task of founding a nation. A palace is great not only because of its large size, but because of its special implications and historical memory. China is the only country in existence with the longest recorded history. The philosophy of the emperors in the past dynasties was that they possessed an undisputable authority over the country. This belief reverberated throughout the centuries.

The concept of combining space and power first matured in the Zhou Dynasty (beginning 7th Century BC), but was implemented comprehensively in the Qin Dynasty (221-207 BC).

Upon unifying the Six States, the First Emperor of Qin (Qin Shihuang) demolished all their palaces and moved the rubble to the capital at Xianyang. At the same time, he ordered 120,000 richest families to move to the capital. Furthermore, he collected metals from all over China to cast into twelve gigantic bronze human figures. Then, he introduced a unified writing to record in Chinese history the first unified governed nation faced with political, economical, military and developmental challenges.

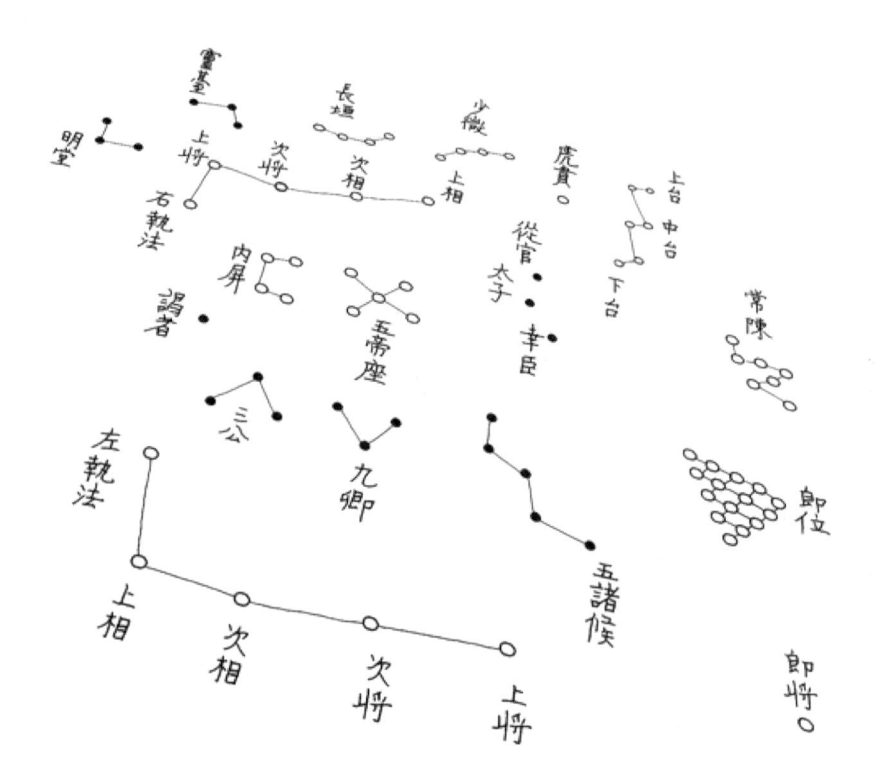

The prowess of the powerful Qin only lasted for two generations. No one can contemplate the extent of the First Emperor's achievements simply by viewing the ruins of the palace of Qin Dynasty — the A-Fang Palace (about 500,000 square meters), which was connected directly with the long Lishange Passageway (corridor built on stilts) 75 kilometers away. The palace and the terracotta warriors shared the same fate. They were created from the yellow earth swiftly and ended up buried not long after.

Qin Dynasty was short-lived and it boasted about its power by having huge quantities of everything ("quantitative" platform). Han Dynasty (206 BC-220 AD) which succeeded later, however, had more time to concentrate on construction and unification of cultural order.

The traditional Confucian philosophy became prominent during this period and was respectfully accepted as the ideology behind establishing rites (li) and prohibitory regulations (fa). It also affected the cultural development of China greatly in the entire feudal era that followed. As a result, the Han Dynasty became the first strong, stable and lasting dynasty and reached the first summit of success in the history of Chinese architecture.

In the Han Dynasty, Xiu He, the prime minister, persuaded Emperor Gaozu to be extravagant in the construction of the Weiyang Palace saying, "... the Son of Heaven rules the earth, his power can only be demonstrated by something magnificent." Emperor Gaozu immediately agreed, and no emperor since had ever disagreed.

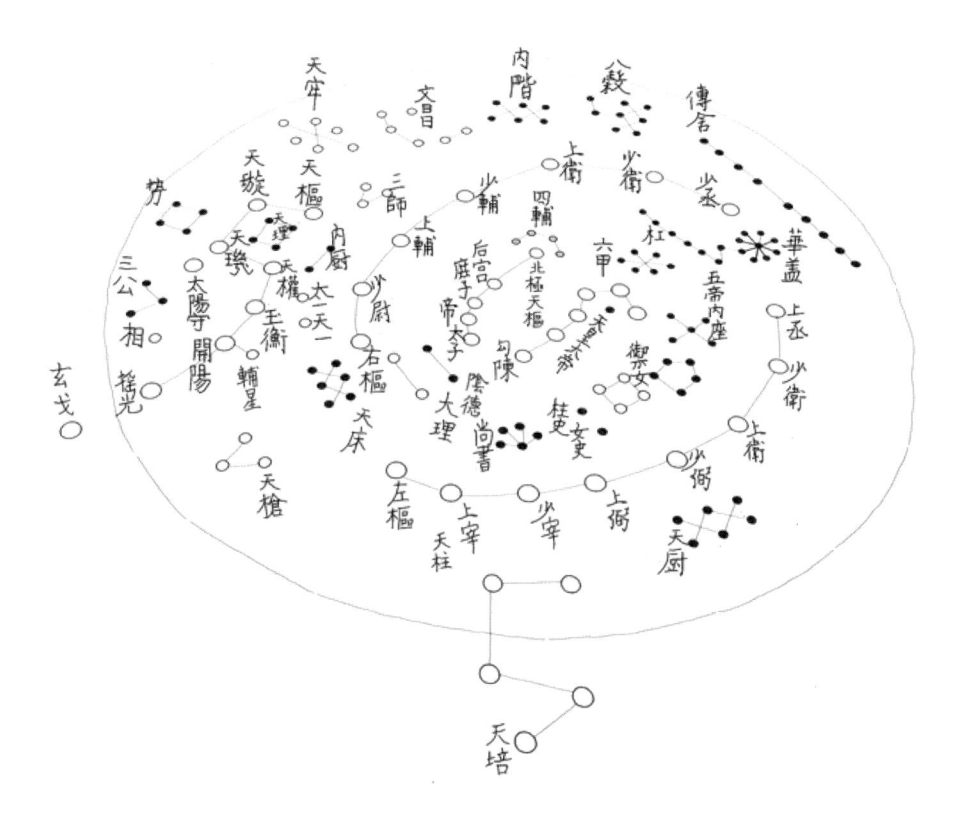

From then on in history, every newly established dynasty continued to follow the ground rules laid down in the Confucian doctrines when planning for imperial constructions. The palatial systems described in the Confucius classic: *The Rites of Zhou* (Zhouli), were used as the basic design, to demonstrate that it is an indisputable fact that the regime is created "by a heavenly mandate".

The architecture of imperial palaces in each dynasty in China is based on conventional concepts of axial symmetry, courtyards and double doors. Special emphasis was placed on the emperor's motto; i.e., "The family is the nation and the nation is the family". This led to a structure which is a practical abode as well as an elaborate display of supreme power and moral order. In the history of architecture, it is not an overstatement to say that the "Study of Palaces" only exists in China. The Ming and Qing dynasties possibly provided the last chapters of this study.

Entering this city of palaces is almost like entering the cultural space of the entire Chinese history. The grandeur of The Imperial Boulevard (Yudao) in front of The Gate of Heavenly Peace (Tiananmen, the largest square in the world today), is the same as that of capitals like Luoyang in North Wei, Changan in the Tang Dynasty, and Kaifeng in North Song. The halls built with yellow tiles and red walls backed by the blue sky originated from royal structures of the Yuan Dynasty. In fact, the "physical" blueprint that people walk on bear all the trademarks of the blueprints of the Yuan, Ming and Qing Dynasties, or even those of the dynasties of

Prologue

Qin, Han, Sui, Tang, Five Dynasties and Song, and *the Book on Craftsmanship (Kao Gong Ji)* [in Chinese] of the Zhou Dynasty. However, erecting chimneys in the back chamber of The Palace of Earthly Tranquility (Kunninggong) in The Inner Court (Neichao), where unauthorized cooking was strictly prohibited, and, furthermore, defying the rules of normal spiral construction of chimneys were definitely Manchurian traditions.

Tadao Ando, a scholar in architecture in Japan, thinks that the huge space in the Chinese palaces makes people feel "at a loss". Indeed, The Forbidden City, with an area equivalent to a small city, is so enormous that visitors will surely feel a bit daunted. In the Ming and Qing Dynasties, people would have experienced this humbling feeling a few kilometers away at The Gate of Eternal Stability (Yongdingmen), and it would have lingered on a few kilometers up to The Bell and Drum Tower (Zhonggulou).

This huge architectural complex of palatial buildings took only fourteen years (1406-1420) to complete. Ten years were spent on project planning but the actual construction took only four years. Such speed was unprecedented. But on the other hand, it took 130 days to produce one tile for the floor of the main palace. Such slow pace was also unprecedented. The brilliance of ancient construction technology in the Ming Dynasty was reflected in these extremities in speed during when executing projects.

To record Chinese history thoroughly and accurately is a monstrous task. However, if one looks closely at the architecture, one may discover some fragmented memories. Every brick and every tile tells a story.

Tourists always indicate their regret about "not having been able to visit the entire City". However, I am afraid that even historically, no one has managed to walk through the entire city. In the old days, officials within or outside the palace had very restrictive movements within the grounds. The hierarchy of ranks was rigid and the rights of the sexes were clearly defined. These rites (li) still form a kind of backbone to our society these days, albeit little remote.

This city of palaces was built according to the most ostentatious ritual and the strictest protocol. It was the last embodiment of the greatest rite conducted through the use of wood, stones, bricks and tiles by our very last feudal regime. It covers an extensive area of 723,633 square meters, pierced through by an axis which takes us from the glorious past to the present and the future, an axis which only an emperor could claim rightful ownership.

CHIU KWONG CHIU
July 2005

/ Background

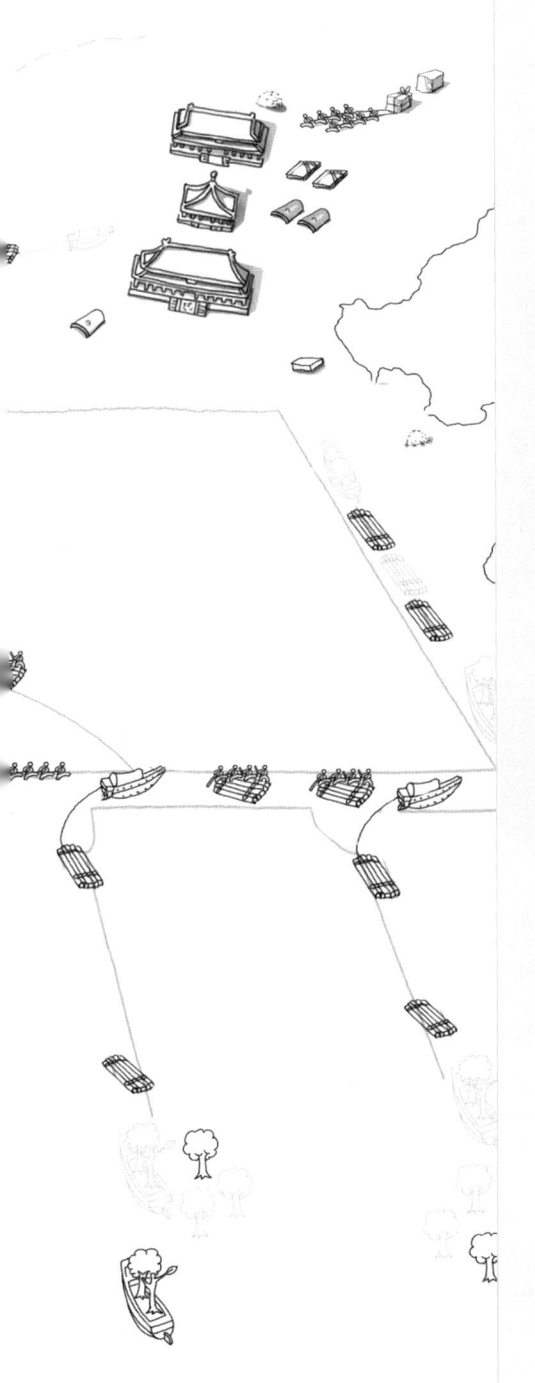

- It was during the period between the 4th and the 22nd year of the Yuan Dynasty (1267-1285) that Beijing was made capital. At that time, the palace was located near the southwestern part of the current City of Beijing. It was then named The Big Capital City (Daducheng).

- After conquering the Yuan Dynasty, the Ming Dynasty set up capital in Nanjing and renamed the Big Capital City "Beiping". Zhu Yuanzhang conferred the title of King of Yan (Yan Wang) to his fourth son, Zhu Di, and stationed him there. Later Zhu Di staged a coup and seized power from Emperor Jianwen (a nephew of Zhu Di), and became Ming Chengzu, the third emperor in the Ming Dynasty. He changed the name of Beiping to Beijing and moved the capital back to his stronghold. He also moved the axis of the original palaces of the Yuan Dynasty to about 150 meters to the east. In order to give the palatial city a more completed look, he removed the West Garden (Xiyuan or Taiyizhi). Superstitious belief stipulated that it would be detrimental to the new dynasty if its main axis overlapped with that of the former dynasty. As a result, the central axis of The Imperial City of the Yuan Dynasty was shifted to the west, making sure that the imperial spirit of the Yuan Dynasty could never be revived.

Background

- Again, with fengshui in mind, over a million cubic meters of soil was excavated from the city moat to form a hill behind the palaces. This was considered to have deterrent and intimidating effects over dark forces.

- The planning of The Forbidden City started in the 6th month, in the 4th Year of Yongle (1406) and the construction was completed on the 4th day of the 11th month, in the 18th Year of Yongle (December 8, 1420). Ten full years were spent on the planning, but the City was completed in merely four years.

- The Qing tribe entered China in 1644 and became the last owners of The Forbidden City. Unlike the new regimes in the past, the Qing Dynasty did not destroy the old palaces. Therefore, even with continued repairs, improvements and extensions, The Forbidden City has basically retained its general appearance from the Ming Dynasty.

- The Revolution of 1911, led by Dr Sun Yat Sen, overturned the Qing Dynasty. On November 5, 1924, the last emperor of the Qing Dynasty, Aisin-Gioro Puyi, moved out of the Qing palaces. In the 500 years prior to that, there were 24 emperors who lived here — 14 in the Ming Dynasty and 10 in the Qing Dynasty.

The Grand Forbidden City — The Imperial Axis

/ Materials

The timber used to build the palaces in the early days of the Ming Dynasty was brought in mainly from Zhejiang, Jiangxi and Sichuan Provinces. Transportation was tricky. For instance, after the timber in the mountains of Sichuan was felled, it was bound together into a raft and pushed into the gullies, waiting for the floods in the rainy season to carry down to the rivers. It was then towed, or pulled until it reached the capital. This could take as long as three to four years. In the early years of the Qing Dynasty, partly because of battles in the southwest (to suppress Wu Sangui) and partly because the quality nanmu [a kind of timber] in Sichuan was almost exhausted, pinewood began to be brought in from the northeast.

Materials

Space, Time
- The central axis of The Forbidden City and the central axis of The City of Beijing are also the meridian of the mid-day sun.

Astronomy
- It can extend to the Supreme Palace Enclosure and Purple Forbidden Enclosure which symbolizes the emperor's seat in Heaven.

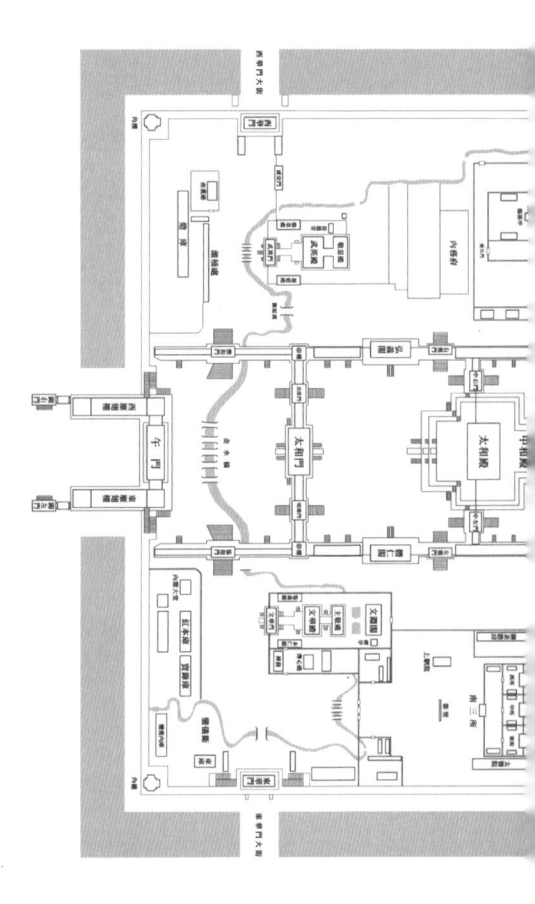

- The red earth used on the walls of the palaces and halls came from Shandong Province.

- The gold clay used to whitewash the walls of the halls came from Xuanhua, Hebei Province.

- The clear mud tiles made from fine soil were manufactured in Linqing, Shandong Province.

- The tiles of highest quality used to decorate the floors of the palaces and halls came from places like Song River, Suzhou.

- A total of over a hundred million tiles were used. This included more than twenty million floor tiles used to cover the courtyards. Eighty million bricks were used to build the city walls, palace walls, and steps.

- The building stones came from Fengshan County, west of the capital. The colored glaze was manufactured near the capital city (known today as Liulichang [Colored Glaze Factory]).

- As a rule, the tile kiln was situated in the southeast to avoid pollution caused by the northwest winds.

- More than 20,000 pieces of rocks weighing almost 10,000 catties [1 catty = 0.5 kg] were laid on The Imperial Boulevard (Yudao) in front of the palaces and halls along the axis extending all the way to The Gate of Heavenly Peace (Tiananmen).

- Building personnel came from all over the country; a total of 100,000 skilled craftsmen and a million labourers.

The Grand Forbidden City — The Imperial Axis

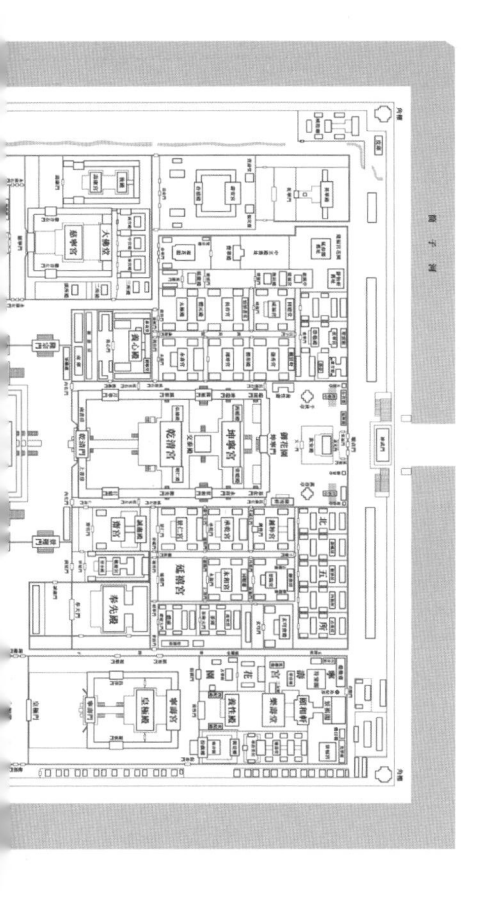

Proprieties
- It can penetrate the strictest protocol of the feudal era.

History
- It can immerse in the rich history of different dynasties.

- The Forbidden City measures 753 meters from the east to the west, and 961 meters from the north to the south, covering an area of 723,633 square meters.

- The city walls are 10 meters high (the base is 8.62 meters wide and the upper part 6.66 meters wide, wide enough for 4 horses to gallop side by side). There is a 52-meter wide moat 20 meters from the wall.

- 980 palatial buildings currently exist, with a total coverage of 8,707 bays (a bay is the space within 4 columns supporting a roof).

- There is a large gate in each of the four directions of east, south, west and north. They are:

  - The Eastern Prosperity Gate (Donghuamen), on the east side
  - The Meridian Gate (Wumen), main entrance in the south
  - The Western Prosperity Gate (Xihuamen), on the west side
  - The Gate of Divine Prowess (Shenwumen), back door on the north side (This was called The Gate of the Tortoise [Xuanwumen] in the Ming Dynasty. Later, because the name consisted of one of the characters in the name of the second Emperor of the Qing Dynasty — Xuanye, it was changed to The Gate of Divine Prowess [Shenwumen]).

P.43

Materials

- Each of the two Imperial Boulevard (Yudao) slabs carved with waves, mountains, clouds and dragons, in the front and back terraces of the Three Large Halls, measures 16.57 meters long, 3.07 meters thick, and weighs about 250 tons (the material in its original state would have weighed at least 300 tons). (The Imperial Boulevard (Yudao) slab in front of The Hall of Supreme Harmony [Taihedian] was erected by putting together 3 pieces of stones following the engraved patterns. The one behind The Hall of Preserving Harmony [Baohedian] was kept intact). More than 20,000 people were employed. They spent 28 days hauling the stones to The City of Beijing from the Fang Hill (Fangshan) nearby.

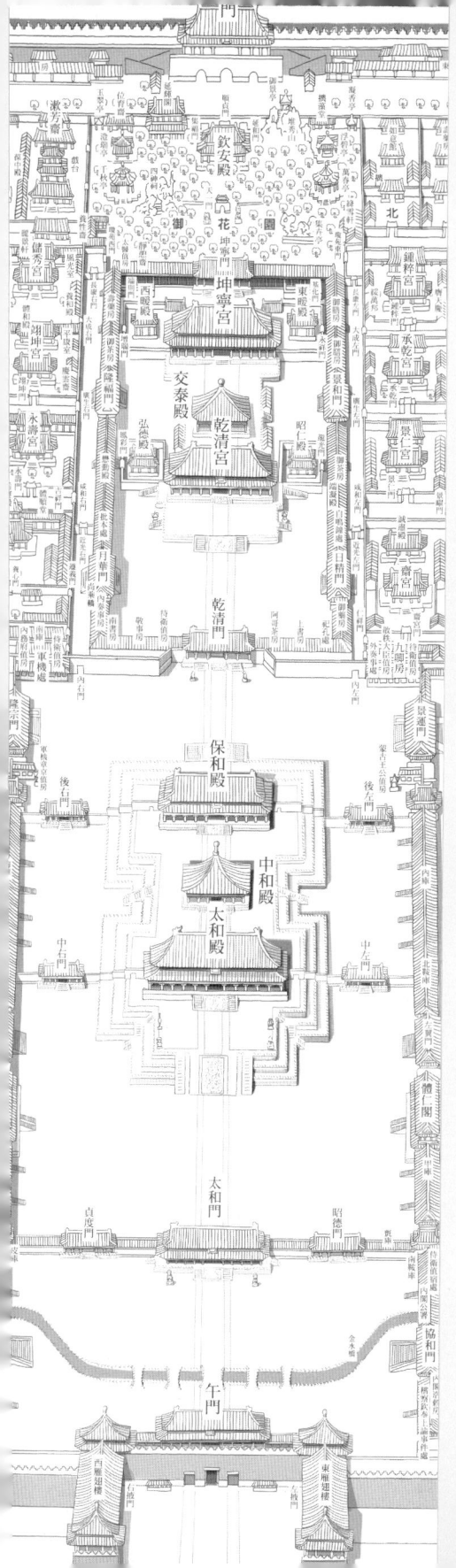

/ The Sacred Axis

According to the Chinese fengshui theories, a vertical space is too powerful. Regardless of whether it is "feng" [wind] or "shui" [water]; if it is dead straight, it will "sever" the energy pod created by the environment like a dagger. The longer the straight line, the greater will be the power of destruction. This is why Chinese gardens promote zigzag designs. Chinese painters also believe that straight lines could devastate the romantic spirit in paintings.

The Sacred Axis

The Hall of Martial Valor (Wuyingdian)

The Meridian Gate (Wumen)

The Gate of Supreme Harmony (Taihemen)

The Forbidden City is located along the central north-south axis of The City of Beijing. (also at the center of the City and even of the nation in those days) The City is incidentally crossed by this most dreaded straight line. This non-negotiable force of nature was something that ordinary people would try everything possible to avoid. It was believed that this force could only be contained by an emperor, who with divine right could transform a destructive straight line into something dignified and honourable.

Apart from privileged buildings like the princes' offices and temples, the general layout of houses is that, the effects of fengshui will be taken into consideration and the main entrance will be positioned in the southeast to avoid the crippling wind blowing directly from the south.

Here is a section of the axis running from the main entrance of The Forbidden City (The Meridian Gate [Wumen]) to the back gate, (The Gate of Divine Prowess [Shenwumen]). The different palatial buildings, flanked by other buildings built on both sides, form a huge palatial complex. Because of their different heights, produce an undulating skyline. Modern architects see the palaces of different heights on the axis as the central spine of the City of Beijing. The ancient Chinese saw them in a mystical light, saying that they were akin to the pulsating vein of the dragon.

Architecture was perceived as an extension of the human

The Grand Forbidden City — The Imperial Axis

The Hall of Supreme Harmony (Taihedian)

The Hall of Preserving Harmony (Baohedian)

The Hall of Central Harmony (zhonghedian)

The Gate of Divine Prowess (Shenwumen)

The Hall of Imperial Peace (Qinandian)

The Palace of Earthly Tranquility (Kunninggong)

The Hall of Union (Jiaotaidian)

The Palace of Heavenly Purity (Qianqinggong)

The Gate of Heavenly Purity (Qianqingmen)

The Hall of Gloy Literary (Wenhuadian)

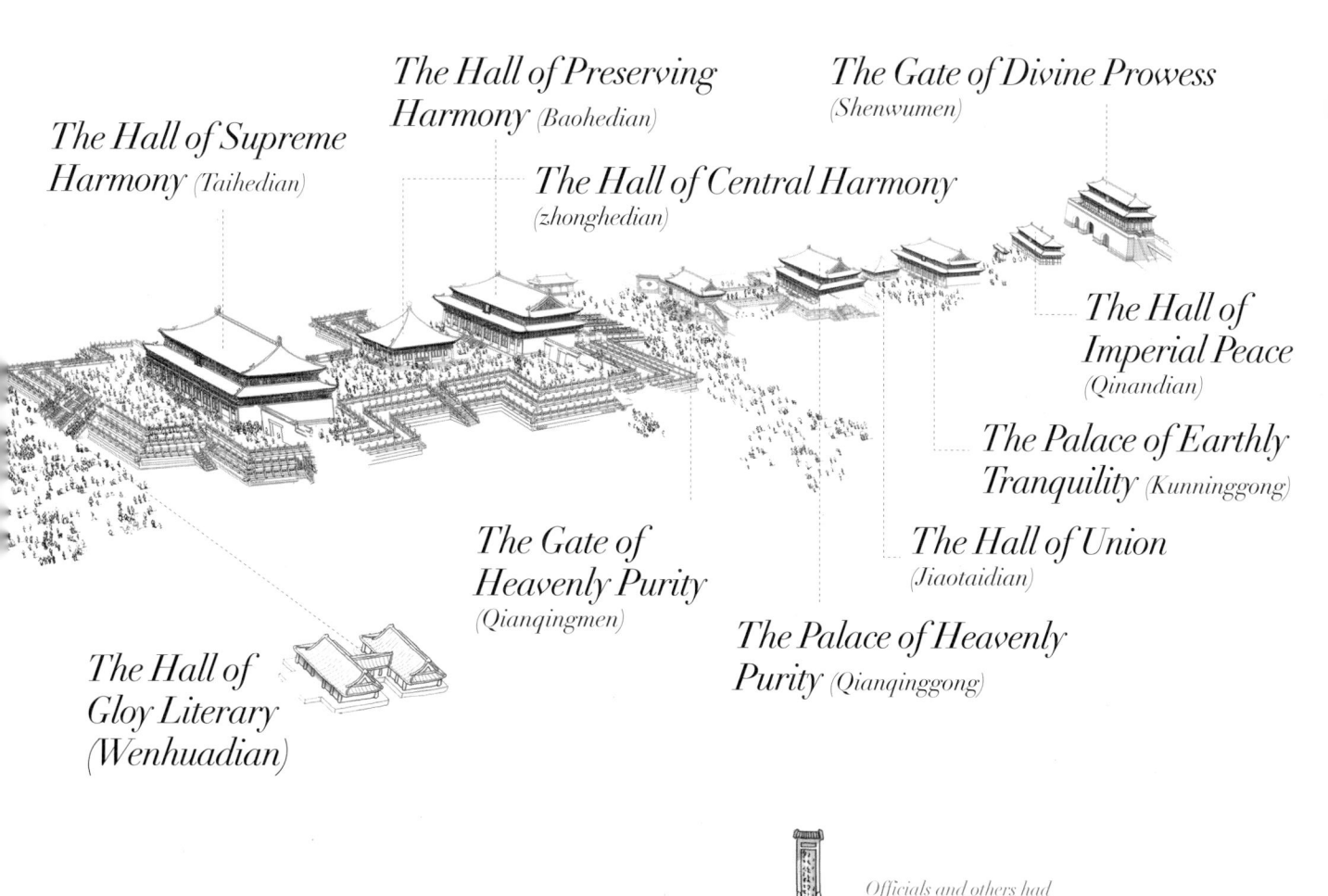

Officials and others had to dismount at this point.

body, and/or the nature. It should, indeed, be in harmony with mankind and nature. Traditional Chinese architecture was appraised on the achievement of an individual building as well as on the inter-connections and arrangements among buildings. This view was particularly popular in the Ming and Qing Dynasties, when the building technology and system achieved a high degree of standardization.

The ancient architects devised some clever and uniquely Chinese methods to lessen the negative effects of the straight lines and verticle space.

1. Build flights of steps and platforms of different heights along the straight line;

2. Vary the widths along different sections of the straight line;

3. Create doorways and gates. This idea of opening up and closing up any space is seen as a kind of symbolic art. It was used in the building of private dwellings, and manifested itself to the highest degree in the construction of imperial buildings.

The traditional imperial prototype was, "The Son of Heaven has five gates and three courts"–that is to say, the palace where the Son of Heaven stays should have five gates and three solemn administrative courts. This was just a general concept of an ideal layout. A huge architectural complex like The Forbidden City boasts thousands of gates and doorways.

"Recently, geographers used advanced technology to take pictures from the sky over the City of Beijing. They accidentally found that the buildings from The Gate of Heavenly Peace (Tiananmen) to the Bell Tower (Zhonglou) form the shape of a dragon. This is a concrete demonstration of the fact that the Chinese emperors considered themselves the Real Dragons and Sons of Heaven, it also reinforces the status of this mythical creature in Chinese culture."

"…apart from the Imperial Ancestral Temple (Taimiao) and the Altar to Worship The Earth and Grain (Shejitan) forming the two eyes of a dragon, and the Bell Tower (Zhonelou) and Drum Tower (Gulou) forming the tail of it, the design also includes a water dragon formed by the Three Seas (Sanhai) and Buddhist Temple Sea (Shicha Hai), giving the impression of two dragons playing with a pearl." (See Reference 16)

/ Five Gates and Three Courts for the Son of Heaven

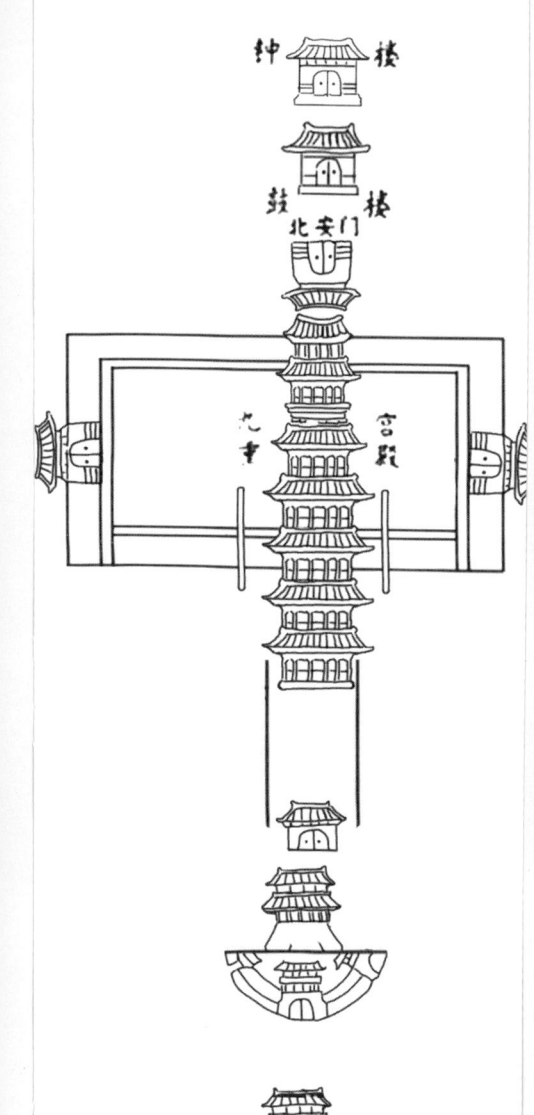

The requirement of "Five Gates and Three Courts" was first recorded in *The Rites of Zhou* (Zhouli). Different degrees of emphasis were placed on it by different dynasties. The basic essence of it, however, was kept intact throughout.

The Gate of Great Qing (Daqingmen, known as The Gate of Great Ming [Damingmen] in the Ming Dynasty, was changed to The Gate of China [Zhonghuamen] in the Republic of China; later demolished), was located roughly where the Monument to the People's Heroes now stands. When the Qing tribe entered the city, they turned the plaque of The Gate of Great Ming (Damingmen) over, wrote on it the three [Chinese] characters standing for The Gate of Great Qing (Daqingmen), and became the new masters of The Forbidden City. It was gesture of "Qing to follow the system of Ming" with no immediate desire to revamp the system or to destroy Ming's legacy.

The outer gate of The Imperial City symbolizes the national gate of the Ming and Qing Dynasties. Whenever the emperor ventured out of the palace, offered of sacrifice to Heaven, or returned from victories in battle, he would pass this gate to enter The Imperial City. Otherwise, the gate would be kept closed unless there were important ceremonies.

The Gate of Great Qing (Daqingmen) and the Thousand-step Corridor (Qianbulang) have been pulled down one after the other in modern times. A solemn and bleak mile long track had disappeared. Between The Gate of Great Qing (Daqingmen) and The Meridian Gate (Wumen) was The Imperial Boulevard (Yudao) where unauthorized access was absolutely denied. (One could only go from the east of the city to the west by passing through the front part of The Gate of Great Qing [Daqingmen])

The Gate of Heavenly Peace (Tiananmen, known as The Gate to Receive Heaven [Chengtianmen] in the Ming Dynasty), is 33.7 meters high, with double eaved gable and hip roof, 9 bays broad and 5 bays deep. There are a pair of stone lions and a pair of Decorative Poles (Huabiao). It was a place where important proclamations were made. In the middle of The External Golden Water Bridge (Waijinshuiqiao), The Imperial Bridge crossing the river has 9 columns on either

Five Gates and Three Courts for the Son of Heaven

The Gate of Heavenly Peace *(Tiananmen)*

The gate where the imperial edicts were promulgated to the world.

The High Gate (Gaomen)
The gate where announcements were made to all the people of the world.

The Gate of Eternal Stability *(Yongdingmen)*

The South Facing Gate *(Zhengyangmen)*

The Gate of Great Qing *(Daqingmen)*

It is 4 kilometers to go from The Gate of Eternal Stability (Yongdingmen) to The South Facing Gate (Zhengyangmen).

On both sides of the long Thousand-step Corridor (Qianbulang) were low-rise corridors adjacent to the chambers. Neither strolling nor hurrying along was permitted. One has to proceed toward the breathtaking Gate of Heavenly Peace (Tiananmen). The Thousand-step Corridor (Qianbulang) was about 500 meters long and 60 meters wide.

There were 144 reception chambers sharing the same ridge, with red columns and yellow tiles.

side and 5 more on the end of each colonnade. This corresponds to the pair of lucky numbers 9 and 5 which symbolises superiority and nobility. This rule is more strictly observed here than at The Golden Water Bridge (Jinshuiqiao) inside The Meridian Gate (Wumen). Whenever there was reading of important imperial edicts (for example, the ascension of the emperor to the throne, the conferment of the title of empress dowager), the ceremony was held in The Hall of Supreme Harmony (Taihedian). The edicts would be read out by the Edict Officer to the officials of all ranks kneeling in the south side of The External Golden Water Bridge (Waijinshuiqiao). At the same time, a gilt bronze phoenix with a copy of the edict in its mouth would be slowly lowered with a rope down the gate tower, symbolizing the promulgation of the imperial edict from the Son of Heaven to all the people in the world. (The golden phoenix was 2 feet and 1.5 inches tall [Chinese measurements], standing on gold-plated clouds.)

The Proper Gate (Duanmen)

The gate for keeping military provisions for palatial guard of honour

The Storage Gate (Kumen)
The supply base for weapons, military provisions and equipment for the guards of honour.

The Gate of Supreme Harmony (Taihemen)

The gate of court discipline.

The Right Gate (Yingmen)
Ying means right. This was the main entrance for people to pay respects. People from other parts of the world would enter through this gate.) This is the gate of discipline, the place designed for ruling and administration.

The moat around The Forbidden City is 19.3 meters wide. More than one million cubic feet of mud had been excavated and transported to the imperial garden at the back of The Forbidden City, to form a hill with its highest peak at about 52 meters. The hill served not only to keep out the chilly winds from the north, but also to suppress the imperial influence of the former dynasty. It also constitutes an ideal fengshui arrangement of having water (The Internal and External Golden Water Rivers (Nei and Wai Jinshuihe)) in front of the building and mountain as a backdrop.

The Meridian Gate (Wumen)

The gate leading to The Imperial Palace.

The Pheasant Gate (Zhimen)
The Middle Gate. The Pheasant Gate offers two views for the emperor. It symbolizes the entrance to the palace where the emperors resides, and where the emperor can look down at his people. The two wing towers extend forward, allowing the emperor to look up to Heaven.

The Gate of Heavenly Purity (Qianqingmen)

The gate of the residence of the Son of Heaven.
In the Qing Dynasty, The Gate of Heavenly Purity was the place where the emperor administered state affairs.

Residence Gate (Lumen)
Lu is the emperor's residence. The Residence Gate (Lumen) is the gate leading to the emperor's bed-chambers. The living space behind the Gate provided the emperor a sanctuary with absolute privacy. What is known as The Great Interior (Danei) refers to this space.

The Gate of Divine Prowess (Shenwumen)

This is the back door of the palatial city. In terms of bearing, the supernatural tortoise (Xuanwu) is situated in the north and provided protection for the Gate thus its original name: The Gate of the Tortoise (Xuanwumen). In the Qing Dynasty, to avoid sharing one of the characters in the name of Emperor Kanxi (Xuanye), its name was changed to The Gate of Divine Prowess (Shenwumen).

P.55

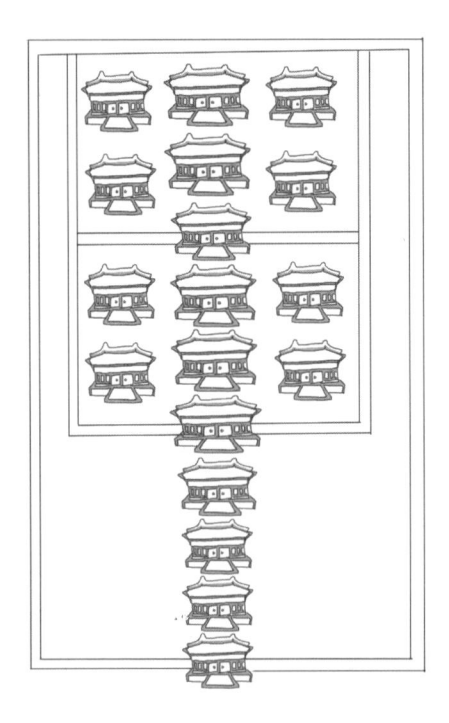

Five Gates and Three Courts for the Son of Heaven

The system of gates as laid down in The Rites of Zhou (Zhouli).

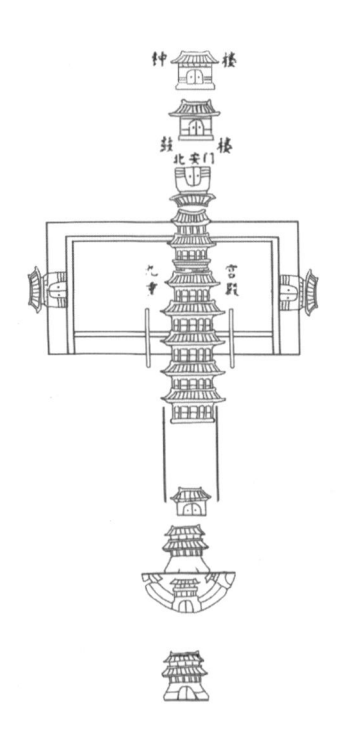

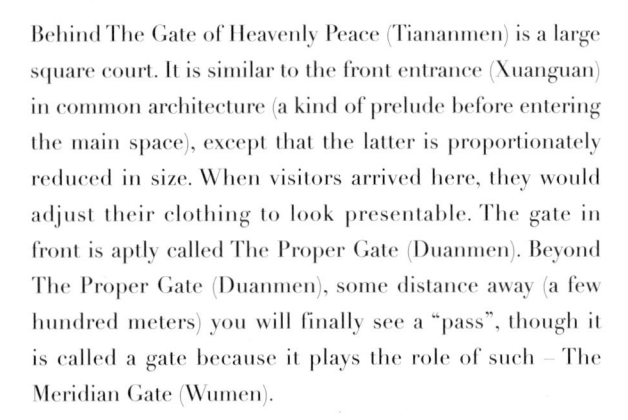

The system of Palatial City Gates in the Ming Dynasty.

Behind The Gate of Heavenly Peace (Tiananmen) is a large square court. It is similar to the front entrance (Xuanguan) in common architecture (a kind of prelude before entering the main space), except that the latter is proportionately reduced in size. When visitors arrived here, they would adjust their clothing to look presentable. The gate in front is aptly called The Proper Gate (Duanmen). Beyond The Proper Gate (Duanmen), some distance away (a few hundred meters) you will finally see a "pass", though it is called a gate because it plays the role of such – The Meridian Gate (Wumen).

Five Gates denotes the most honorable spatial order. In the studies of Yin-Yang, even numbers belong to yin (kun), odd numbers belong to yang (qian). The emperor represents "qianyang". "5" is the middle odd number out of the five (1, 3, 5, 7, 9), symbolising that the "emperor occupies the central position". "9", on the other hand, is the biggest odd number (after 10, the counting starts from 1 again). Thus "9, 5" has become the symbol of an emperor. This is evident everywhere in the whole of The Forbidden City. A width of 9 bays (one bay is the space between two timber columns), and a depth of 5 bays is the most important dimensions used for building palaces. Similarly, the dragon representing the emperor has 5 claws.

There are also scholars who consider 9 sets of gates as a symbol of the "Son of Heaven residing in the 9th Heaven", the most sacred part of Heaven.

/ The Meridian Gate (Wumen)

This Gate is as huge as a pass with two extensions stretching forward, like the letter "U". It is well known that "courtyards" provide the earliest memory of space in Chinese architecture and this huge "U" symbol is an evidence of the earliest "huge gate" in imperial buildings.

The two lofty gate towers are observatory towers for the emperors to "cast his eyes over" his people under Heaven. They are not connected horizontally to form a watch tower. The space in between is open and uncovered, known as "Imperial Palace" — The Meridian Gate (Wumen), the main gate of The Grand Forbidden City.

The Meridian Gate (Wumen)

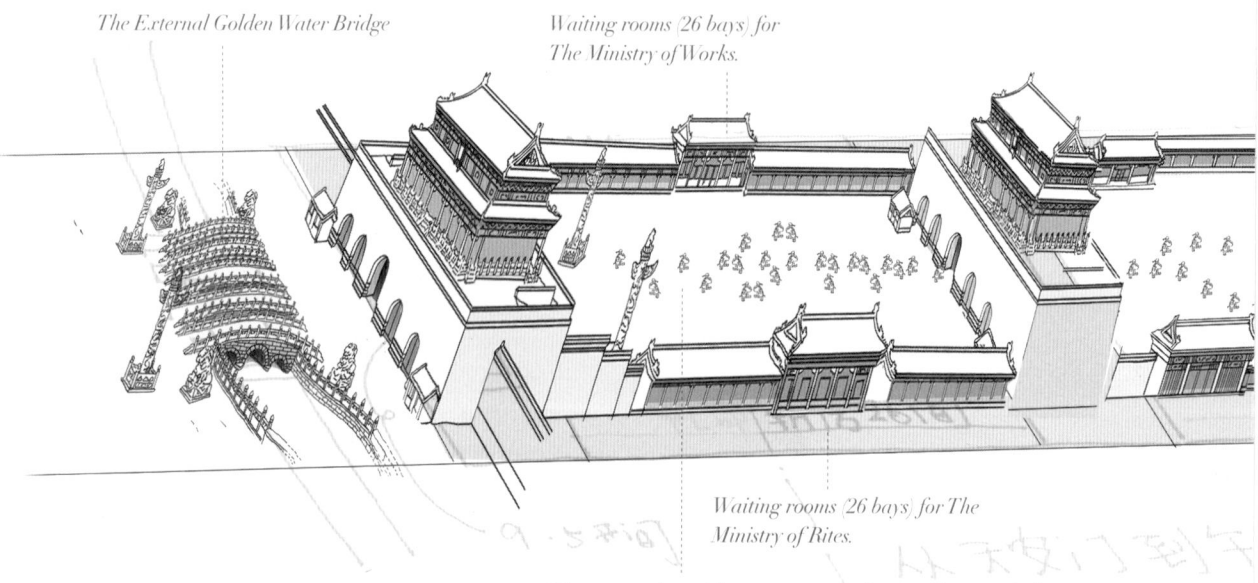

The External Golden Water Bridge

Waiting rooms (26 bays) for The Ministry of Works.

Waiting rooms (26 bays) for The Ministry of Rites.

The square-shaped Square serves as the reception area before entering the main enclosure.

(Bracket)

The Main Gate of The Forbidden City

Double-eaved hip roof, covered with yellow glazed tiles, *width*: 9 bays (60.055 meters), *depth*: 5 bays (25 meters), *height*: 37.95 meters.
Along The Imperial Boulevard (Yudao) leading to the gate, there is a sundial on the left and a jialiang [a copper cast standard scale] on the right. Time as well as weights and measures are important matters in a farming society, and they are also symbols of ancient imperial power.

The Meridian Gate (Wumen) rests high above the foundation of the city. It is the tallest structure in the entire palatial city and also the only one of the four gates where brackets were used. Though it was built with the most ideal measurement of 9 by 5 bays, its two sides have no verandahs under the eaves. Its status was still inferior to the main hall (The Hall of Supreme Harmony [Taihedian]).

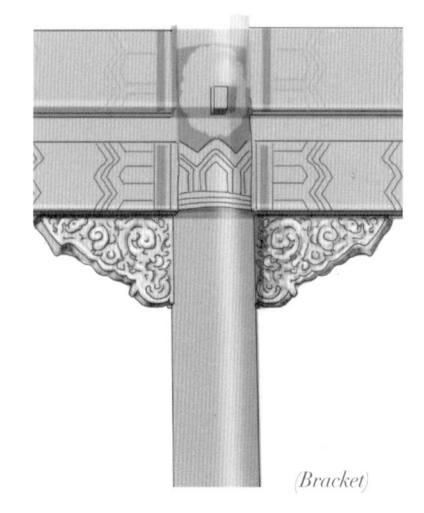

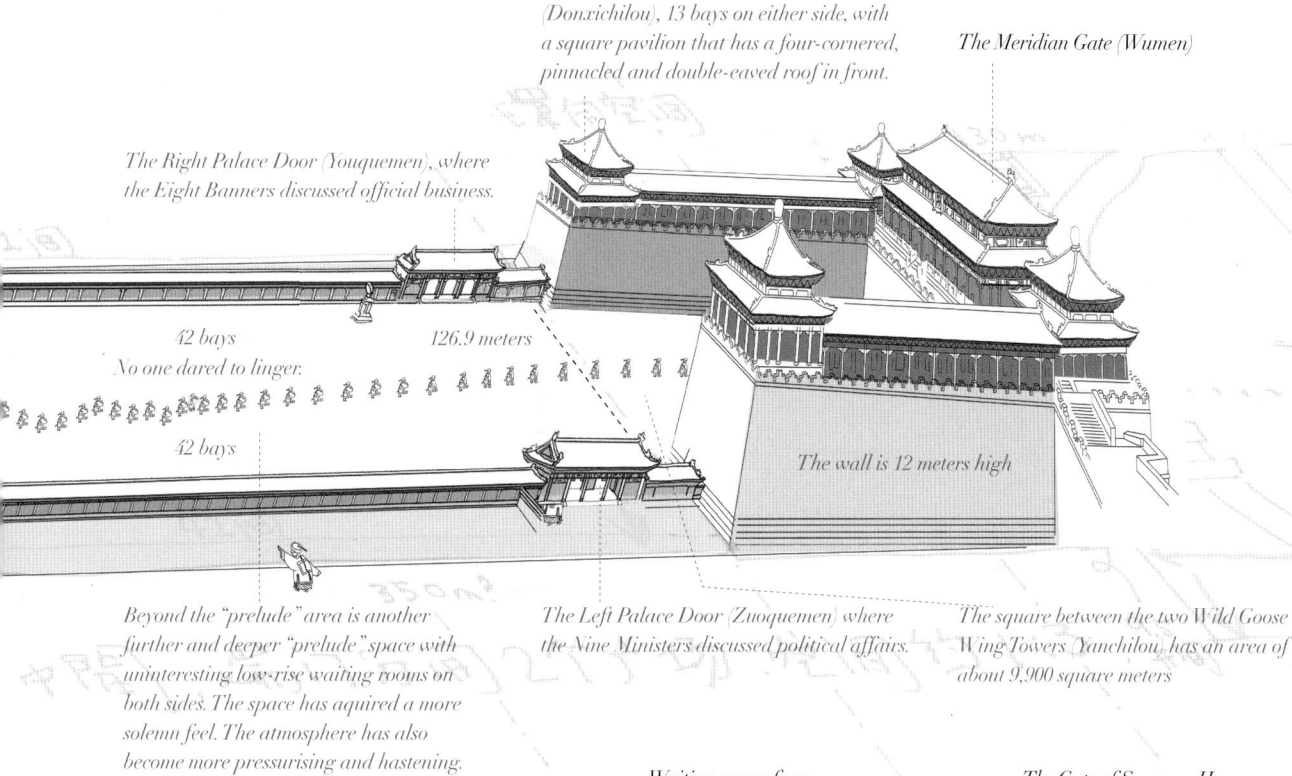

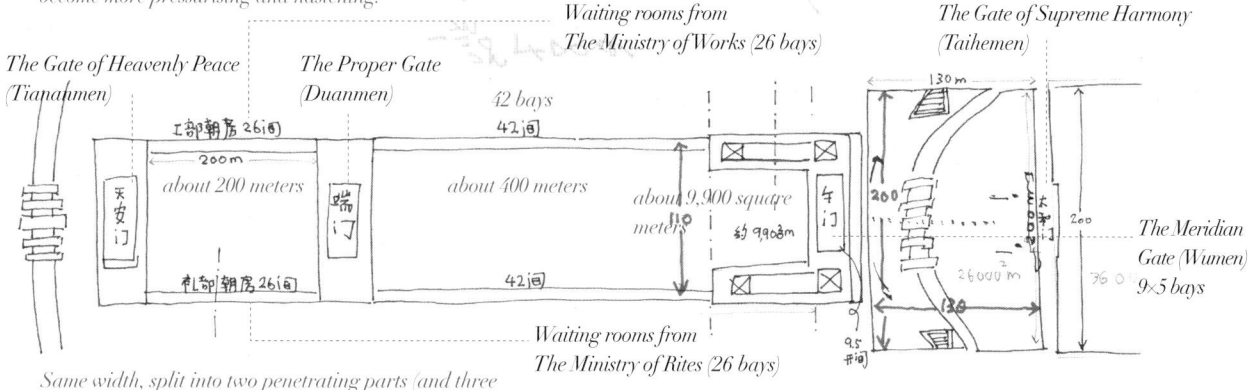

The East and West Wing Towers (Donxichilou), 13 bays on either side, with a square pavilion that has a four-cornered, pinnacled and double-eaved roof in front.

The Meridian Gate (Wumen)

The Right Palace Door (Youquemen), where the Eight Banners discussed official business.

42 bays
126.9 meters
No one dared to linger.
42 bays

The wall is 12 meters high

Beyond the "prelude" area is another further and deeper "prelude" space with uninteresting low-rise waiting rooms on both sides. The space has aquired a more solemn feel. The atmosphere has also become more pressurising and hastening.

The Left Palace Door (Zuoquemen) where the Nine Ministers discussed political affairs.

The square between the two Wild Goose Wing Towers (Yanchilou) has an area of about 9,900 square meters

Waiting rooms from The Ministry of Works (26 bays)

The Gate of Supreme Harmony (Taihemen)

The Gate of Heavenly Peace (Tiananmen)

The Proper Gate (Duanmen)

42 bays

about 200 meters

about 400 meters

about 9,900 square meters

The Meridian Gate (Wumen) 9×5 bays

42 bays

Waiting rooms from The Ministry of Rites (26 bays)

Same width, split into two penetrating parts (and three palatial reception spaces with different atmospheres).

In the square in front of The Meridian Gate (Wumen), apart from The Imperial Boulevard (Yudao), there are no "centers of interest" like a sculpture, a pond, or a pillar which are common in modern plazas or courtyards. Therefore, there is no encouragement for people to congregate. The soldiers were guarding in the front, the red walls were standing tall on three sides, and more soldiers were casting their watchful eyes from the watch towers. These transformed the square into a space of "pressure" where one felt the need to move on. However, the irony is that people could not move freely because everywhere was heavily guarded and everyone was being watched.

In those days, there were always two red poles kept at The Meridian Gate (Wumen) by the guards. They were specifically used to beat anyone who tried to enter without authorization. Even those from the imperial household would not be spared. Just compare the mental states of visitors of the older days and tourists nowadays. The contrast is incredible.

P.61

The Meridian Gate (Wumen)

Symbols and Metaphors

The Han civilization originated in the north of China. The higher classes enjoyed better living accommodation that "faced the south" (to avoid the north wind). Bearings were first used for practical reasons, and were gradually elevated to the higher status of symbols for worship and power. The Son of Heaven would "face south and rule" because "facing north" has the implication of succumbing to someone's power.

The "Wu" or "Meridian" faces directly south in terms of bearings. From The Proper Gate (Duanmen) to The Meridian Gate, one was encouraged to conduct himself properly before arriving at the main entrance of the palatial city.

Bearings in China have unique meanings. While in harmony with the five elements [metal, wood, water, fire and earth], they are also guarded by mystical animals. They can act directly as symbols of conquest (against unfavorable elements) or luck. There is a green dragon in the east, and a white-headed tiger in the west. In the north there is a black sacred tortoise and in the south a red phoenix.

There was "The Pheasant Gate (Zhimen)" recorded in *The Rites of Zhou (Zhouli)* as one of the "Five Gates of the Son of Heaven". The phoenix is sometimes called a pheasant and sometimes a rosefinch. The Meridian Gate (Wumen) was looked upon as an equivalent of the "Pheasant Gate (Zhimen)". (In the Tang and Song Dynasties, The Imperial Boulevard [Yudao] in front of the palatial city gate was called Rosefinch Boulevard.) The five lofty towers standing on the "U" shaped foundation with their roofs slightly tilted upwards were described as five phoenixes spreading their wings — The Five-Phoenix Towers (Wufenglou).

This architectural language is like a riddle (its complexity is directly proportional to its formality). The metaphors and symbols implied may not be easily construed by a lay person. In the Western world, similar situations would have only occurred probably during the creation of religious paintings and in sculptures in churches in the Middle Ages. It is obvious that in the Western world, the highest architectural skills were devoted to serve the churches; whereas in traditional China, the highest architectural skills were devoted to the imperial state.

When you are on The Imperial Boulevard (Yudao) admiring the skyline of The Pheasant Gate (Zhimen) (The Meridian Gate [Wumen]), the 9,900 square meter Square between The East and West Wing Towers (Dongxichilou) is huge. You are so dwarfed by it, the skyline becomes less impressive as you get near the enormous structure. The color of a "rosefinch" is red; the south side of The Meridian Gate (Wumen) belongs to "fire" in the five elements, and thus also red. The Square is surrounded by three red walls and gives a solemn ending to the road of pilgrimage which starts with The Gate of Great Qing (Daqingmen) — Welcome to the city of palaces!

The Grand Forbidden City — The Imperial Axis

A bell and a drum were installed on The Meridian Gate (Wumen). Officials rang the bell and beat the drum to proclaim the superiority of the empire to the world. The bell was rung when the emperor was departing or entering the palace, or when he offered sacrifices to The God of The Earth. The drum was beaten when he offered sacrifices to The Imperial Ancestral Temple. Generally speaking, the emperor only appeared at The Meridian Gate (Wumen) when there were solemn ceremonies like triumphant returns from battles and acceptance of prisoners of war (Emperor Qianlong did this 4 times, and no emperor ever did since).

The imperial government also made its annual promulgation of the almanac (li-shu) for the forthcoming year here. (During the reign of Emperor Qianlong, because his name Hong-li contained the character "li", the li-shu had to be renamed xian-shu, or constitutional book.)

As for the phrase "Beheaded at The Meridian Gate (Wumen)", it is more a novelist's flight of fancy than anything else. This practice did not factually exist. Instead, when the ministers in the Ming Dynasty offended the emperor, they might have to face the punishment of being "flogged with a pole at court" in front of The Meridian Gate (Wumen). While originally intended as a punishment to slight one's "dignity", it became a deadly savage torture in the Ming Dynasty.

The Final Imperial Examination took place once every three years and results were announced officially. The top three candidates (First Place Scholar [zhuangyuan], Second Place Scholar, [bangyan], Third Place Scholar, [Tanhua]) were given the special permission to leave the palace through the middle door of the Meridian Gate. This was the highest honour a scholar could receive.

During imperial marriage ceremonies, the imperial sedan chair carrying the empress also entered the palace through the middle door. Otherwise, only the emperor himself could enter or leave the palace through this door.

During the imperial marriage of Emperor Tongzhi (reigned from 1862-1874), all people wearing colorful clothes were allowed to come here. At that time, visitors turned up in large numbers, wearing colorful "disposable clothing". Because the visitors came from all walks of life, some vagrants exploited the situation and stole treasures from the palace. Thus, during the imperial marriage of Emperor Guangxu (reigned from 1875-1908), entrance control was reinstated. (See Reference 11)

五帝座

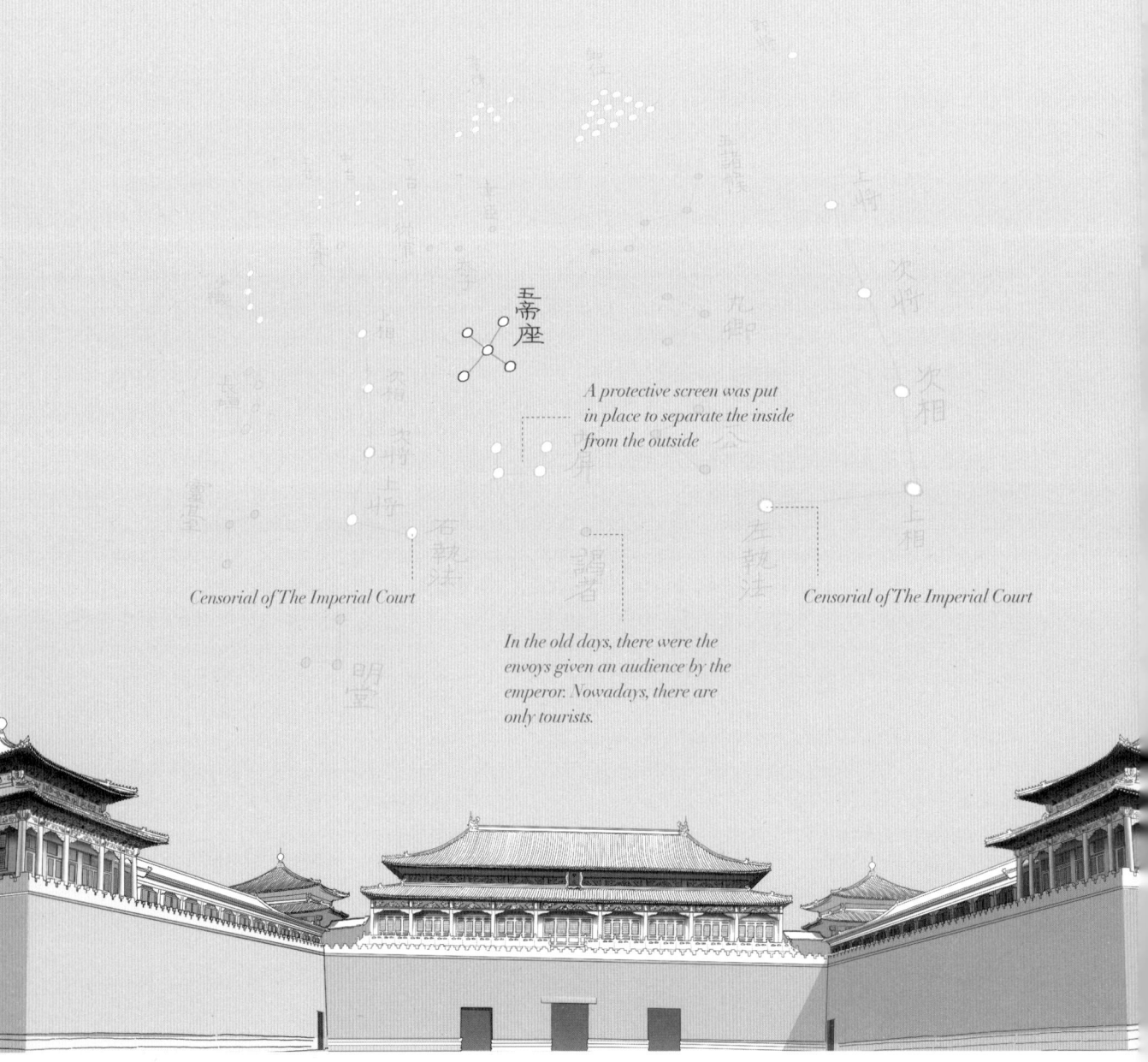

A protective screen was put in place to separate the inside from the outside

Censorial of The Imperial Court

Censorial of The Imperial Court

In the old days, there were the envoys given an audience by the emperor. Nowadays, there are only tourists.

/ The Corner Tower (Jiaolou)
Strict Restrictions - Outstanding Designs

Each of the four corners of The Forbidden City has a tall watch tower. Normally, they were built according to the standard design and for decoration purposes than for functional needs. (If enemies were spotted within the observation range of the corner tower, it might be too late for any viable defence.) Therefore, it demanded exhaustive planning to build these corner towers while adhering to the strict requirements of palatial construction.

The Corner Tower (Jiaolou)

Firstly, every corner tower should be able to provide a panoramic view of all directions (security function). Secondly, there should be a balanced elevation on all four sides to give the stately appearance of a palace. Among the traditional styles, only the hip roof, helmet-shaped roof and pyramidal roof could satisfy both of these requirements. The hip roof to be adopted was of the highest standard of all. Once moved to the side, the entire spatial order would be in chaos (upset). If the helmet-shaped roof was used here, then it would either look too superior (like The Hall for Prayer for Good Harvest of The Temple of Heaven [Tiantan Qiliandian], which was for the purpose of offering sacrifices), or too casual (the pavilion in a garden as an example). The four cornered pyramidal roof was adopted in The East and West Wing Towers (Dongxichilou) of The Meridian Gate (Wumen). The circular roof would have contradicted with the square and rigid nature of the palatial structures, and thereby lessened the orderly solemnity here.

(See pg 144 -145 of this book for different patterns of roofs.)

Example:
In ancient Greek architecture, the Doric order for columns applied to all sides of buildings. One grade lower was the Ionic order. The design of the corners of the Holy Temple really demanded a lot of careful thinking. The Corinthian order was the last to come on the scene. It was the most decorative but was seen as the lowest grade.

In terms of column order, the bracket system in the Chinese architecture bracket set or dougong provides one complete solution to the "design" problem of the Greek column orders.

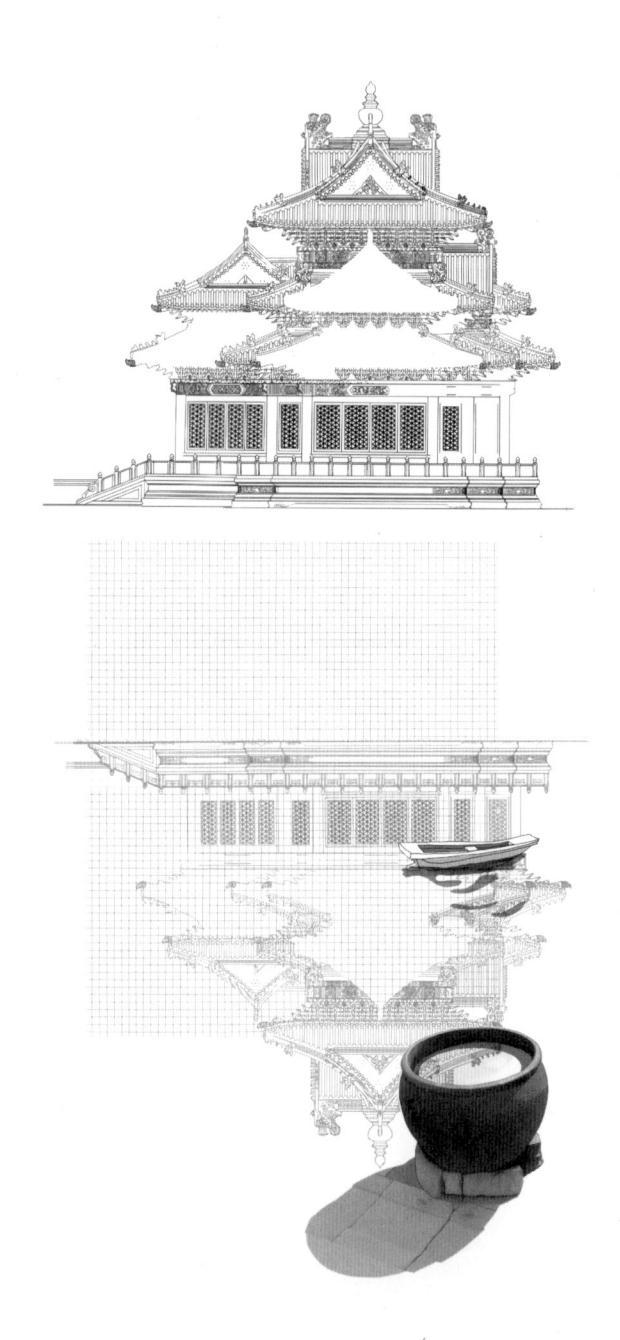

Since there were no precedents of any established and standardized style to follow, the design of the corner tower became very difficult. What finally came out was the model that everyone sees now, which is both within the league (grade control), and simply exquisite (dignified and rich in décor). This complicated structure did appear before in some old paintings such as the famous Tower of the Yellow Crane (Huanghe Lou). Folklore has it that the craftsmen at that time did not have the technique, not until the spirit of Luban (the great master of woodwork during the period of BC722-BC481) appeared and gave them instructions to solve the problem. (It is said that Luban was holding an ornate cricket cage and gave building tips to the craftsmen).

With the corner towers as backdrop, the gates of The Forbidden City, particularly the most significant Meridian Gate (Wumen), look even more powerful and solemn. The corner towers stand high on top of the city wall. They are elaborate on top and simple at the base. If you look from afar, they make the two ends of the skylines (the 753-meter long line from north to south and particularly the 961-meter skyline on the side) merge and become delicately raised. In terms of visual effect, it is the same as the slightly tilted eaves corner of a single building. It is aesthetically beautiful anytime of the day.

The structure of each tower was adjusted with different right angle planes according to its positions. This made the originally four independent city walls which varied in length and width, blend with the overall structure of The Forbidden City. In the face of such strict limitations, it was unbelievable that there could still be such a ingenious design. Each of the four corner towers of The Forbidden City is grand enough to stand as an imperial palace on its own.

The Corner Tower (Jiaolou)

753 meters wide from the east to the west.

961 meters from the north to the south.

Limitations lead to design.

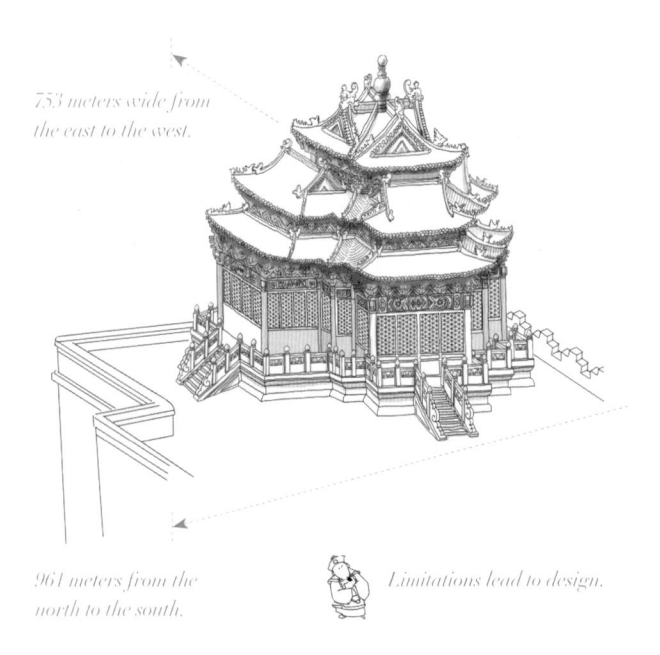

The Corner tower was the strategically important station for observation, watch and defence. There is one on each of the four corners of The Forbidden City, sitting high on top of the 10-meter high city wall (16.81 meters high measuring from the floor of the tower platform). It is composed of six intermingled gable and hip roofs. The three-level eaves have a total of 28 wing corners. There are 10 pieces of pediments, 72 ridges, and a total of 230 ridge-end animal sculptures. The common saying has it that there are "nine beams, 18 columns and 72 ridges".

/ The Gate of Supreme Harmony Square
(Taihemen Guangchang) - *The first courtyard*

The courtyards in The Forbidden City are customarily called Squares because they are enormous..

This is the first courtyard in the palaces of The Forbidden City and I find it most tricky to describe.

As it played the role of the front yard of the largest powerhouse historically, it may not be appropriate to describe it as beautiful. It may be described as solemn, but there are signs of unusual tenderness everywhere.

The Gate of Supreme Harmony Square
(Taihemen Guangchang)

The Gate of Supreme Harmony Square (Taihemen Guangchang)

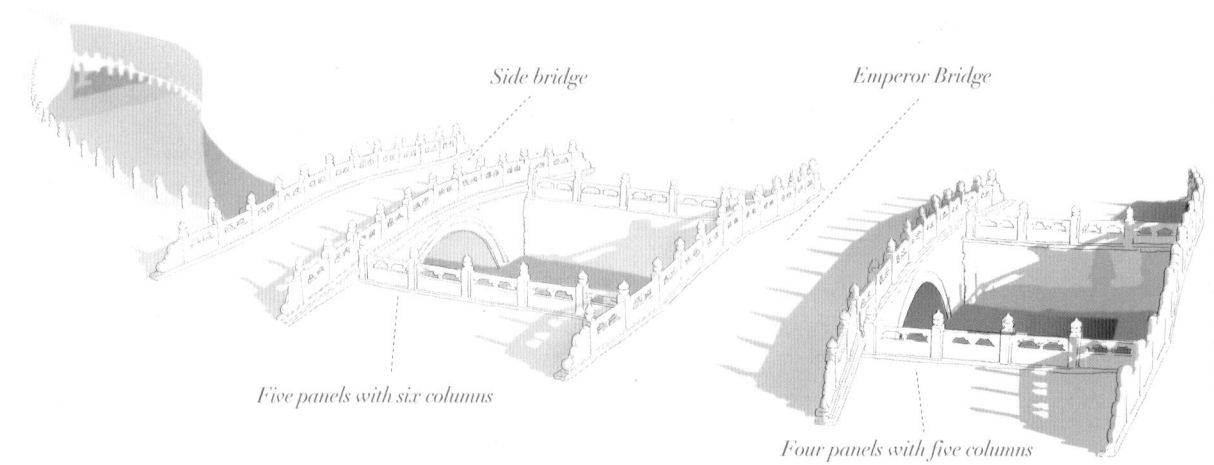

Side bridge

Emperor Bridge

Five panels with six columns

Four panels with five columns

The Internal Golden Water Bridge (Neijinshuiqiao) is slightly smaller than The External Golden Water Bridge (Waijinshuiqiao). Water-lilies were planted here in the Ming Dynasty. The river fulfilled simultaneously the functions of zoning, drainage, water supply (building work) and fire-prevention, as well as decoration. Originally, it was a ditch, but after some arrangements, it became more spectacular.

It almost seems unfitting to find "a small bridge with water running underneath" in the front yard of the largest dynasty in recent history. (In the Ming Dynasty, lilies were planted and fishes were kept.) May be, the honorable layout arrangement in fengshui of "having water in front and backed by a mountain" could provide the justification. The small river comes in from the west, (the position of Metal or Gold in the Five Elements, wuxing), so it was named The Golden Water River (Jinshuihe). It meanders to avoid flowing in a deadly straight line, broadening out gradually in the center of the square in the shape of a crescent moon. It is "shaped like a jade belt, with five bridges flying over it".

Apart from this, there is nothing else in this 26,000 cubic meters courtyard.

The traditional Chinese-style square (courtyard) does not promote a center of interest.

Imperial Bridge

Emperor Bridge

Side Bridge

Five panels with six columns

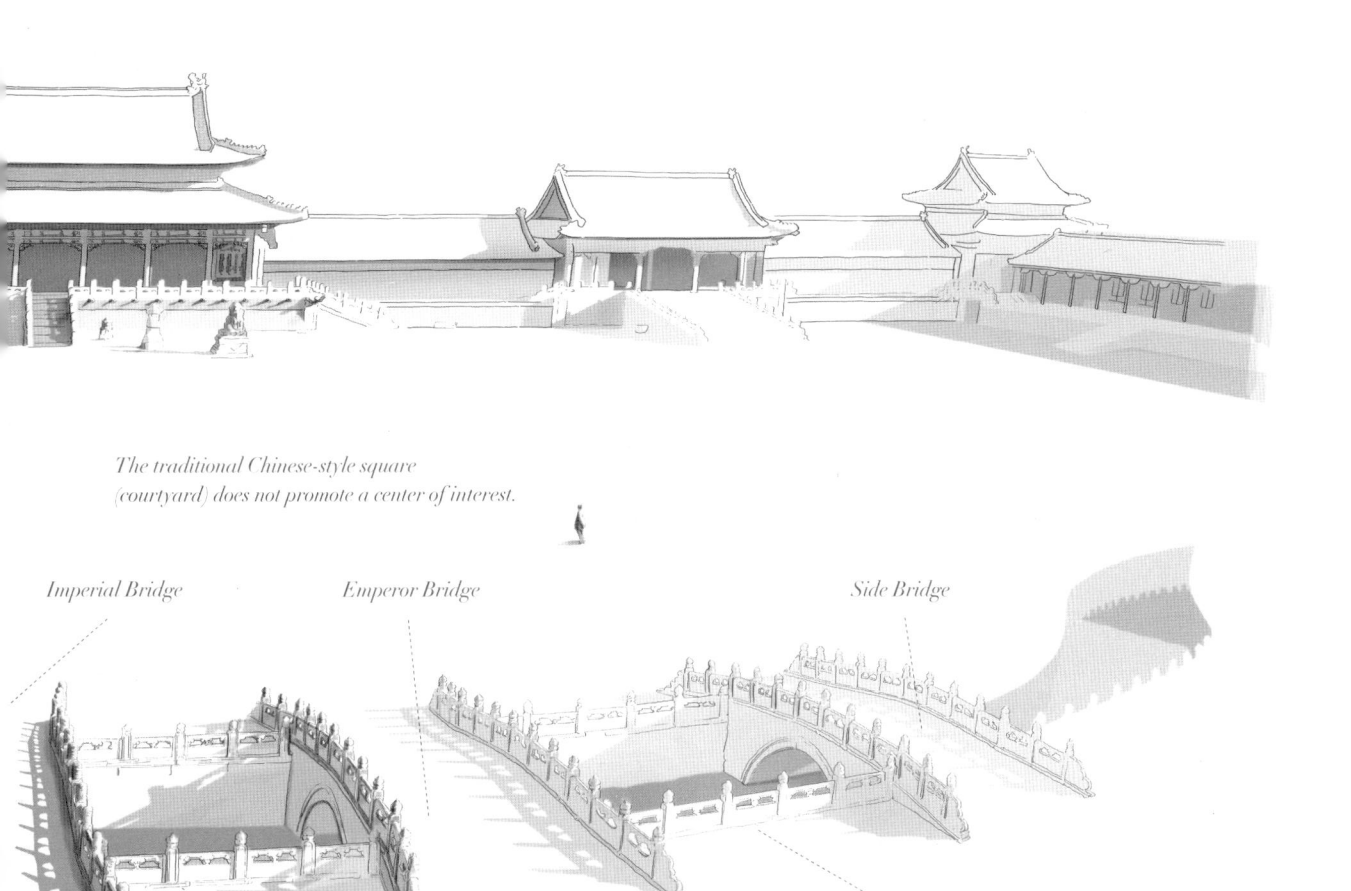

Four panels with five columns

The baluster columns of The Imperial Bridge have dragon carvings. There are seven railing panels crossing over the river and an extra three railing panels, with wavy end boards, on each side of the banks. Each of the four remaining bridges has two panels and end boards.

This place looks as if it was the front foyer of a super theater, graceful and dignified as well as magnificent and benevolent. Ironically this largest political stage in the old days is no longer in action when thousands of visitors could be the audience! It is difficult to describe probably because of these mixed feelings that accompany us while we enter this ancient palace with a gradually intensifying sense of history.

The Meridian Gate (Wumen) is the gate of the palatial city. The Gate of Supreme Harmony (Taihemen) confronting us is the real gate of the palace. "Supreme" is more significant than "big". Behind this gate is the place with the greatest harmony between Heaven and Earth.

/ The Gate of Supreme Harmony (Taihemen)

The few large gates in front follow the model of city gates (connected to the city wall or palace wall, and are tower and pavilion structures). The Gate of Supreme Harmony (Taihemen), on the other hand, follows the model of a palace gate. It is the grandest hall type of palace gates, at 9 bays wide and 4 bays deep, with double-eaved gable and hip roof. It rests on a platform of white marble, with the largest male and female bronze lions in the country standing respectively on its left and right.

Here is where the emperors of the Ming Dynasty were worshipped and imperial edicts were issued. This process was called "administering state affairs at the imperial gate". Hundreds of civil and military officials came here every day in the early morning to carry out the rites of early court (whether or not the emperor presided).

After The Hall of Heaven Worship (Fengtiandian, known as The Hall of Supreme Harmony [Taihedian] in the Qing Dynasty) was completed in the early years of the Ming Dynasty, it was soon destroyed by fire. The main hall had been damaged and repaired many times (the concept of fire-prevention in the Ming Dynasty fell far behind that in the Qing Dynasty). Nevertheless, the tradition of administering state affairs at The Gate of Heaven Worship (Fengtianmen, known as the Gate of Supreme Harmony [Taihemen] in the Qing Dynasty) commenced. The Gate of Heaven Worship (Fengtianmen) had since played an important role in administration and ceremonies.

In order to centralize power, Emperor Taizu of the Ming Dynasty abolished the position of the prime minister and replaced it with a team headed by the scholars of the Cabinet. The cabinet was set up outside of The Left Gate of Success (Zuoshunmen). Reviewing and discussing documents as well as issuing of imperial edicts were very efficiently carried out. The Ming Dynasty was another era of unification after the Tang Dynasty. When it was first founded, its people followed a healthy code of etiquette.

The close proximity and efficiency between The Gate of Heaven Worship (Fengtianmen, known as the Gate of Supreme Harmony [Taihemen] in the Qing Dynasty) and the cabinet contributed to the very powerful national strength of the Ming Dynasty in its early years. On the other hand, The Gate of Heaven Worship (Fengtianmen) was far away from The Inner Court (Neichao). After a few generations, the emperors enjoying a long span of peace became complacent . Some emperors did not attend the court for long periods, resulting in a deserted cabinet. The management of the state affairs ultimately taken over by the eunuchs, who were originally messengers.

In September, 1644, the six-year old Fulin ascended to the throne here as the first generation of emperors (Emperor Shunzhi) after the Manchus became the new masters of the Central Plains [middle and lower reaches of the Yellow River]. General Wu Sangui of the Ming Dynasty was appointed King of Pacification of the West (Pingxiwang) by the Qing Dynasty after being previously conferred the title of Earl of Pacification of the West by Emperor Chongzhen of the Ming Dynasty at the beginning of the same year.

The Gate of Supreme Harmony Square (Taihemen Guangchang)

The Gate of Congeniality
(Xihemen, known as The Right Gate of Success [Youshunmen] in the Ming Dynasty)

This agency looked after the translation of Manchurian/Han languages as well as the recording of the daily words and deeds of the emperors. (The Translation Room (Fanshufang) and Records Office on Daily Life (Qijuzhuguan) were located on the south side of The Gate of Congeniality (Xihemen). The agency was also responsible for relating to the emperors the literary classics on Confucianism.

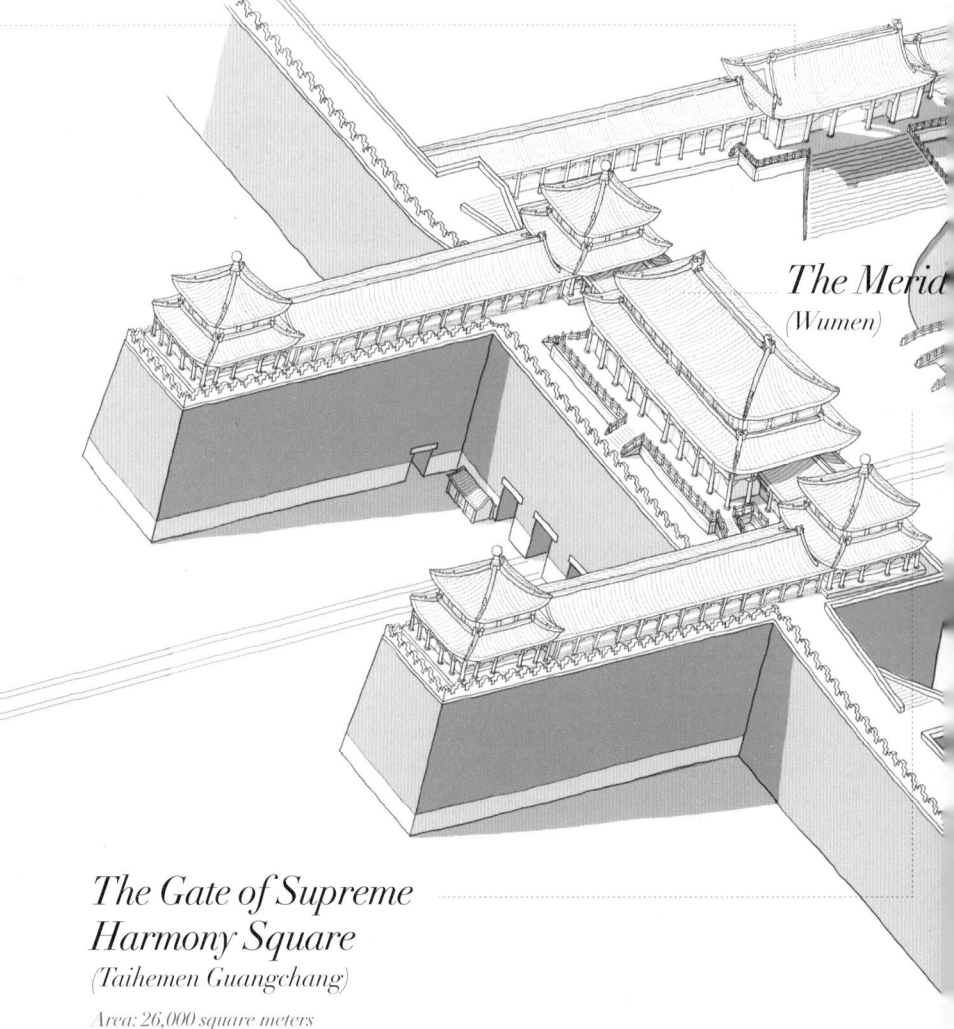

The Meridian Gate
(Wumen)

The Gate of Supreme Harmony Square
(Taihemen Guangchang)

Area: 26,000 square meters

The Grand Forbidden City — The Imperial Axis

The Gate of Supreme Harmony *(Taihemen)*

(The Gate of Heaven Worship [Fengtianmen] in the Ming Dynasty, and its name was changed to The Gate of Imperial Supremacy [Huangjimen] during the reign of Emperor Jiajing)

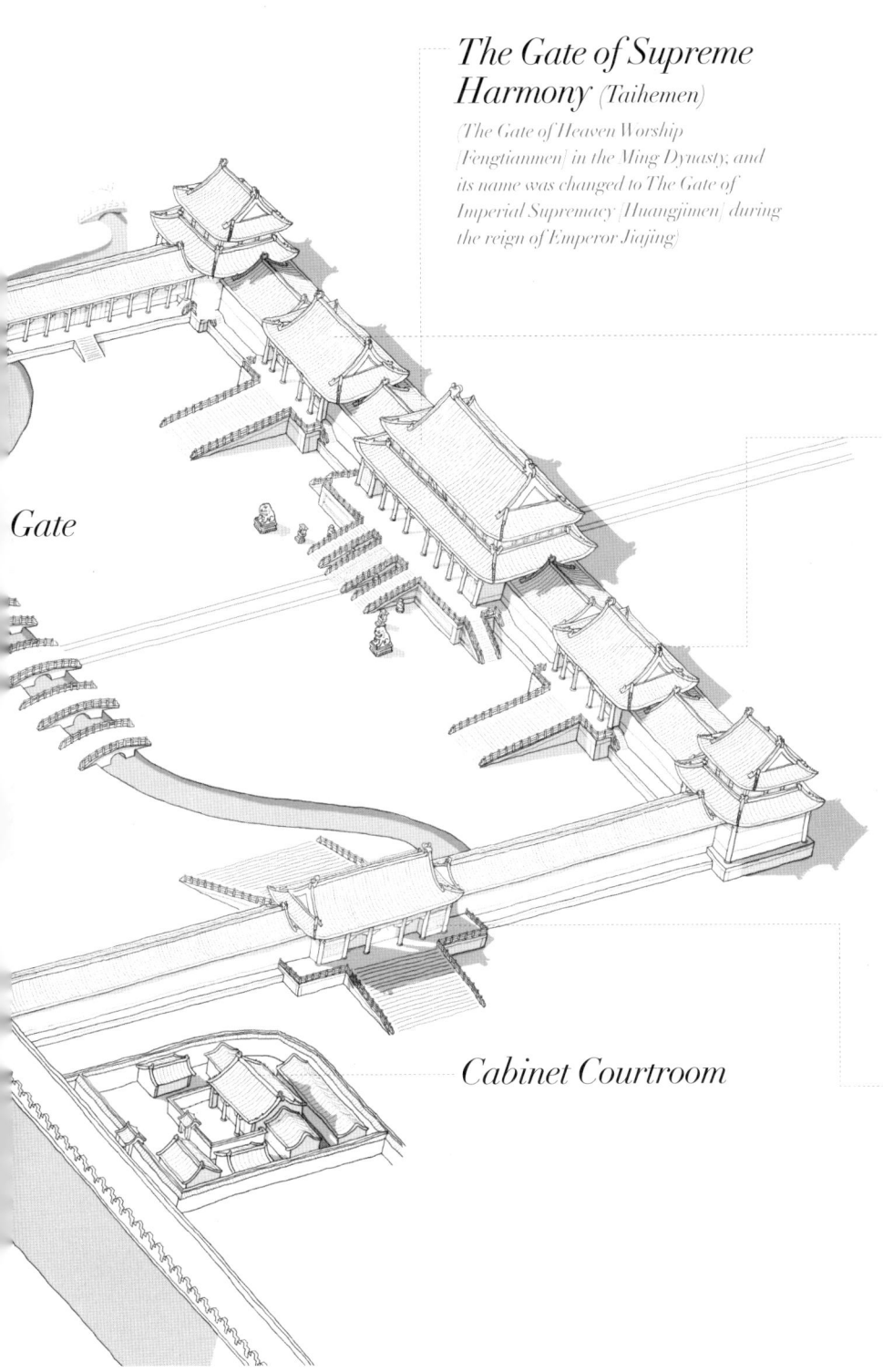

The Gate of Steadfast Virtue *(Zhendumen)*

(The Western Corner Gate [Xijiaomen] and The Gate of Proclamation [Xuanzhimen] in the Ming Dynasty)

The Gate of Inspiring Virtues *(Zhaodemen)*

(The Eastern Corner Gate [Dongjiaomen] and The Grand Government Gate [Hongzhenmen] in the Ming Dynasty)

The Big Protest related to Rites in the Ming Dynasty
(The 15-year old Emperor Jiajing ascended to the throne in his capacity as a feudal lord. When he insisted on posthumous recognition of his biological father as emperor, he started bitter debate on the issue. More than 200 cabinet ministers knelt incessantly in protest in front of the The Left Gate of Success [Zuoshunmen]. Some were screaming and crying uncontrollably. Jiajing ordered 130 ministers to be tied up and pushed out to The Meridian Gate [Wumen] to be flogged. Seventeen of them were beaten to death on the spot.)

Gate

Cabinet Courtroom

The Gate of Blending Harmony

(Xiehemen, known as The Left Gate of Obedience [Zuoshunmen] in the Ming Dynasty)

Office for the Senior Confidential Officials. (Office for Overseeing Matters related to Imperial Edicts and Room for the Imperial Mandates of the Cabinet)

P.79

The Gate of Supreme Harmony Square (Taihemen Guangchang)

The spatial design of The Gate of Supreme Harmony Square (Taihemen Guangchang)

At a glance, there seems to be no special arrangement. However, if one looks closer, there is such ingenious spatial design that no courtyard of any other palace in this world could even compare.

When a large courtyard is opened up, it can enclose a larger courtyard, or even a square.

Foreign envoys who paid homage to the emperors for the first time, had to follow the protocol and entered the palace through The Gate of Great Qing (Daqingmen). From The Gate of Heavenly Peace (Tiananmen) to The Meridian Gate (Wumen), they walked for about 1,700 meters along the narrow and long straight passageway flanked by reception rooms on both sides. They then passed through an even narrower and longer opening of The Meridian Gate (Wumen) to enter the palace. This "penetrating" dramatically led to a vast open space. Their bodies and minds might feel liberated but because they had been apprehensive and cautious, the enormity of the square could plunge them into a state of "submission".

The door opening in The Meridian Gate (Wumen)

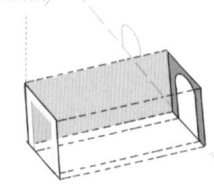

Square for Earth

The Chinese architecture has a strong amorphous flavor. Different components of a structure can be linked up or detached to give different outlooks.

When a small courtyard formed by winding corridors is opened up, for example, it can enclose a large courtyard.

The Gate of Supreme Harmony Square (Taihemen Guangchang) has a total of 10 doors (5 open to entry from The Meridian Gate (Wumen)), providing easy access from all directions. There is however, only one destination, The Gate of Supreme Harmony (Taihemen) in the north.

The Gate of Supreme Harmony (Taihemen)

Circle for Heaven

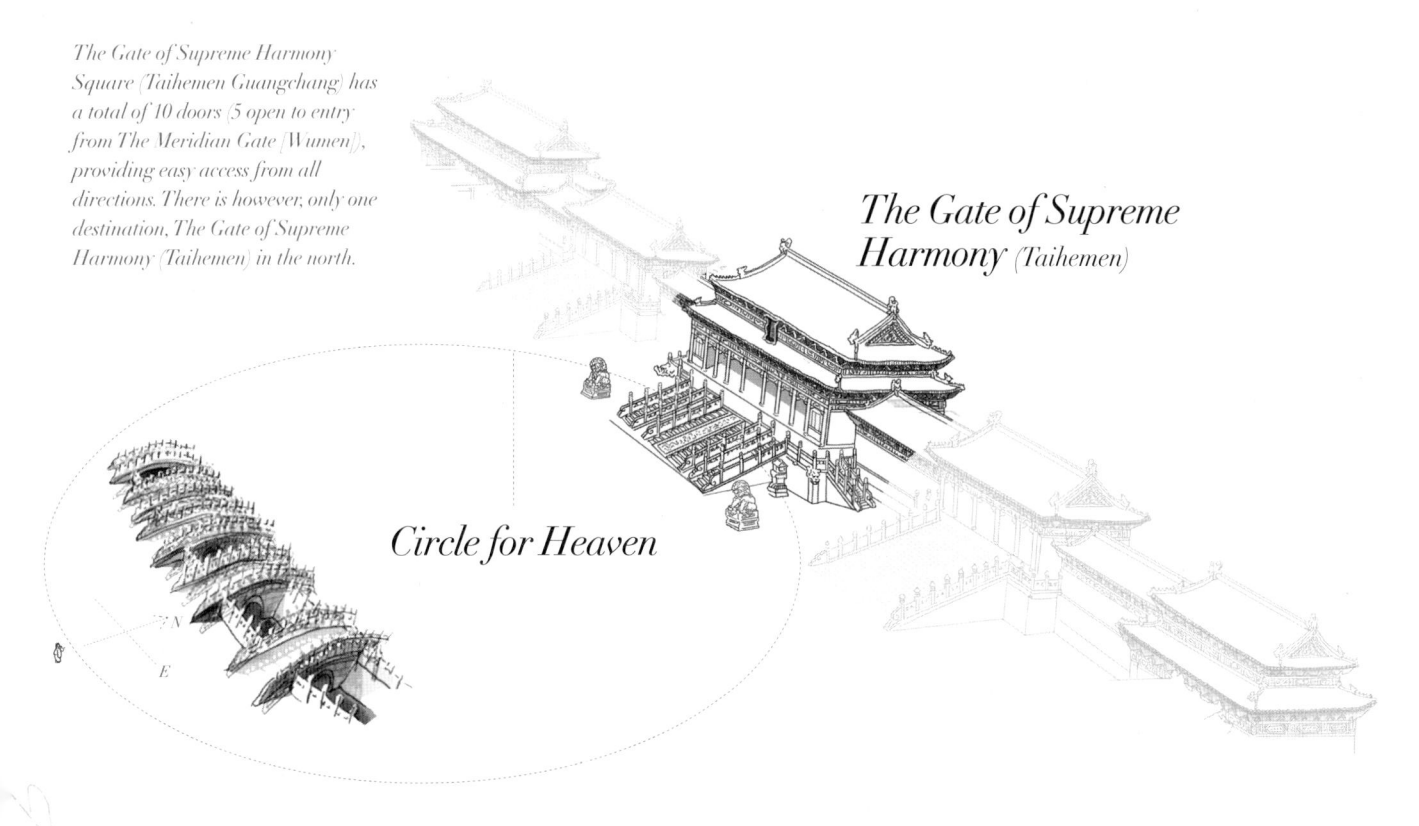

Square and Circle

The square-shaped entrance to The Meridian Gate (Wumen) seen from outside of the palace became a archway when viewed from the inside. It is said to be the traditional symbol of "Circle for Heaven and Square for Earth" (in this instance, it is laid level on earth). In those days, people who were fortunate enough to enter The Forbidden City where the Son of Heaven resided would see the journey as traveling from the earth (square) to heaven (circle). The Meridian Gate (Wumen) became the transition between heaven and earth. Walking over a few exquisite white marble bridges, and crossing into the circular inner river in the Square, was like entering the heavenly palace from the secular world.

Density

The baluster columns and railing panels between The Imperial Bridge and the side bridges on its left and right gradually increase in width along the river. The middle part of the river course also widens correspondingly (in the shape of a crescent moon). The horizontal spacing out (the railing panels) and the vertical widening (the river course) emphasize the ranking of the bridges. Visually speaking, apart from making the radian of the river look more pronounced than in reality, the end boards sprawling out from the two ends of the small bridges would have seemed inviting for the officials walking on them to proceed in directions commensurate with their own hierarchical ranking.

The Gate of Supreme Harmony Square (Taihemen Guangchang)

Resist and Lead

The width of the serpentine Golden Water River (Jinshuihe) gradually increases in the center of the Square, in the shape of a crescent moon. The radian is in the shape of a drawn bow which implies resistance but somehow expresses a certain degree of tenderness at the same time. Several beautiful marble arch bridges dexterously stride across the river as if they were ushers leading the way.

Under the atmospheric force of acceptance and resistance, everyone present in this Square has to keep on moving. In the old days, the hundreds of officials who came to pay homage would not linger. Visitors nowadays may think they are free to wander. In fact, they are subconsciously being drawn towards the gate leading to the most brilliant palace of the nation — The Gate of Supreme Harmony (Taihemen).

A Ramp that is Rarely Seen

The Ming emperors administered state affairs at The Gate of Heaven Worship (Fengtianmen, known as The Gate of Supreme Harmony [Taihemen] in the Qing Dynasty). The Golden Water River (Jinshuihe) became the boundary between the inside (north) and the outside (south) districts. It helps to visually remove the two doors on the east and the west which are situated in the central point of the Square from the main focal point, and presents them as part of the outer district. The stair passageways leading up to the doors on the left and the right were arranged in an unusual manner. The irregular oblique angles not only facilitated the movement of the imperial carriage (to adhere to the requirements of the court protocol of the Ming Dynasty), but also served to direct the officials which paths to follow.

Grandeur

The Gate of Supreme Harmony (Taihemen, known as The Gate of Heaven Worship [Fengtianmen] in the Ming Dynasty) was built very near The Meridian Gate (Wumen). If no thoughts were given to the design, the characteristics of the two gates might have been too similar. The gates could have looked bleak and uninteresting. To have the imposing outlook of being the first large gate of the palaces, the Meridian Gate, with the corridors on its left and right, was rested on a platform about two meters above the ground level (even higher than the highest point of the span of the most significant Imperial Bridge). The whole extensive courtyard of 26,000 square meters was placed at a level below its steps. The "watchful" atmosphere outside The Meridian Gate (Wumen) which could be intimidating, suddenly changes and visitors are encouraged to look up and admire.

Although the magnificent Gate of Supreme Harmony (Taihemen) is a lower structure than The Meridian Gate (Wumen), with a foreground of rivers, white marble bridges and corridors on its left and right, and, furthermore, with it being guarded by two bronze lions which are the largest in the nation, it has added impressive grandeur to the city.

The ramps in front of The Gate of Congeniality (Xihemen) and also The Gate of Collaborative Harmony (Xiehemen) are rare.

The river splits the Square into inner and outer districts for imperial court rites. It helps to visually remove the east and west entrances from the central position and presents them as part of the outer area.

Instead of placing the two largest bronze lions in the nation in a usual manner — i.e., at The Imperial Terrace (Danbi) of the imperial gate. They were placed further apart on the left and the right, dividing the inner area of the circle into superior and inferior sections.

The Gate of Congeniality (Xihemen)

The Ming emperors administered state affairs here at this imperial gate.

Right Wing Gate

Out   In

The Gate of Supreme Harmony (Taihemen)

The Meridian Gate (Wumen)

Left Wing Gate

The Gate of Blending Harmony (Xiehemen)

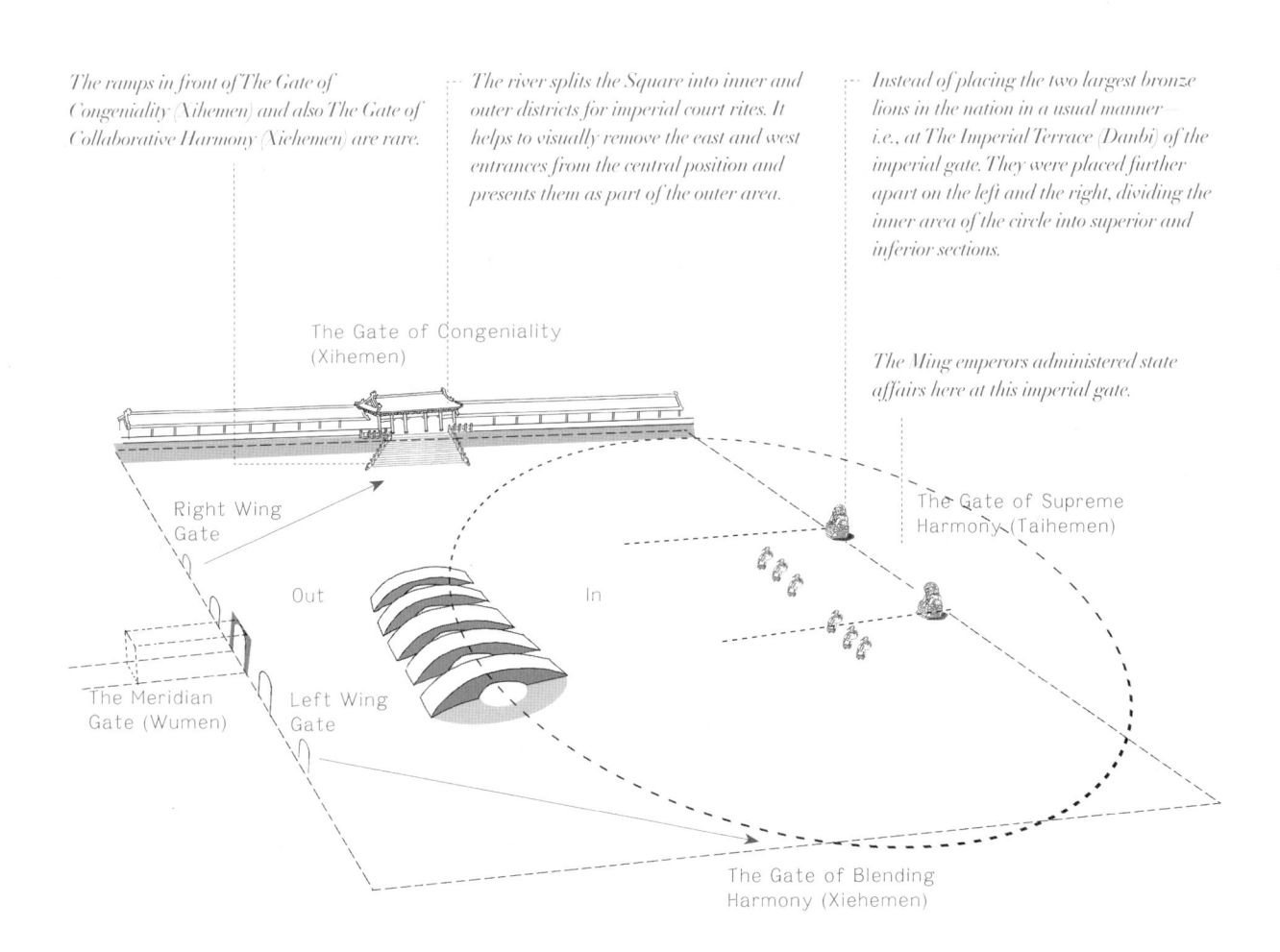

All that civil and military officials could observe from their position between the left or right side doors and The Gate of Collaborative Harmony (Xiehemen), or The Gate of Congeniality (Xihemen), were narrow, sharp corners. Even an official who had spent all his life in The Imperial Court might not have an opportunity to get a full front view of this enormous space.

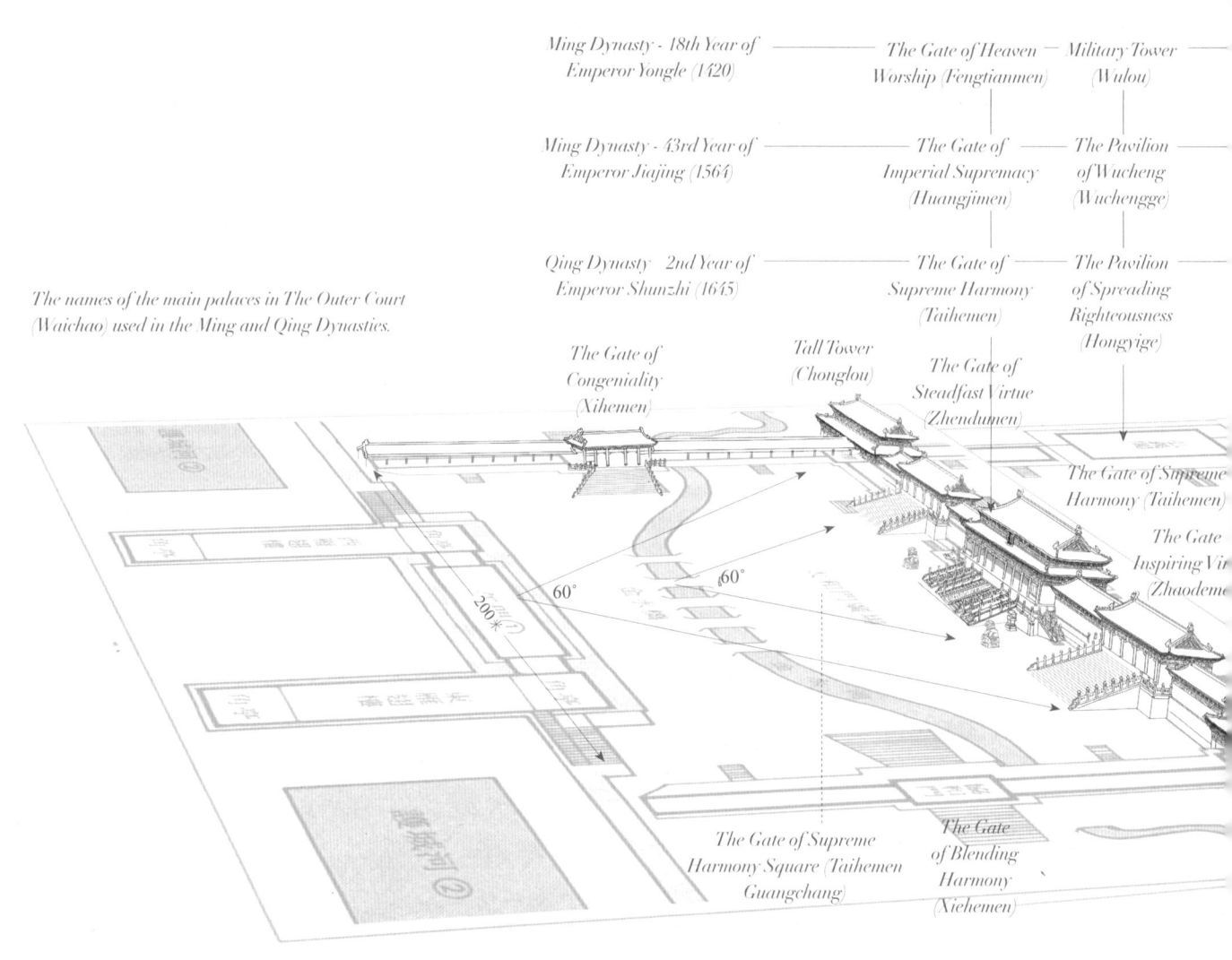

The Gate of Supreme Harmony Square (Taihemen Guangchang)

Ming Dynasty - 18th Year of Emperor Yongle (1420) — The Gate of Heaven Worship (Fengtianmen) — Military Tower (Wulou)

Ming Dynasty - 43rd Year of Emperor Jiajing (1564) — The Gate of Imperial Supremacy (Huangjimen) — The Pavilion of Wucheng (Wuchengge)

Qing Dynasty - 2nd Year of Emperor Shunzhi (1645) — The Gate of Supreme Harmony (Taihemen) — The Pavilion of Spreading Righteousness (Hongyige)

The names of the main palaces in The Outer Court (Waichao) used in the Ming and Qing Dynasties.

The Gate of Congeniality (Xihemen)

Tall Tower (Chonglou)

The Gate of Steadfast Virtue (Zhendumen)

The Gate of Supreme Harmony (Taihemen)

The Gate Inspiring Virtue (Zhaodemen)

The Gate of Supreme Harmony Square (Taihemen Guangchang)

The Gate of Blending Harmony (Xiehemen)

Field of Vision

Based on the calculation that the best field of vision within a 120-degree range in normal vision is 60 degrees, this constitutes the field of vision of the emperor on The Imperial Boulevard (Yudao).

Once a person enters The Meridian Gate (Wumen), he/she can see due north the entire facade and skyline in the north, suspended on the five delicate, white marble bridges.

When one reaches The Imperial Bridge in the middle, one can fully admire the most glamorous gate in the nation — The Gate of Supreme Harmony (Taihemen). The emperor could also have had a clear panoramic view of the whole set up as he came out of The Gate of Supreme Harmony (Taihemen).

The practice of keeping space design in harmony with vision started in fact with The External Golden Water Bridge (Waijinshuiqiao) in Tiananmen. This was adopted again and again in the main palaces along the central axis inside The Forbidden City.

The Grand Forbidden City — The Imperial Axis

Civil Tower — The Hall of — The Hall of — The Hall of
(Wenlou) Heaven Worship Overwhelming Glory Personal Prudence
 (Fengtiandian) (Huagaidian) (Jinshendian)

The Pavilion — The Hall of — The Hall of — The Hall of People
of Wenzhao Imperial Supremacy Central Supremacy Sovereign (Jianjidian)
(Wenzhaoge) (Huangjidian) (Zhongjidian)

The Pavilion — The Hall of — The Hall of — The Hall of Preserving
of Practice of Supreme Harmony Central Harmony Harmony (Baohedian)
Compassion (Taihedian) (Zhonghedian)
(Tirenge)

Tall Tower
(Chonglou)

The Hall of Supreme Harmony Square
(Taihedian Guangchang)

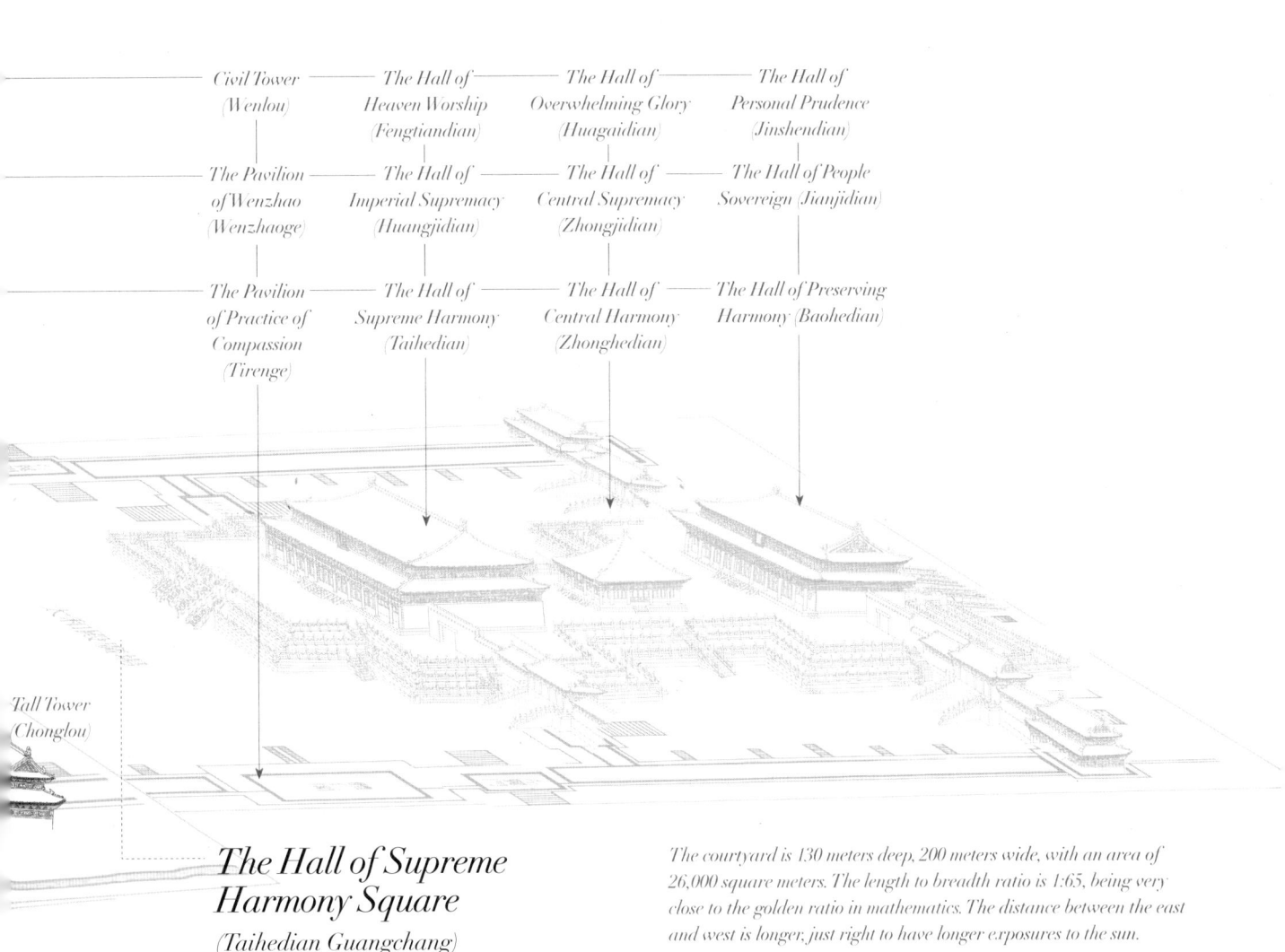

The courtyard is 130 meters deep, 200 meters wide, with an area of 26,000 square meters. The length to breadth ratio is 1:65, being very close to the golden ratio in mathematics. The distance between the east and west is longer, just right to have longer exposures to the sun.

Relativity

Having passed through The Gate of Supreme Harmony (Taihemen), one then arrives at the largest square in The Forbidden City. It is also the largest square within a building structure in the world (with a total area of over 30,000 square meters) — The Hall of Supreme Harmony Square (Taihedian Guangchang).

In terms of overall arrangement, this is the second courtyard with the same width in The Outer Court (Waichao) along the central axis. In terms of spatial units, its unique status within imperial court rites is heralded by four tall towers. Also, there are two yellow-tiled red walls separating the front yard from the back yard. Otherwise this square would be even larger than what we see.

The Gate of Supreme Harmony Square (Taihemen Guangchang)

We mentioned before (on pg 56-57) the versatile use of "gates". The Meridian Gate (Wumen) is the solemn and ceremonial "gate of the palatial city", and The Gate of Supreme Harmony (Taihemen) is the most honorable "palatial gate" that is "both a gate and a house". It dominates the entire space of the front yard but in the first inner courtyard, it immediately becomes subordinate to The Hall of Supreme Harmony (Taihedian, facing the main Hall and facing north in the bearings of The Forbidden City). Even though the ancient Chinese had never placed architecture on the pedestal with regards to culture and art, architecture has in fact incessantly reflected the Chinese cultural and artistic traditions. The following was recorded (see Reference 11):

"During a devastating spell of drought, Emperor Kanxi led his officials on foot from The Gate of Supreme Harmony (Taihemen) to The Temple of Heaven (Tiantan) located in the south of The City of Beijing. He prayed to Heaven for rain and blessings for his people, which was answered before Kanxi reached the Bridge of Heaven. Emperor Qianlong who saw Kanxi as his inspiration, also prayed for rain during another drought, and the results was just as pleasing."

The emperor was above everything. He "faced south" to rule. Under extraordinary circumstances, he would join his people (standing in the forefront, of course) to "face north" and worship. (During important ceremonies, the emperor, who was carried around on the sedan chair even during daily activities inside the palace, would walk to The Temple of Heaven [Tiantan]. He would "face north" and walk piously on the Sacred Boulevard for a few hundred meters to carry out the ceremony of offering sacrifices to Heaven. If he went to the distant Taishan to "worship Heaven and Earth", it was strictly a private affair between the emperor and Heaven.)

- Heaven -
- Emperor -
- People -
An Intricate and Inter-reliant Relationship.

The common people put their faith in the emperor. The emperor puts his faith in Heaven. The emperor was seen as the middleman by the border between Heaven and people. The heart of the border is The Hall of Supreme Harmony (Taihedian). The emperor does not lose his status by "worshipping". (On the contrary, the image of an emperor pleading for his people is all the more conspicuous.) In this Square, the exquisite Gate of Supreme Harmony (Taihemen) does not appear to lack lustre at all by becoming a subordinate.

The Grand Forbidden City — The Imperial Axis

/ The Hall of Supreme Harmony Square
(Taihedian Guangchang)

The hall of Supreme Harmony is the major main hall of The Outer Court (Waichao), forming a triangle with The Hall of Martial Valor (Wuyingdian) and The Hall of Literary Glory (Wenhuadian).

The double-eaved hip style is the most honorable class of roofing in ancient Chinese architecture. It is 9 bays wide (60.01 meters, 11 bays if the two side corridors are included), 5 bays deep (33.33 meters), covering an area of 2,377 square meters. It is 35.05 meters high. Like the other two main halls, it rests on three-tier foundation with white marble stairs that has a total of 28 steps and measures more than 8 meters.

1. Imperial Officer Grade One
2. Deputy Imperial Officer Grade One
3. Imperial Officer Grade Two
4. Deputy Imperial Officer Grade Two
5. Imperial Officer Grade Three
6. Deputy Imperial Officer Grade Three
7. Imperial Officer Grade Four
8. Deputy Imperial Officer Grade Four
9. Imperial Officer Grade Five
10. Deputy Imperial Officer Grade Five

The Gate of Supreme Harmony *(Taihemen)*

Imperial Officer, The Ministry of Rites

Prince, Beile (Manchurian rank below prince)

Guard of Honor for the Imperial Carriage

The Right Gate of the Middle Court *(Zhongyoumen)*

Officer-in-Charge, The Ministry of Rites

The Officer of Ceremonies, Censorate *(Duchayuan)*

The Gate of Steadfast Virtue *(Zhendumen)*

The Gate of Supreme Harmony *(Taihemen)*

(For order arrangement in paying respect, see Reference 20.)

11. Imperial Officer Grade Six
12. Deputy Imperial Officer Grade Six
13. Imperial Officer Grade Seven
14. Deputy Imperial Officer Grade Seven
15. Imperial Officer Grade Eight

16. Deputy Imperial Officer Grade Eight
17. Imperial Officer Grade Nine
18. Deputy Imperial Officer Grade Nine
19. Guard of Imperial Officer, The Ministry of Rites
20. The Officer of Cermonies, The Ministry of Rites
21. The Grand Imperial Orchestra

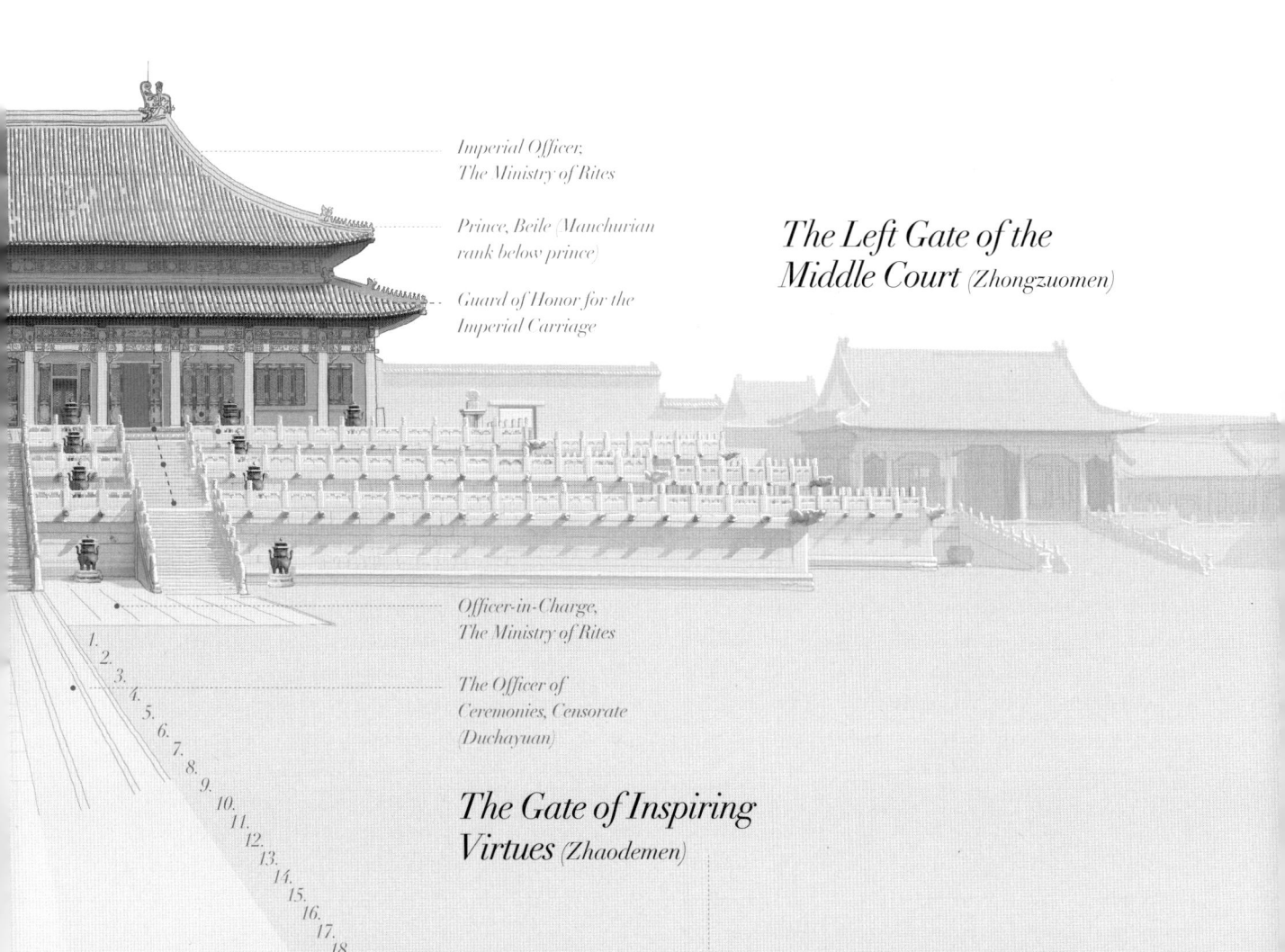

Imperial Officer, The Ministry of Rites

Prince, Beile (Manchurian rank below prince)

The Left Gate of the Middle Court (Zhongzuomen)

Guard of Honor for the Imperial Carriage

Officer-in-Charge, The Ministry of Rites

The Officer of Ceremonies, Censorate (Duchayuan)

The Gate of Inspiring Virtues (Zhaodemen)

The Hall of Supreme Harmony Square (Taihedian Guangchang)

This square is the largest internal square in the world that is located within a building structure (with a total area of over 30,000 square meters). It is all covered with tiles (seven layers in all). In the past, when there was a grand court ceremony, the square would be filled with civil and military officials, standing or kneeling there according to their ranks. On ordinary days, no one was allowed to enter. This was a place assigned for very important ceremonies and it served very few practical purposes.

The podiums on which the guards of honor on duty stood arise from the floor on both sides of The Imperial Boulevard (Yudao). When there was a grand court ceremony the civil and military officials would kneel to pay respect to the emperor in accordance with their ranks. The grandest ceremonies held in The Hall of Supreme Harmony (Taihedian) included: the emperor's ascension to the throne, imperial marriages, conferment of the title of empress dowager, appointment of empress and designation of the crown prince, the launch of the imperial army against enemies, the first day of each year, winter solstice, and Long Life Festival (Wanshoujie or the birthday of the emperor). The system of designating the crown prince was abolished in the Qing Dynasty. When a juvenile emperor became an adult and started personally administering state affairs, the relevant ceremony was also held in The Hall of Supreme Harmony (Taihedian).

Before the 54th Year of Emperor Qianlong (1789), the nation's highest level examination for the selection of the number-one scholar zhuangyuan (Hall Examination) was held here. The venue was later moved to The Hall of Preserving Harmony (Baohedian). The announcement ceremony of the First Class Scholar (zhuangyuan) (known as Chuanlu [reading out names from the emperor's edict]) was, however, still held in The Hall of Supreme Harmony (Taihedian).

Nowadays, some hidden corners which are less frequented by the tourists might see the growing of weeds and grass. This is a scene that would have been unimaginable in the days of the emperors. According to the Chinese concept of the Five Elements, the emperor is at the central core, belonging to "earth". The "earth" will not subject itself to the domination of "wood" (vegetation). Thus, no grass was allowed to grow on the ground. The drainage system of the entire palatial city is extremely remarkable, and water retention would basically not be a problem for the Square. If you visit the place today when it is raining, and if the rain is heavy enough, you may be able to see the spectacular view of a thousand dragons ejecting the excess water. If you happen to see water puddles in the Square, they probably are the result of the flat floor having fallen into bad repair over the course of time, or they may be caused by inappropriate method of maintenance.

The Hall of Supreme Harmony Square (Taihedian Guangchang)

Military officers on duty without swords.

Painting of the Imperial Wedding of Emperor Guangxu *(repainted)*

This is a grand imperial wedding scene that rarely happened in the Qing Dynasty. The painting shows part of The Hall of Supreme Harmony Square (Taihedian Guangchang). The line of Guards of Honor extended all the way beyond The Gate of Heavenly Peace (Tiananmen). The wedding ceremony was very expensive. Thereafter, The Imperial Court no longer had the financial resources (and also no opportunity) to fund celebrations of a similar scale.

This painting is believed to have been done by a painter who was not familiar with the architecture of the palatial court. On the two sides of the main hall there are no doors leading to the two halls behind. The number of large tripods (ding, two are missing) on display at The Imperial Terrace (Danbi) and the number of Propitious Vats (bronze water vats) are incorrect. Whether or not there had been changes after the ceremony is an area for experts to research further.

One of the two groups of "military officers on duty" do not carry swords. The artist might have simply overlooked. However, it may also, albeit slightly, reflect the fact that in the late years of the Qing Dynasty, the palatial court rules were not as strict as those in the early years.

The inscribed plaque hung above the main entrances of The Hall of Supreme Harmony (Taihedian) originally had the name of the building written in both the Han and Manchurian languages. It was taken down when Yuan Xikai declared himself emperor. After the downfall of Yuan, the plaque was lost. Today there is only an inscribed plaque in Han characters.

P.94   The Grand Forbidden City — The Imperial Axis

P.95

The Hall of Supreme Harmony Square (Taihedian Guangchang)

/ The Layout of The Outer Court (Waichao)

The Pavilion of Spreading Righteousness *(Hongyige)*

This Pavilion of Spreading Righteousness (Hongyige) was used as national coffer after the reign of Emperor Qianlong.
Along the corridors on both sides of the Pavilion were storerooms for imperial articles for use. The Office of Internal Affairs (Neiwufu) was in charge of the storerooms.

The Hall of Martial of Valor *(Wuyingdian)*

The Gate of Martial of Valor *(Wuyingmen)*

The West Route of The Outer Court *(Waichao)*
as a supplementary axis

From The Gate of Steadfast Virtue (Zhendumen), one can only see the sharp corners of the platform of the main hall and cannot see The Inner Court (Neichao).

The Gate of Supreme Harmony *(Taihemen)*

The main axis runs through The Forbidden City, the Imperial City, and the entire City of Beijing.

From The Gate of Inspiring Virtues (Zhaodemen), one can only see the sharp corners of the platform of the main hall and cannot see The Inner Court (Neichao).

The Hall of Literary Glory *(Wenhuadian)*

The Gate of Literary Glory *(Wenhuamen)*

The East Route of The Outer Court *(Waichao)*
as a Supplementary Axis

The central axis of the Square is The Imperial Boulevard (Yudao) which in the past, only the emperors could use. On both the east and west sides of the palatial district of The Outer Court (Waichao) there are groups of palaces. The Hall of Literary Glory (Wenhuadian) is in the east and The Hall of Martial Valor (Wuyingdian) in the west, each forming a shorter axis and acting as an accessory on the left and right of the main axis. At the same time, they form an isosceles triangle with The Hall of Supreme Harmony (Taihedian). In terms of arrangement, this has a symbolic meaning of national stability and long-lasting reign of an emperor. It also helps to manifest the grandeur of the wide and spacious Outer Court (Waichao).

The Golden Water River (Jinshuihe) flowed in from the northwest of The Forbidden City and out toward the southeast. (Previously we have already admired the ingenious arrangement of the river course in The Gate of Supreme Harmony Square [Taihemen Guangchang]). When it flowed past The Hall of Literary Glory (Wenhuadian) in the east and The Hall of Martial Valor (Wuyingdian) in the west, it was deliberately split into two parts, in front of and behind the Hall. Experts say that when The Hall of Literary Glory (Wenhuadian) was first built, it was

The Hall of Supreme Harmony (Taihedian)

From The Right Gate of the Middle Court (Zhongyoumen), one cannot see The Gate of Supreme Harmony Square (Taihemen Guangchang).

The Hall of Preserving Harmony (Baohedian)

The Hall of Central Harmony (Zhonghedian)

The Left Gate of the Middle Court (Zhongzuomen) was the place where The Final Imperial Examination (dianshi) papers were sealed. The names of candidates were concealed to prevent bribery or favoritism. From The Left Gate of the Middle Court (Zhongzuomen), one cannot see The Gate of Supreme Harmony Square (Taihemen Guangchang).

The Pavilion of Literary Source (Wenyuange)

The Complete Works of the Four Bibliographic Categories compiled under the order of Emperor Qianlong in his 37th Year are stored here.

The Hall of Respect (Zhujingdian)

The Pavilion of Embodying Benevolence (Tirenge)

In the early years of the Qing Dynasty, the two reigns of Emperors Kangxi and Yongzheng, the "erudition" examination which was used to offer amnesty to the scholars of the Ming Dynasty was held here. Talented scholars recommended by local governments of the nation came here to be examined personally by the Emperor. Most of those who succeeded were conferred the title of Member of the Imperial Academy and asked to compile the history of the Ming Dynasty. This Pavilion was used for storing treasures instead after the reign of Qianlong.

the main hall for a prince. (Therefore dragons did not form part of the decoration. It was only in the 15th Year of Emperor Jiajing of the Ming Dynasty that its roof was covered by yellow tiles and became the feasting hall for the emperor.) Because of this, the river course went round the back, showing that the ranking of this Hall was outside of the main hall. On the other hand, The Hall of Martial Valor (Wuyingdian) was used previously as an emperor's office, thus the river flowed past the front of the Hall.

Putting together the two side halls, Wen (literary) on the left and Wu (martial) on the right, will form a Taiji symbol. However, there could have been in deeper meaning.

The Hall of Supreme Harmony Square (Taihedian Guangchang)

Only courts of the highest grade have doors on all four sides. The several sections of the courtyard in The Outer Court (Waichao) are separated by door after door. Furthermore, apart from the important doors along the central axis, it was deliberately designed that no two doors in between the sections face each other.

This deviation would have made it impossible for the guards on duty by each door, or the officials who attended the court, to have a peep at whatever was going on behind the door in front.

This design might have had something to do with taboos in fengshui. And precisely because of this, whether it was the guards on duty or the officials attending court; they could only have a line of vision which commensurate with their status in the palace.

Let us revisit the idea that 'the emperor's land is in the center'. The platform in the north of The Hall of Supreme Harmony Square (Taihedian Guangchang) is shaped like the Chinese character Tu (土, or land) and probably is the largest in the world (with an area of 26,000 square meters). It is so large that from any courtyard one can only see part of the three-tier white marble steps which forms part of the character. On the platform, tall and proud, stands the most gigantic palace within the palatial city.

The great hall rises 35.05 meters above the ground level, 37.44 meters if the owl-tail ridge ornament is counted in. The foundation of the platform is again several tens of meters deep below the ground level. Whether there was any other profound theory in the depth of the foundation, is so far still a mystery. The solid foundation, however, was sufficient to ensure the palaces on the platform stood intact and survived past earthquakes. The emperor, who was held in the highest honor, is positioned on the border between Heaven and people. The core of the border is The Hall of Supreme Harmony (Taihedian). The Son of Heaven or Emperor of the People, therefore, viewed from whichever direction, seemed to always rule from a centralized position. He received the officials who faced north to pay respect, and had the panoramic view of The Gate of Supreme Harmony (Taihemen).

The height of the platform of the three main halls almost reaches the level of the overhanging eaves of the corridors around them. As a result, the main halls spread magnificently above, and the corridors seem to cower below them, looking up timidly at the stately demeanor of the main halls.

The stately demeanor not only came from the traditional consciousness of heaven granting the powers to the emperor, but also from the remarkable decoration of the palace itself.

/ A Glimpse of Palatial Decorations within The Hall of Supreme Harmony (Taihedian)

The emperor was more amazing than the animal tamer in the circus. He spent his days living with tens or even hundreds of animals. Here is a portrait showing Emperor Xiaozhong of the Ming Dynasty in his court robes (see pg 104). In the portrait alone, there are a total of 56 dragons, (57 if the Emperor himself is counted as one).

The emperors in the past dynasties all posed similarly in portraits. One quick look at the portrait and one can tell that it is a portrait of an emperor.

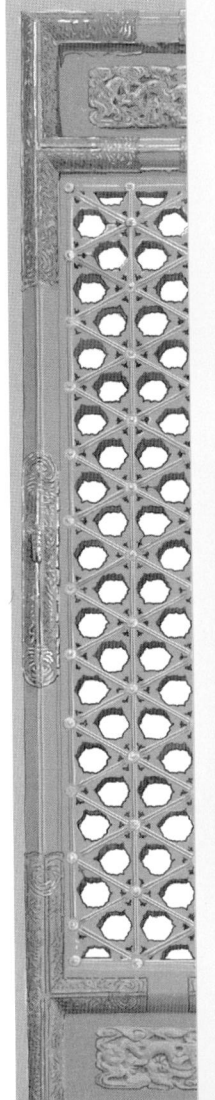

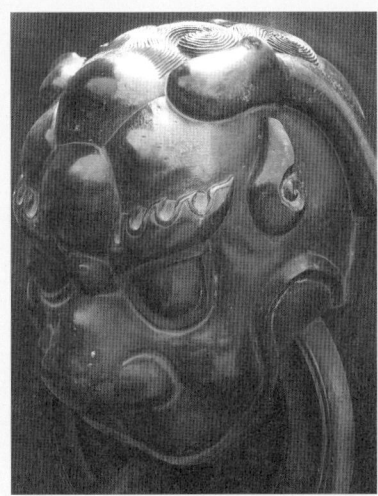

P.101

Emperor Xiaozhong of the Ming Dynasty

Emperor Qianlong (Gaozhong) of the Qing Dynasty

A Glimpse of Palatial Decorations within
The Hall of Supreme Harmony (Taihedian)

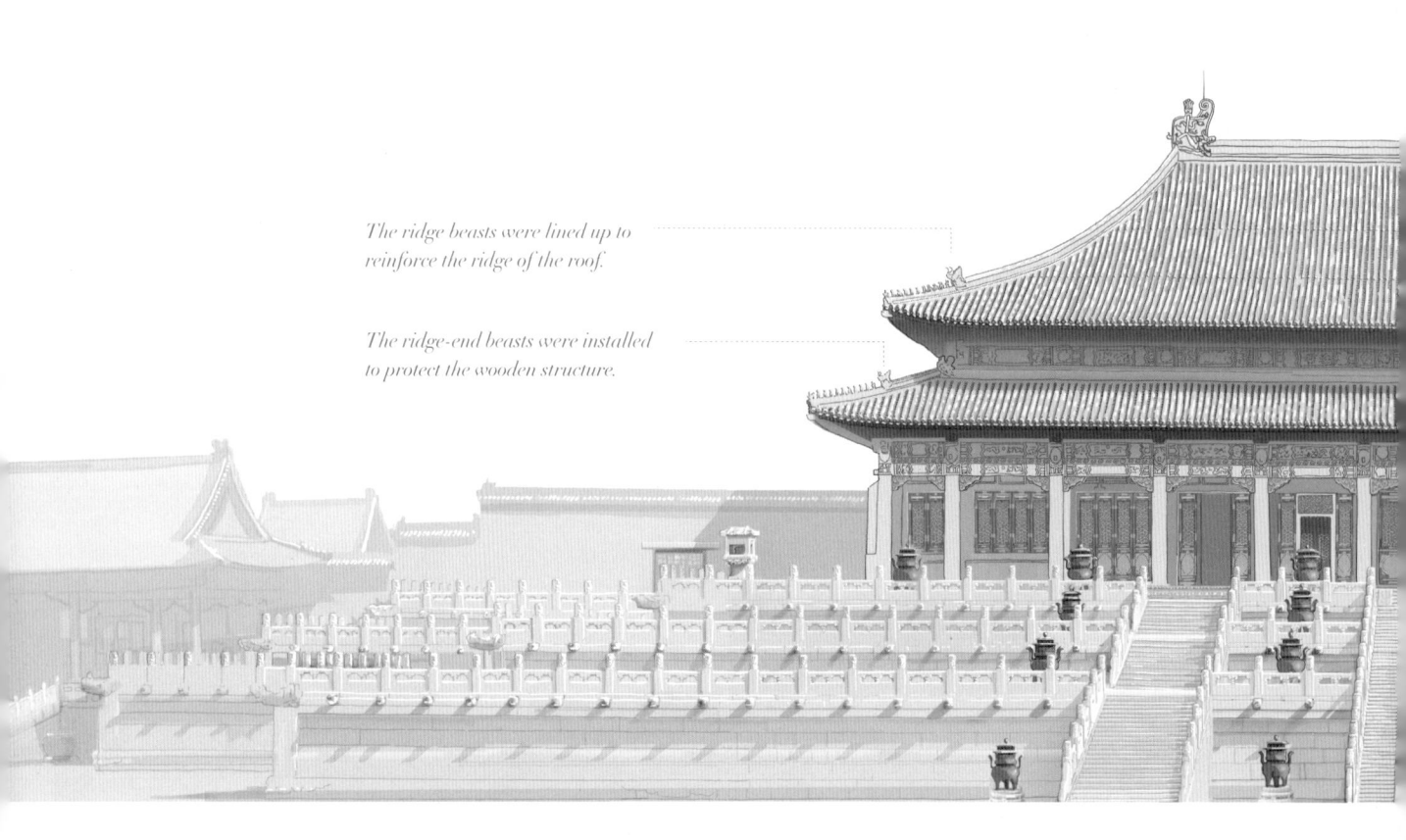

The ridge beasts were lined up to reinforce the ridge of the roof.

The ridge-end beasts were installed to protect the wooden structure.

The Hall of Supreme Harmony (Taihedian) has 13,433 dragons of all kinds. It would far exceed that number if the dragons hidden under the eaves were all included as well! Furthermore, the image of a dragon is made up of quite a number of animals put together. If they "reverted" back to their original forms, the number of these animals may perhaps be in the tens of thousands! They had all been created solely for the emperor.

It was probably after the industrial revolution of the 18th Century that, as a response to the question started off by mechanical production, "is sheer decoration beautiful ?", that decoration was seen as an art. It seems to be about the same time when decoration and art began to disunite. "Is sheer decoration art?".

Traditionally, the meaning of decoration in the eyes of Chinese is "to adorn", a natural phenomenon of cultural development. While it is true that adornment is not the equivalent of culture, it can reflect the likes and dislikes of an ethnic group. Also, decoration cannot fully demonstrate the beliefs of an ethnic group, but it can reveal its character.

The Chinese idiom "To conceal faults and gloss over wrongs" means to cover up flaws and defects. This is not a good thing and is the worst strategy that could be adopted when decorating. The traditional Chinese decoration skills are consistent with what all artists pursue: "the true, the good and the beauty". The "true" refers to the knowledge of the nature of substance (materials). The "good" refers

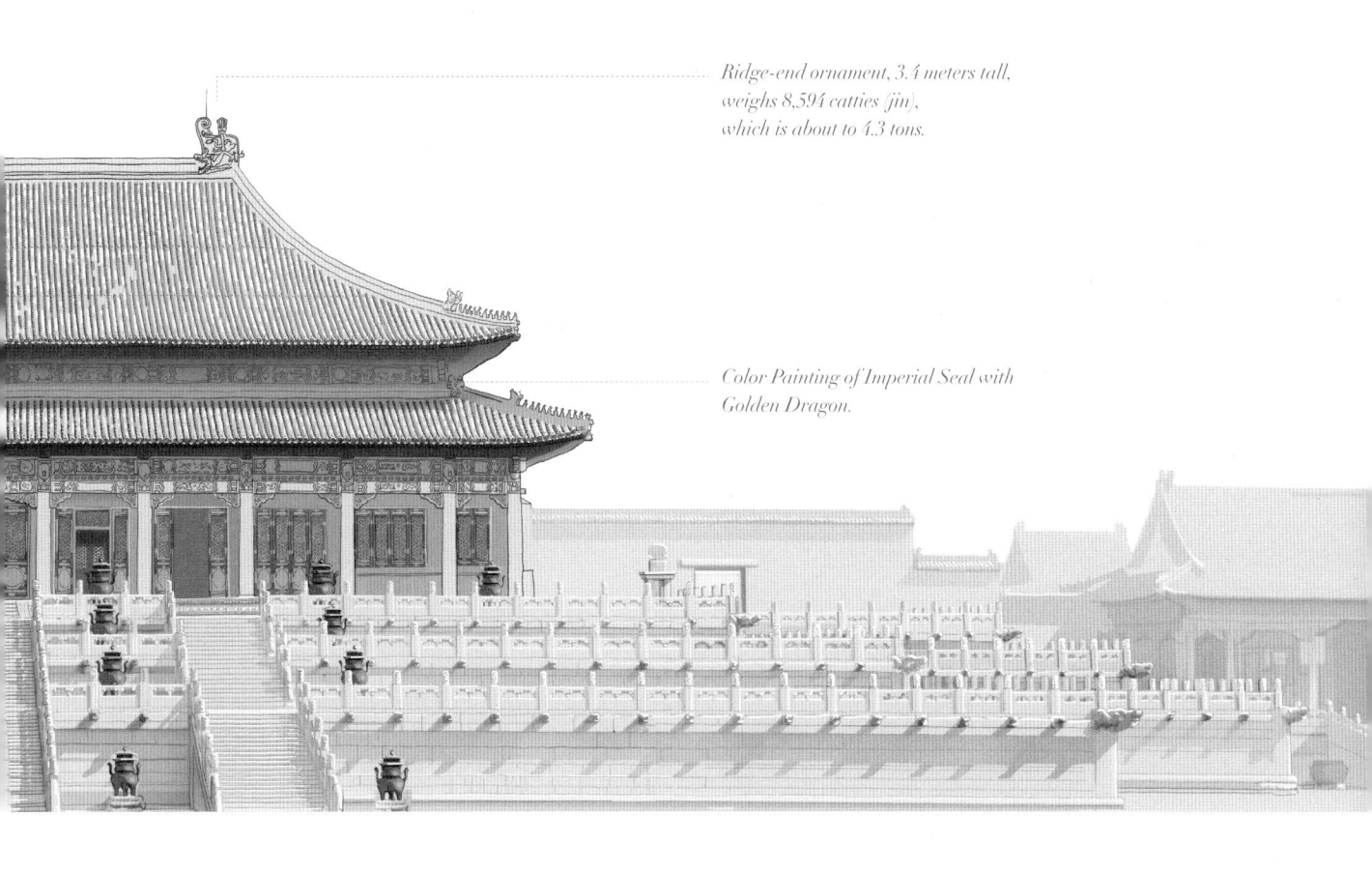

Ridge-end ornament, 3.4 meters tall, weighs 8,594 catties (jin), which is about to 4.3 tons.

Color Painting of Imperial Seal with Golden Dragon.

to exemplification of various functions (including moral). The "beauty" refers to the appreciative value resulting from the achievement of the "true" and the "good", and also the feeling of self-contentment.

The Forbidden City has numerous examples of the above in both simple and complicated forms. The portrait of Emperor Xiaozhong of the Ming Dynasty is typical of extreme complexity.

An emperor needs to exuberate a stately and almost godly appearance. The more dragons there are, the stronger the indication of royalty. This is just like the main palaces along the central axis in the palatial city.

The more magnificent they are, the less chance they get utilized or occupied. The highest grade of windows in a palace is called the water-caltrop flower pattern window, with 3 criss-cross bars and six bowls. It requires the most ingenious decorative skills. Yet its photopermeability is the lowest (only half as much photopermeability as an ordinary window). They had to be extra special because they were windows installed in The Hall of Supreme Harmony (Taihedian).

*Humble and Subtle Design
for Ventilation*

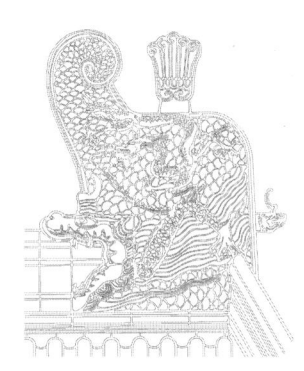

*A Glimpse of Palatial Decorations within
The Hall of Supreme Harmony (Taihedian)*

*The ridge-end ornaments of
The Hall of Supreme Harmony
(Taihedian).*

By the same token, this brick is not just any brick. It is a golden brick that took 130 days to make. This painting is not just any painting. It is an Imperial Seal with a Golden Dragon, a color painting that only appeared in a hall where an emperor's ascension was held and where he administered state affairs.

The tiles laid on the floors of the main palaces in The Forbidden City were tiles of the highest grade. They were produced in Suzhou and the production process was very complicated. First, soil of the best quality was selected. Water was then added and it was trampled and pounded continuously until the mixture became a thick liquid. This was then strained and poured into moulds. When they had been dried in the shade, they were put into the kiln. There they were smoked with chaff for 30 days, followed by burning; with thin pieces of firewood for 30 days, with dried-out firewood for 30 days and finally with pine branches for 40 days. Altogether, the burning and refinement process took 130 days. After leaving the kiln, the tiles were polished in a pit. (For the high-grade floors and walls, tiles had to be sanded down to ensure tight-fitting joints and smooth surfaces. Before the tiles were laid, they had to be submerged in tung oil so that they looked lubricated and shiny. These tiles were very expensive to make, and when rapped produced a melodious sound like metal. Hence, they were known as "golden tiles". They were also known as "capital brick (jingzhuan)", because they were made especially for usage within the capital.

The Grand Forbidden City — The Imperial Axis

The ridges of the highest ranking halls have 9 auspicious animals (only The Hall of Supreme Harmony (Taihedian) has 10). The number of animals decreases with lower ranks.

1. Heavenly Being (ren)
It is said that this represented King Qimin during the period of the Eastern Zhou Dynasty (770-255AD). He was defeated by the famous General Leyi of the Yan State and was looking everywhere for a place to hide. Finally he fled to a roof ridge. While he was feeling distressed for arriving at a dead end, a divine phoenix suddenly appeared and King Qimin was able to ride on it and flew away into the clouds. This obviously has the implication that even though the end might seem imminent, life is full of hope.

2. Dragon (long)
It can swim and fly at its will. It is the most honorable among all heavenly beasts. It is stated in The Book of Changes (yijing), "The dragon in heaven is called the Flying Dragon. Before acquiring the flying skills, it roams on the ground and is called a coiling dragon (panlong)."

3. Phoenix (feng)
King of all birds. It lands only on treasures and its presence is highly auspicious.

4. Lion (shizi)
King of all animals. His one single roar can scare away all other animals. It is also the Defender of Buddha's teachings in Buddhism.

5. Heavenly Horse (tianma)
A divine beast that can travel a thousand miles a day. (Thus the saying tianma-xingkong, i.e., like a heavenly steed soaring across the skies! (meaning powerful and unrestrained))

6. Auspicious Seahorse (haima)
An auspicious beast in the sea with immense courage and power.

7. Mythical Lion (suanni)
A beast of prey which has a particular taste for tigers and panthers (like Heavenly Horse and Auspicious Seahorse, it is considered an incarnation from the offsprings of a dragon).

8. Wind and Storm-Summoning Fish (yayu)
An auspicious animal which is half-fish and half-beast.

9. Courageous Goat-Bull (xiezhi)
It is staunch and upright, and has a sense of righteousness. It uses its horn to attack liars and dishonest people without mercy. Thus, it is always on display to guard courts of law (yamen).

10. Evil Dispelling Bull (douniu)
It can devour clouds and exhale mist. (Thus the saying qitun-douniu; i.e., be imbued with a spirit that can swallow the Evil Dispelling Bull (which means be full of boldness).) It guards the palaces.

11. Immortal Guardian (xingshi-(No. 10)).
This was said to be The Son of Thunder (Leizhenzi), holding a precious pestle in hand to protect from thunder. It is believed that when the craftsmen were compiling a book on building standards, they named it "Number 10" as they could not see the immortal guardian very clearly from afar. It is an isolated example found only on the ridge of The Hall of Supreme Harmony (Taihedian).

Below: The sun-dial in front of The Hall of Supreme Harmony (Taihedian) does not have much carving decoration.

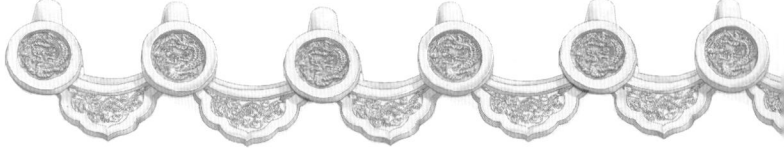

Furthermore, on the roof there are ridge-end and ridge beast sculptures arranged in order along the hanging ridge to seal off the roof from rain as well as to reinforce the roof ridge; glazed tile work to make the roof more watertight; tile ends to hold the tiles from slipping off, nail caps on the tile ends, and driptiles in the shape of an ornamental scepter at the front end of each row of tiles. The beasts encased under the eaves were installed to protect the wooden components, and the colored painted patterns which brighten up the area beneath the large eaves, were originally meant to serve as a protective layer against dampness and pests (the paint was poisonous!) The door pins above the lintel are large wooden nail caps to further strengthen the heelposts on both sides of the door. On each panel of the large door, the ornamental cover on the door nail, developed from nailing tight the panel boards, is said to be the son of a dragon, Jiaotu, who is an introvert. The door knockers are necessary to open, close, lock, or bolt up the doors. All these decorations were designed to serve practical functions, and at the same time, considerations were duly given to the hierarchy of different building forms.

The Grand Forbidden City — The Imperial Axis

Nail cap

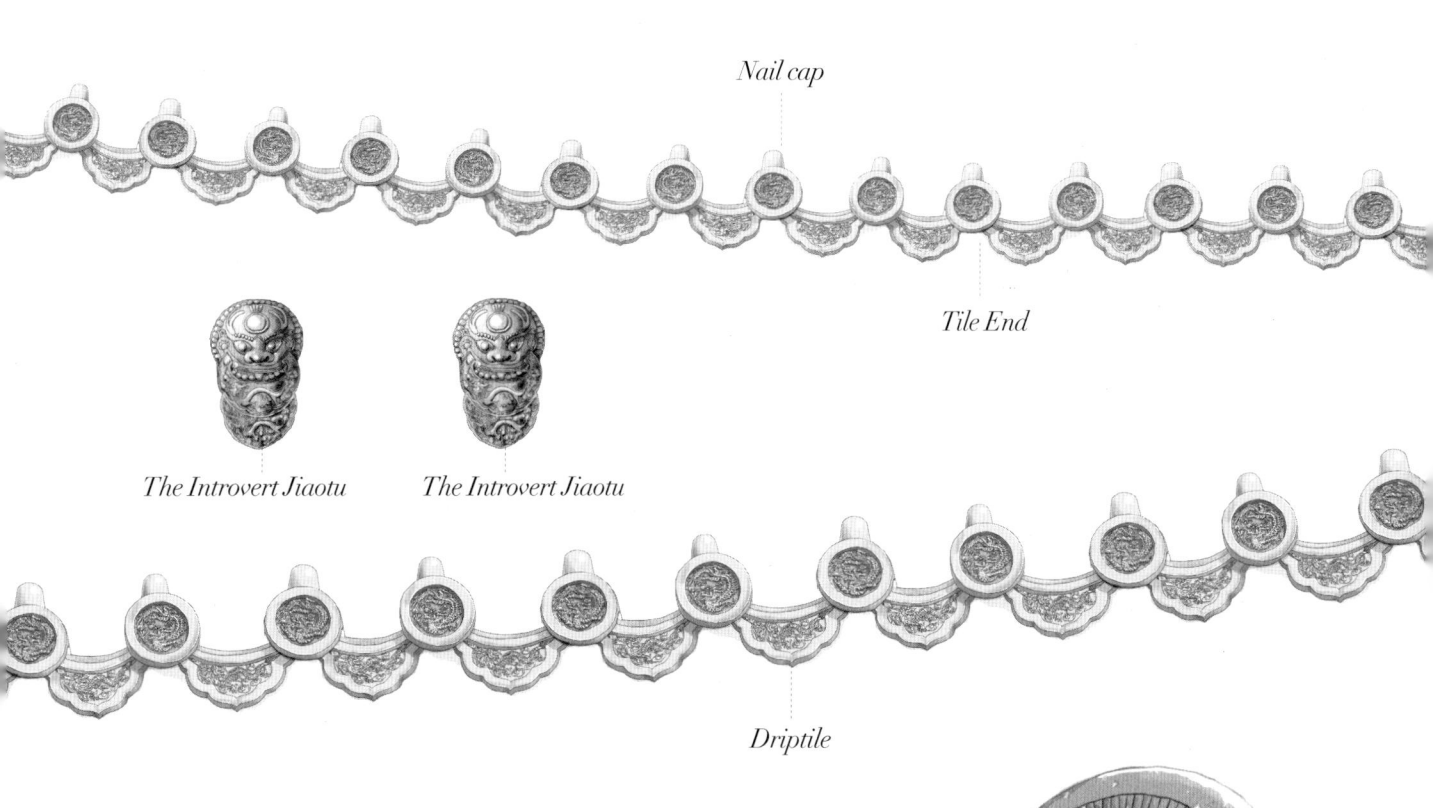

Tile End

The Introvert Jiaotu   *The Introvert Jiaotu*

Driptile

Above: This is the exquisite and delicate sundial in front of The Hall of Cultivating One's Character (Yangxingdian) inside The Palace of Tranquility and Longevity (Ningshougong) district along The East Route.

A Glimpse of Palatial Decorations within
The Hall of Supreme Harmony (Taihedian)

The doors of the imperial palaces are the biggest in size and use the largest number of nails, developing into the highest specification of 9 rows and 9 columns (81 nails).

What were originally intended as the cover pieces of the tile work, each stood proudly as the rare and sacred beasts on the ridge. They effortlessly reinforced several large drooping ridges, and guarded the masters of the palaces. In the past, to show respect to all these beastly sculptures which were believed to be living, people would not say "move [them]", but "invite [them]". Furthermore, they would not say "display [them]" but "consecrate [them]".

In terms of structure, the fist-shaped beam head is doubtlessly the only huge tenon which can take on the task of holding in place the corner column of the palace. The bracket set layers under the eaves, which have always been the important component in supporting the roof, are the signature characteristics of large scale wood work. In the hall structures developed from the Song Dynasty, the weight of the roof was shared by part of the column frame. In the Ming and Qing Dynasties, the gable on two sides and the back wall provided additional support. Apart from the function of supporting the extended eaves, the bracket set no longer played the role of being the main weight-carrying component, but were used to identify important building structures.

The railing on the three-tier white marble flight of steps (which were designed to raise the entire wooden building from the dampness near ground level), and the 1,453 baluster columns, display different moods of lights and shades during different season and weather. On the railing panels are meticulous carvings. There are 1,142 overflows all around, with the sprinkler dragon head [head of the hornless dragon, chishou]. These create a spectacle when it rains. The rainwater ejected is "like a white piece of silk in heavy rain and icicles in light rain".

What follow are decorations which can be classified as "much restrained", though there were all the means to go extravagant. Examples include the plain red columns, the pillar base using the simplest overturned saucer design; the red walls with one single color and the ventilation on the walls (the vents for airing the wooden columns in between the walls). If this construction was done in the south where brick carving and clay sculpture were prevalent, it would probably have been pursued on a grand scale and elaborate style. In this palace, however, only one small piece of carved brick was used.

Let us look again at the two large ridge-end ornaments on the chief roof ridge of the main hall, which consist of 13 pieces of glazeware. They are 3.4 meters tall and weigh 3,650 kilograms. They hold together the most important joints of the four huge sloping faces on the roof. Even the dagger nailed on the back serves a functional purpose (to reinforce : having been lodged into the main post). When the emperors in the Ming and Qing Dynasties built their palaces, they especially revered this sacred wonder [ridge end ornament]. When the production procedure were complete, they would send an important court official to the kiln to collect it with respect. There would also be a grand ceremony with kneeling worshipers and burning incense. All these fits in well with the saying that "the more solemn the ceremony, the more longlasting the memory of the people that I, the emperor, am the world".

The Hall of Supreme Harmony (Taihedian) is the largest in the nation. The two ridge end ornaments are also the largest. In the book on standards, however, they were only called "second tile". The "First" existed but was not recorded, and the "Tenth" was recorded but did not exist. There were no extremities known as the smallest, nor the largest. Even for someone as honorable as the emperor was no exception.

This aspect is not within the realms of decoration. However, it touches on the Chinese mentality towards decoration. It is like the saying "when nothing is impossible, just do not push things too far".

*(If you would like to know more about traditional Chinese architecture, please refer to my other book **Beyond Chinese Wooden Architecture**, published by Joint Publishing [H.K.] Co., Ltd., see Reference 13.)*

/ Accompaniment for Ceremonies

Solidified music has now become one of the most popular architectural aesthetics terms. It was first used to describe the achievements of Parthenon in ancient Greece in the art of architecture. In those days, large scale activities of worship were held in the open space in front of the Parthenon, with the "solidified music emerging from the background (the façade of the Parthenon).

Yet in China, even before the Shang Dynasty (16 century-11 century AD), courtyard architecture (convenient for clans to get together) had already started to appeared. Walls and doors created courtyards with their own individual stretch of sky. The main house formed the central core (In the palace, it would be the main hall). The most formidable man-made structure was covered by the most remarkable roof. It was said that in the middle of this roof which separated you from the sky was the road leading to heaven. To further explain may be slightly cumbersome. Ritual makes you believe that what you can see is inferior to what you cannot see. Traditionally the Chinese architecture is a "three-dimensional ritual". The "solidified music" comes from the inside of a building, and is the accompaniment for rituals. The spirit of rituals is "ceremony".

Accompaniment for Ceremonies

In the middle of the roof of the hall, there is a tee.

The Hall of Central Harmony (Zhonghedian)

In the upper part of the hall, there is the caisson ceiling.

The Gate of Supreme Harmony (Taihemen)

The Hall of Supreme Harmony (Taihedian)

Under the roof leading to heaven is an extraordinary caisson ceiling. Originally it was a usable passageway that led to the outside. In old Chinese, the character "cong", or chimney, refers to a window opening for light and ventilation. Situated in the center of a room, it was called "zhongliu". Later the position of the window opening was lowered when the wall was raised, Now everyone looks upon it as decoration and the "cong" has become a symbol in our cultural memory.

The caisson ceiling of The Hall of Supreme Harmony (Taihedian) is located a little to the front above the throne of the emperor, "overseeing" the overall management of the imperial court. The Chinese name for it is a fire prevention blessing for the entire wooden structure. In the middle of the caisson ceiling hangs a precious pearl called "Xuanyuan Mirror". Folklore has it that on one hand, this pearl protects the Son of Heaven, and on the other, it is there to pound on the Sons of Heaven who are not truly deserving. There is no record of any emperor being pounded on the head; but in the Ming and Qing Dynasties, there were emperors who did not attend court for years on end. Needless to say, they were fatuous and lazy. Maybe they did not attend court because they tried to avoid being pounded!

P.114   The Grand Forbidden City — The Imperial Axis

Tall Tower (Chonglou)

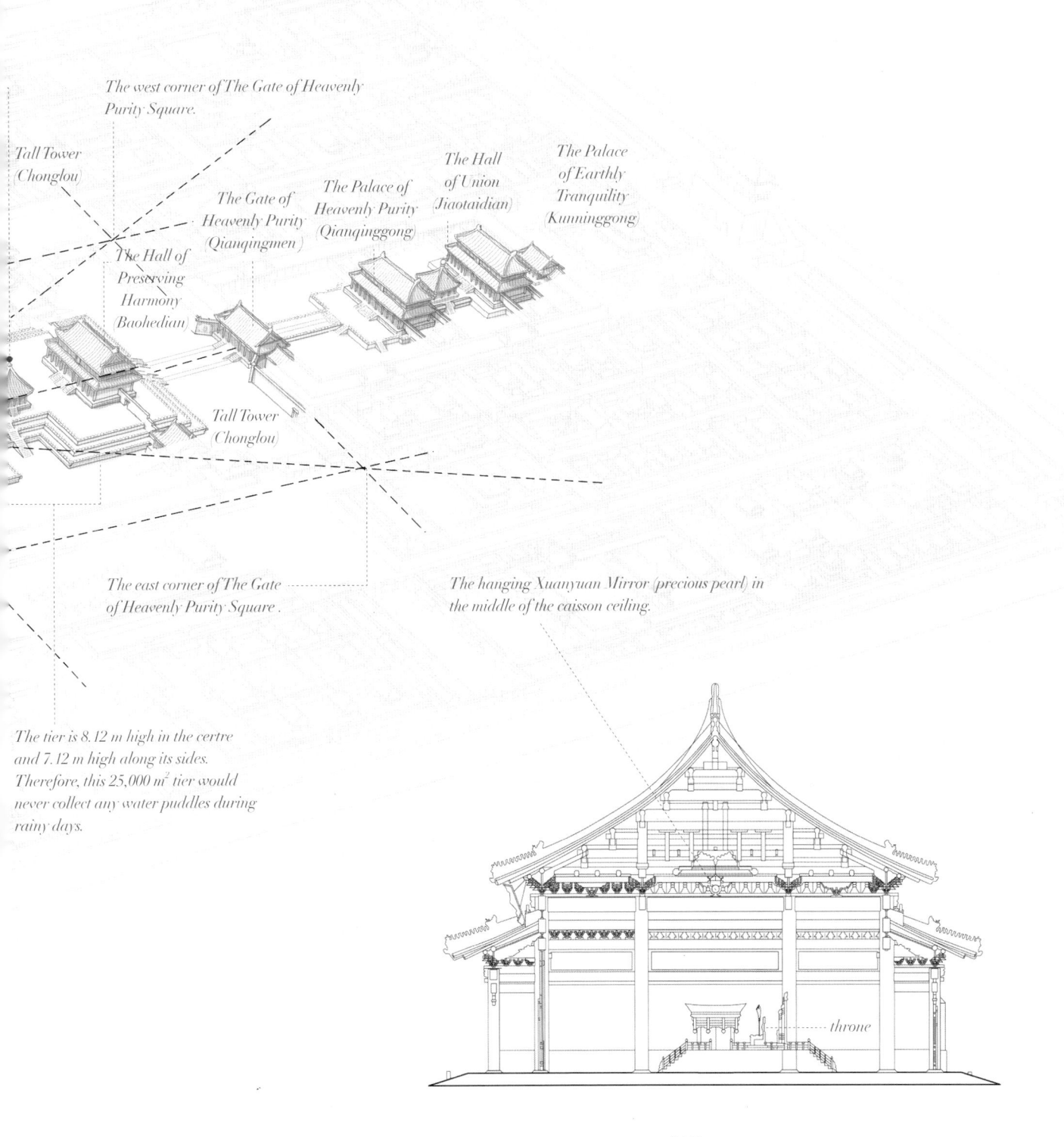

The west corner of The Gate of Heavenly Purity Square.

The Hall of Preserving Harmony (Baohedian)

The Gate of Heavenly Purity (Qianqingmen)

The Palace of Heavenly Purity (Qianqinggong)

The Hall of Union (Jiaotaidian)

The Palace of Earthly Tranquility (Kunninggong)

Tall Tower (Chonglou)

The east corner of The Gate of Heavenly Purity Square.

The hanging Xuanyuan Mirror (precious pearl) in the middle of the caisson ceiling.

The tier is 8.12 m high in the centre and 7.12 m high along its sides. Therefore, this 25,000 m² tier would never collect any water puddles during rainy days.

throne

P.115

Accompaniment for Ceremonies

The location of The Hall of Central Harmony (Zhonghedian) and The Hall of Preserving Harmony (Baohedian) had been moved back slightly. Therefore, the stairs are not in line with the stairs of the three-tier marble terraces.

The Hall of Supreme Harmony (Taihedian)

The Gate of Supreme Harmony (Taihedian)

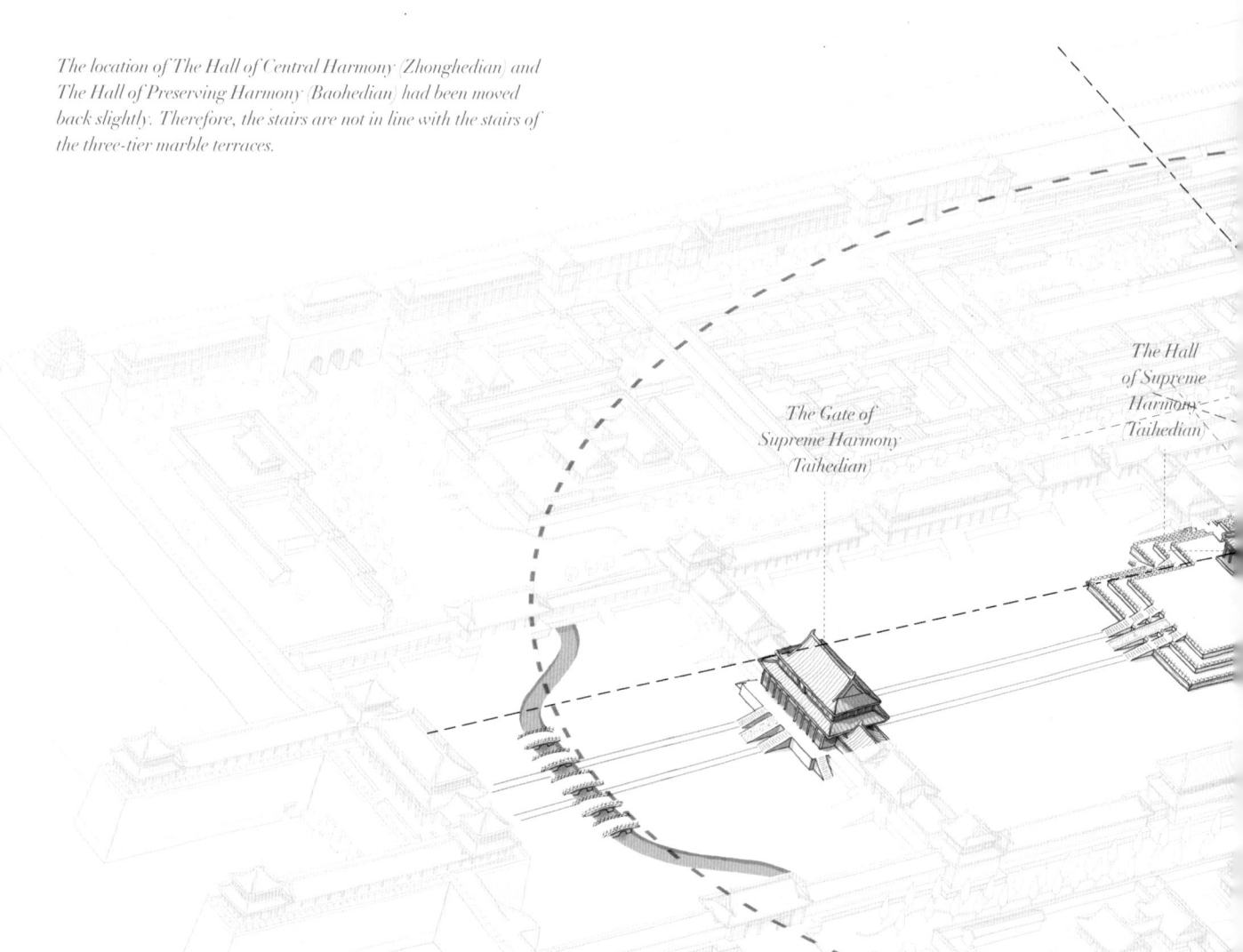

The precious pearl dominates the roof and embraces the boundless sky, giving a greater meaning to the Universe. This is called a "tee", whose creation is the most important and laborious task in the completion of a square or circular pyramidal roof structure. The sealing cover on this tee ensures a watertight roof. The tee is supported by a short column (the supporting framework centralized around this short column) called "*leigongzhu*" [the Column of the Thunder God, or suspended column]. It is vulnerable to lightning strikes. By inviting the Thunder God to reside here, with a "beam of peace" underneath, they hoped nature and the structure could co-exist harmoniously.

Our focus is now on the second palace on the three platforms — The Hall of Central Harmony (Zhonghedian). Tired visitors, who have passed through the grand Hall of Supreme Harmony (Taihedian), may easily overlook this Hall which is significantly smaller.

Among the Three Large Halls, The Hall of Supreme Harmony (Taihedian) comes first, followed closely by The Hall of Central Harmony (Zhonghedian) and The Hall of Preserving Harmony (Baohedian). They are generally called The Halls of Golden Chimes (Jinluanbaodian) and looked upon as the ultimate blueprint in traditional

P.116

The Grand Forbidden City — The Imperial Axis

The Hall of Central Harmony (Zhonghedian) is 27.83 meters high, resting on a level and square plane with each side of the base measuring 24.15 meters.

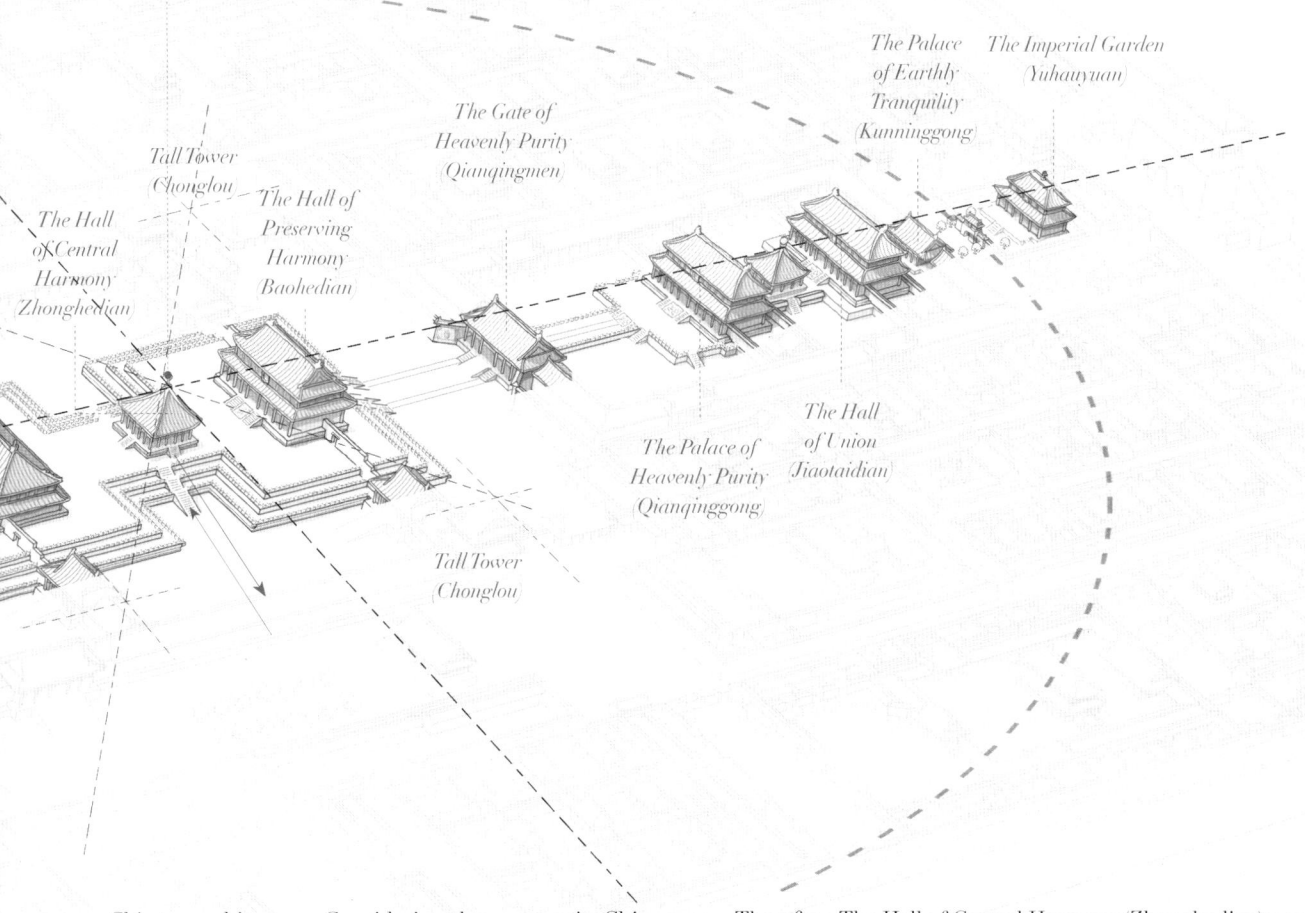

The Hall of Central Harmony (Zhonghedian)

Tall Tower (Chonglou)

The Hall of Preserving Harmony (Baohedian)

The Gate of Heavenly Purity (Qianqingmen)

The Palace of Earthly Tranquility (Kunninggong)

The Imperial Garden (Yuhauyuan)

The Palace of Heavenly Purity (Qianqinggong)

The Hall of Union (Jiaotaidian)

Tall Tower (Chonglou)

Chinese architecture. Considering the concept in Chinese architecture that a group is bigger than a unit, we could consider the three palaces together as "one" Hall of Golden Chimes (Jinluanbaodian). Before each large audience was held in The Hall of Supreme Harmony (Taihedian), the emperor would first go to The Hall of Central Harmony (Zhonghedian) to accept salutation from senior officials. Furthermore, before leaving the palace to worship his ancestors, offering sacrifices to Confucius, or declaring the commencement of farming, the emperor would first examine the ceremonial scripts here.

Therefore, The Hall of Central Harmony (Zhonghedian) was like the backstage, for the preparation of various imperial court rites. In other words, without the presence of The Hall of Central Harmony (Zhonghedian), no ceremonial activities could possibly be smoothly carried out.

The Hall of Central Harmony (Zhonghedian) as the Central Point. If one looks closely, one will find that the flights of steps on the east and west side of The Hall of Central Harmony (Zhonghedian) are slightly out of sync with the flights of steps of the three-tiered marble terraces. This is because in the Qing Dynasty, The Hall of Central

P.117

Accompaniment for Ceremonies

Harmony (Zhonghedian) and The Hall of Preserving Harmony (Baohedian) had been moved back slightly. (The stairs on the side of the Hall do not directly face the bay of the main hall. However, this rearrangement makes the space in front of the Halls more prominent.)

Even so, this hall which rests on a square plane is situated roughly in the central position in this section of the courtyard. It is a typical "centrally located" arrangement (This arrangement is not rare in China, but is more popular in the Western world). It allows people to walk around the main building, and observe the independent, self-contained sculptural structure unit. What is more special is that The Hall of Central Harmony (Zhonghedian) belongs to the four-cornered pyramidal pattern. All four sides have penetrating partition doors to dissipate any claustrophobic atmosphere. The Hall appears to be a magnificent pavilion house, just like the traditional "hallway pattern". When it was first built in the Ming Dynasty, its name was The Hall of Magnificent Canopy (Huagaidian). Rising between the sloping roofs of the great halls, whether it is a bright gold pearl or merely a surging drop of golden water. I'll leave it to your imagination!

The symmetrical elevations on the four sides subtly divided the hall into two administrative districts of different natures. The map of The Forbidden City shows that if you go from The Hall of Central Harmony (Zhonghedian) back to The Golden Water Bridge (Jinshuiqiao) where it has just passed The Meridian Gate (Wumen), and apply the same distance to the north, it will hit the entrance to The Imperial Garden (Yuhuayuan). Within this middle section of the central axis, there is no vegetation at all. This could be for security reasons (to prevent intruders using trees as cover), but it is generally believed that builders were aware of the mutual restriction of the Five Elements. Since the "yellow earth (which the emperor belonged) is in the center", earth-breaking vegetation needs to be strictly limited. But, beyond this section, it is full of "organic and volatile" elements.

*The Hall of
Central Harmony
(Zhonghedian)*

*The Hall of
Preserving Harmony
(Baohedian)*

In the early years of the Qing Dynasty, The Inner Court (Neichao) was seriously dilapidated. The Gate of Heavenly Purity (Qianqinggong) had to be renovated thoroughly. The Hall of Preserving Harmony (Baohedian) also became the emperor's resting place in the two reigns of Shunzhi and Kangxi.

The Hall of Preserving Harmony
(Baohedian)

In the early years of the Ming Dynasty, it was named The Hall of Personal Prudence (Jinshendian). In the 43rd Year of Jiajing (1564), it was rebuilt and renamed The Hall of Establishing Supremacy (Jianjidian). When the Qing Dynasty usurped power, its name was changed to The Hall of Preserving Harmony (Baohedian).

Ceremonial rituals involved dining. Apart from being used for ceremonial activities related to administration, the Three Large Halls were also used to hold sumptuous banquets for the officials. These were often held in The Hall of Preserving Harmony (Baohedian). The "column reduction" method was used in the construction of this hall, leaving the hall wide open and was therefore an ideal venue to hold banquets. During the years of Jiajing in the Ming Dynasty, the imperial kitchen had 4,100 cooking staff. You can imagine how pompous the imperial banquets were! Here in The Hall of Preserving Harmony (Baohedian), banquets were granted to feudal lords, princes, and civil and military ministers to celebrate seasonal festivals and birthdays. Family banquets were held in the palaces of The Inner Court (Neichao).

After the 55th Year of Qianlong (1790). The venue for the highest-level selective imperial civil examination (The Final Imperial Examination [dianshi]) was changed from The Hall of Supreme Harmony (Taihedian) to The Hall of Preserving Harmony (Baohedian). In ancient China, the studious trend was prevalent. The examination system was already well established in the Sui and Tang Dynasties (589-905). Such a system basically continued without interruption except under unusual circumstances (outbreaks of wars or invasions from foreign tribes). Up to the beginning of the Qing Dynasty, the education system was more advanced than that of other nations. In the Qing Dynasty, the different levels of examination were generally as follows:

Accompaniment for Ceremonies

Tongsheng — for anyone, without age limit, who is not a qualified student of a school formally recognised by the nation.

Xiucai — for those who have passed the examination at the county level.

Juren — for those who have passed the triennial provincial level examination after having obtained the Xiucai qualification. In the national government bureaucracy, Juren is entitled to receive a stipend.

Gongshi — for Jurens who have passed a joint examination held triennially in the capital. Held in the Fall, it was also known as The Fall Imperial Examinaiton (qiuwei).

The Final Imperial Examination (dianshi) — Gongshis are automatically qualified to sit the highest level of examination held in the following spring in The Hall of Golden Chimes (Jinluanbaodian) inside The Imperial Palace. This is also known as The Spring Imperial Examination (chunwei).

The process of The Final Imperial Examination (dianshi) is generally as follows:
In the Qing Dynasty the examination period usually started on April 21. The Gongshi would don their court attire (as stipulated by court rules), follow the officials of The Ministry of Ceremonies and The Ministry of Rites, and enter The Forbidden City through the left and right side doors of The Meridian Gate (Wumen). When they reached The Imperial Terrace (Danbi) of The Hall of Preserving Harmony (Baohedian), they waited until the end of the ceremonies held inside the Hall was finished. Then they would go inside the Hall to sit the examination. The examination papers had to be submitted before sunset.

The completed examination papers were then sent immediately to The Left Gate of the Middle Court (Zhongzuomen) beside The Hall of Supreme Harmony (Taihedian) and sealed by specially appointed officials. (The examination papers were sealed along with the names to avoid fraud). Then they were packed in boxes and sent to the reception room inside The Meridian Gate (Wumen), where grading ministers would spend two days checking the examination papers.

In early hours of the third day, the grading ministers would present the top ten examination papers to the emperor, who would personally choose the three best scholars and award them what is commonly known as Number One Scholar (zhuangyuan), Number Two Scholar, (bangyan), and Number Three Scholar (Tanhua).

After thanking the emperor, the three newly awarded top scholars would proudly leave the palace through the middle door opening of The Meridian Gate (Wumen), bathing in the Spring breeze.

There are three grades in the central selection of successful candidates:
Grade One is called Successful Candidate with a Good Pass (Jinshijidi); usually there are three: Number One Scholar (zhuangyuan), Number Two Scholar, (bangyan), and Number Three Scholar (Tanhua).
Grade Two is called Successful Candidate with a Pass, (Cijinshijidi).
Grade Three is called Equivalent to Successful Candidate with a Pass, (Citongjinshijidi).

/ The Three Large Halls under the Sky

The Three Large Halls occupied the most important position in the large central axis. The courtyards followed an absolutely symmetrical format to symbolize the perpetuity of the imperial power. The first one, The Hall of Supreme Harmony (Taihedian), built near the end of the 17th Century and rebuilt in the early years of the Qing Dynasty; was constructed in accordance to the most honorable specifications. The structure fastidious and orderly. Inside the Hall stand 72 huge columns, demonstrating the most honorable grandeur belonging to the Son of Heaven.

The Hall of Preserving Harmony (Baohedian, built around early 17th Century, in the second half of the Ming Dynasty) adopted the "column reduction" approach as described in the "Construction Specifications" (Yingzhaofashi) of the Song Dynasty. Six wooden columns that were to be placed in the middle front portion of the Hall were eliminated from the heavy and thick beam frame structure. Massive space was created without the slightest effect on the overall structure of the Hall. This achievement was outstanding.

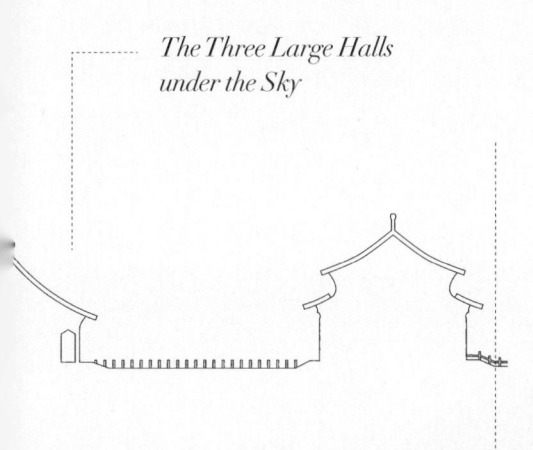

The Three Large Halls under the Sky

The component parts of the tee at the top of The Hall of Central Harmony (Zhonghedian)

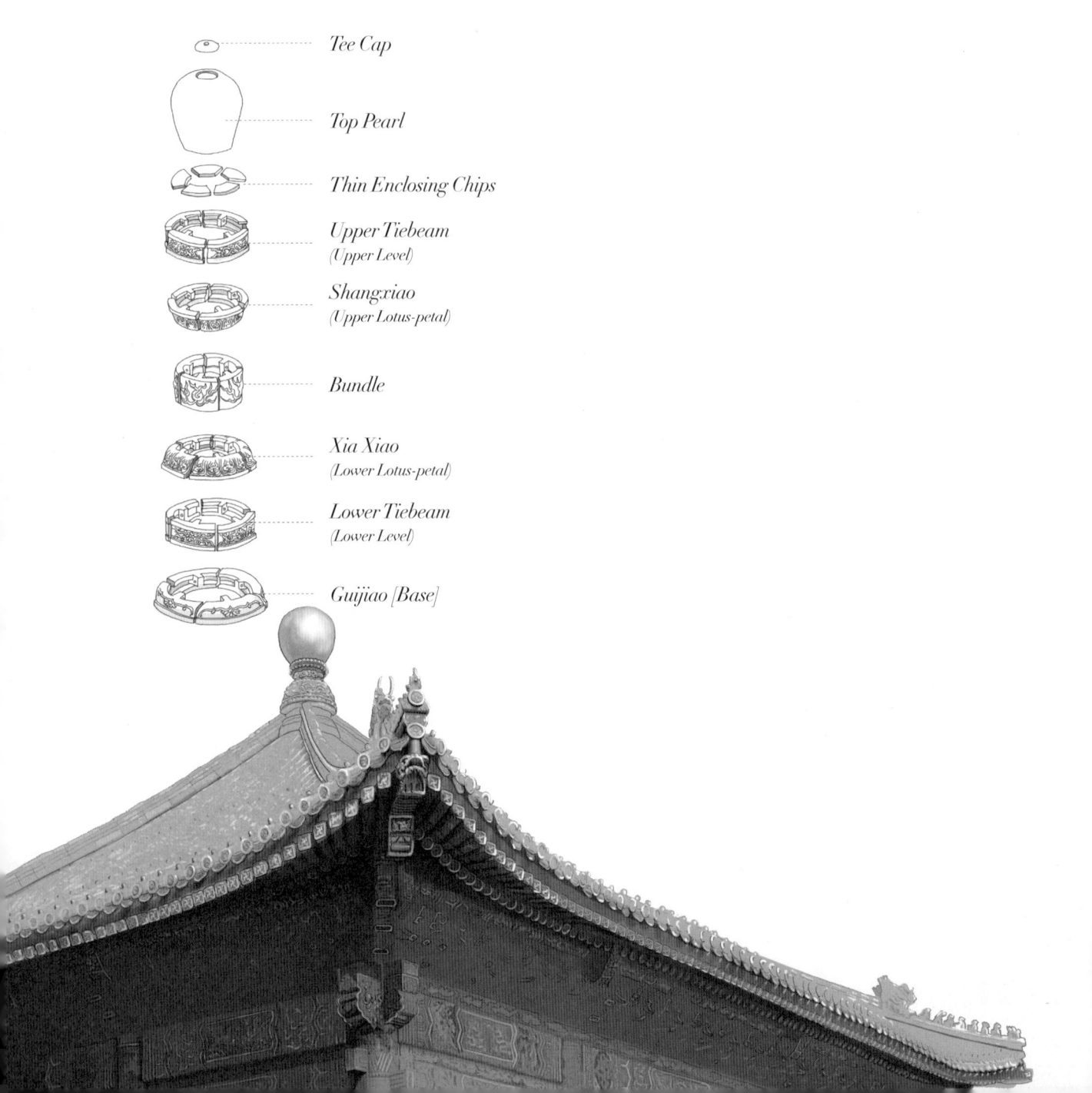

Tee Cap

Top Pearl

Thin Enclosing Chips

Upper Tiebeam
(Upper Level)

Shangxiao
(Upper Lotus-petal)

Bundle

Xia Xiao
(Lower Lotus-petal)

Lower Tiebeam
(Lower Level)

Guijiao [Base]

The different heights of the halls create a high-low-high (a horse-shoe shaped) rhythm resembling the movements of fish and dragon.

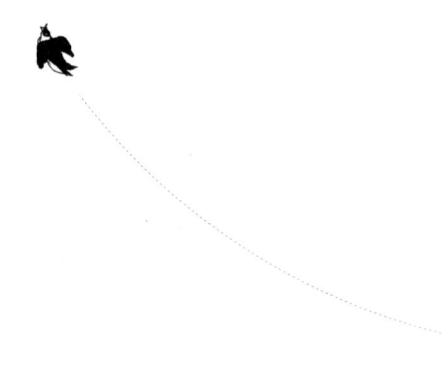

Horizontally the Three Large Halls are a smaller square in between two rectangles.

An outstanding structure with "column reduction".

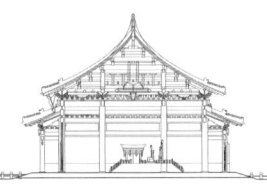

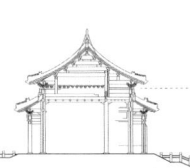

The Tee

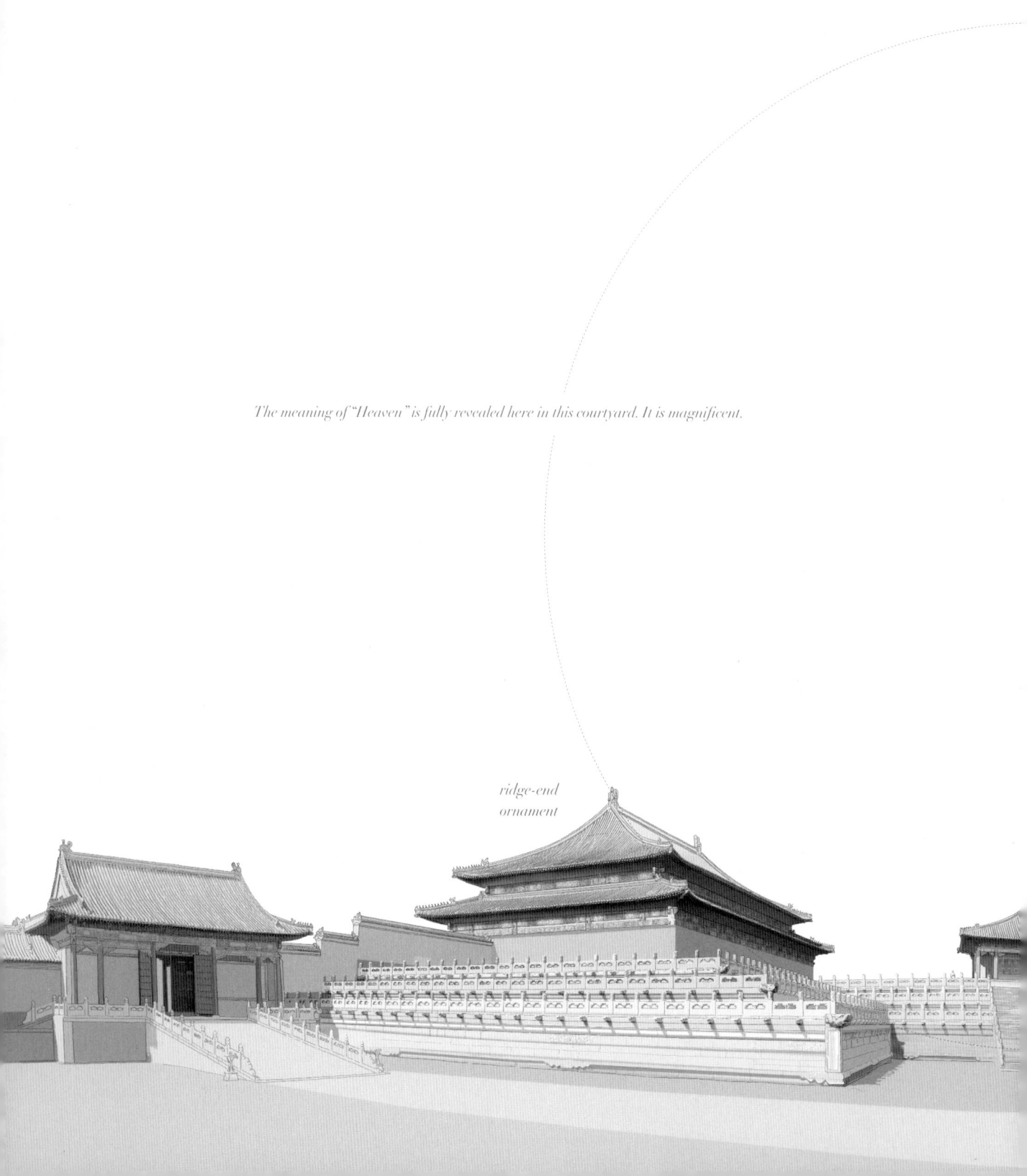

The meaning of "Heaven" is fully revealed here in this courtyard. It is magnificent.

ridge-end ornament

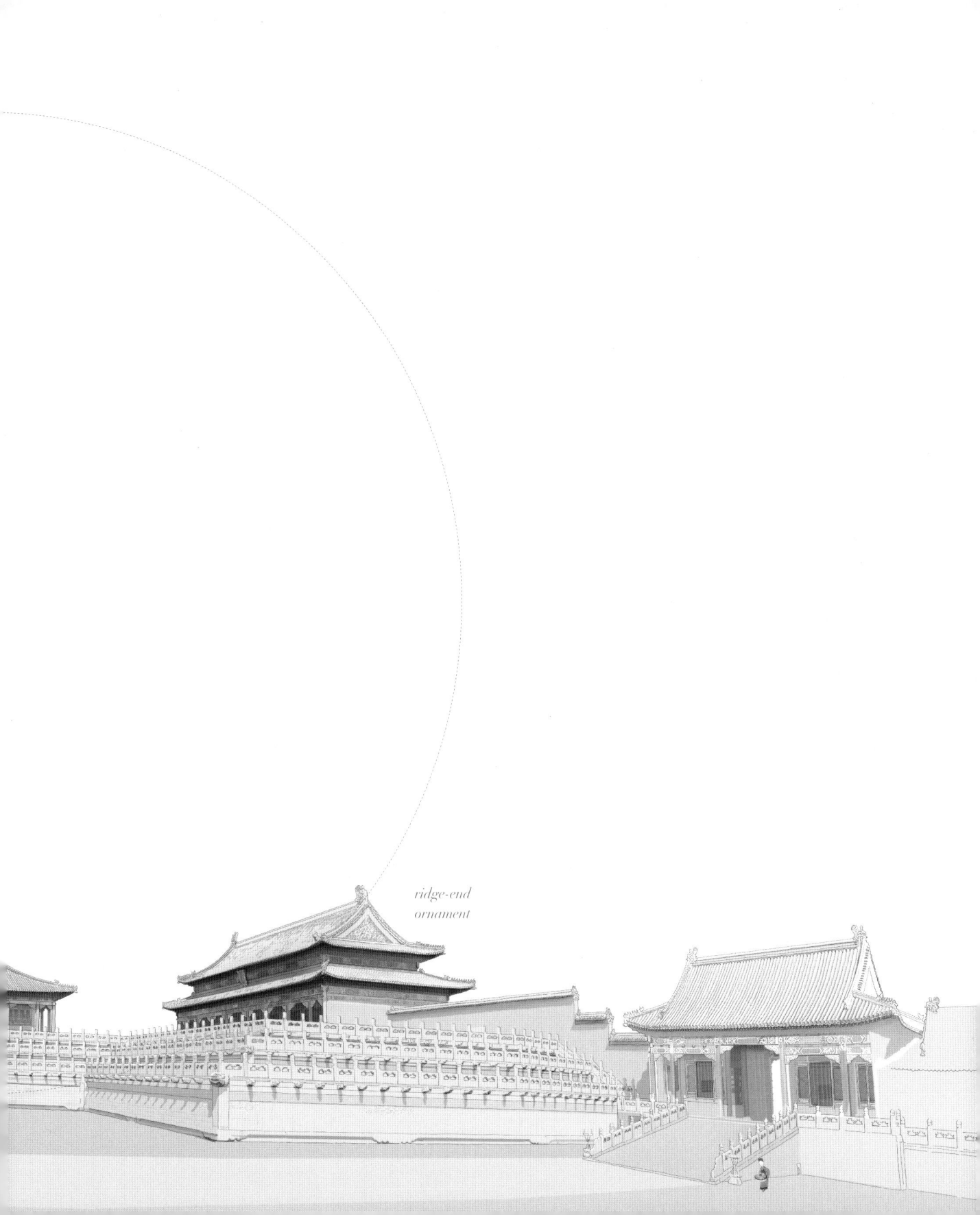

ridge-end ornament

The Three Large Halls under the Sky

If we view this courtyard from the two side-corridors at the bottom of the platform, the size and height of The Hall of Central Harmony (Zhonghedian) are obviously inferior to the halls in front of and behind it. All these form a very unusual "centrally located" arrangement. Considering the fact that the nation's largest ridge-end ornament on the ridge of The Hall of Supreme Harmony (Taihedian) was considered as "second grade", the inferiority seems to show that the real pinnacle in architecture is not in the building itself, but in the space created. It is true that the roofs of the Three Large Halls all seem to be within the control of an invisible space rhythm. What is worth noting is that the corridors at the bottom of the platform were for the use of the attending officials. Even inside the palace, the emperor was carried on a sedan chair, and would only walk on the path known as The Imperial Boulevard (Yudao). He would not compromise his dignity without a cause by coming to this part of the palace. However, it was not the emperor who built the palace, but his lowly subordinates who worshipped him at the bottom of the platform. Like The Hall of Central Harmony (Zhonghedian), the more modest it appears on the platform, the greater it seems from the bottom. After all, the reflection and aspiration of the entire bureaucracy are symbolized by this imperial and godly space.

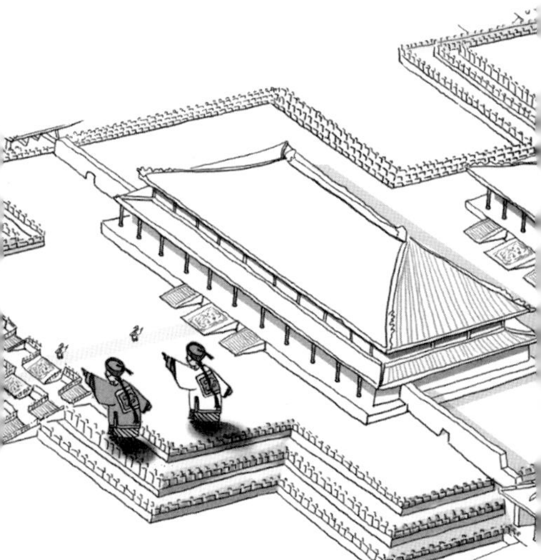

/ The Hall of Supreme Harmony (Taihedian) - *Revisited*

The people in the West say that the ancient Greeks were first to convert beauty into data (The ancient Egyptians would definitely disagree). The people during the Renaissance Period tried to convert all beauty into data. Whether or not the quality of beauty is equivalent to its quantity is a question that probably only experts in all three areas of philosophy, science and art can answer. Here is an attempt without actual data. Perhaps each tourist can make his/her own attempt.

The "cosmic" scene of the The Hall of Central Harmony (Zhonghedian) reminds us that the different courtyards of the Three Large Halls were originally a complete unit separated by red walls, but then reunited by an enormous platform. After all, will this magnificent feeling of space also control, in the same way, the largest hall in the nation, The Hall of Supreme Harmony (Taihedian)? Let us return to The Hall of Supreme Harmony Square (Taihedian Guangchang) and see if we can have yet another understanding...

According to the current theory on modern visual art and space design, when our eyes view certain objects, apart from subjective preferences and natural choices, environmental arrangements can also be employed to guide our line of vision .(This is commonly applied in architecture and exhibition halls). The theory is based on "The principle of arranging the space of vision in accordance with the height multiples of an object (or a building).

The Hall of Supreme Harmony (Taihedian)

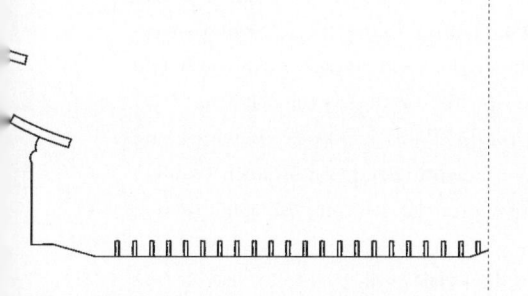

The Hall of Supreme Harmony (Taihedian)

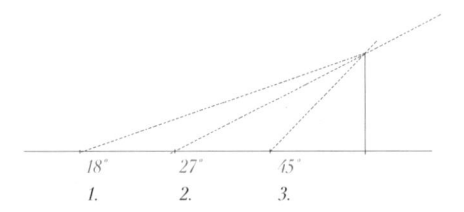

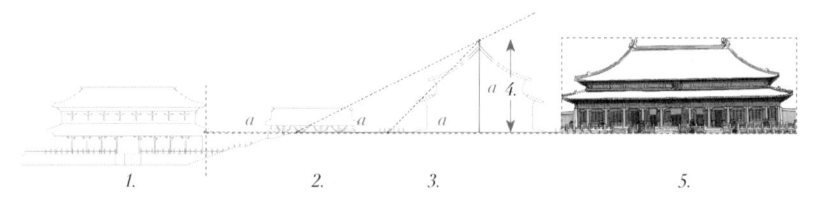

General Principle

1. When the distance is three times the height of an object, (18 degrees), it provides the best field of vision of the relationship between the object and its environment.
2. When the distance is twice the height of an object, you can admire the whole object (an independent image).
3. When the height to distance ratio is 1:1, the observer can clearly appreciate the more detailed parts and the texture of material used.

Let us apply this principle to The Hall of Supreme Harmony *(Taihedian)*

1. The Main Hall stands upright on a tall platform 8 meters high. The 3:1 distance does not actually exist (the height has become that of the Main Hall plus the platform).
2. At the 2:1 distance, the Main Hall looks impressive and full of grandeur but the entire elevation is hardly visible.
3. At the 1:1 distance, one can see only the small section under the eaves.
4. The height of the Main Hall itself.

The Grand Forbidden City — The Imperial Axis

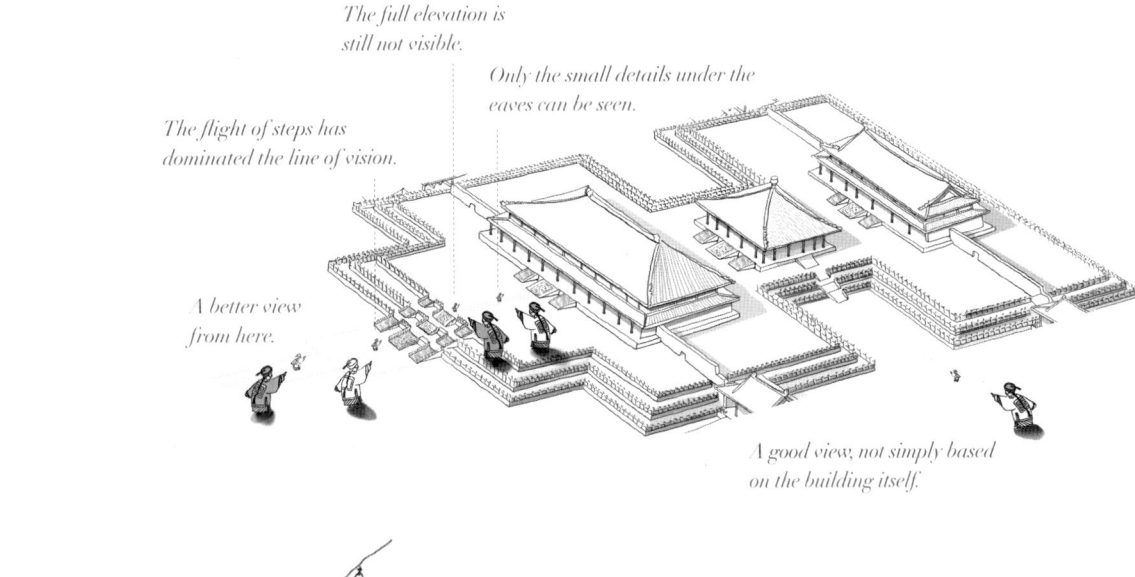

The full elevation is still not visible.

Only the small details under the eaves can be seen.

The flight of steps has dominated the line of vision.

A better view from here.

A good view, not simply based on the building itself.

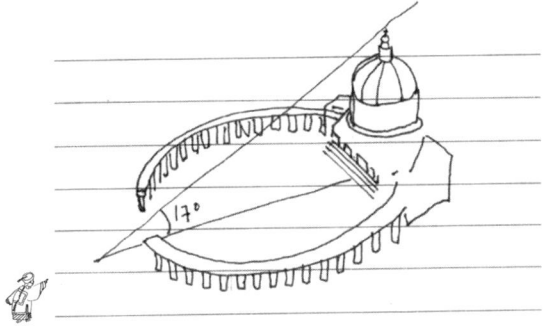

For example: when one stands at the entrance to the square of the St Peter's Basilica in The Vatican, one can, at about 17 degrees, see the large sphere on its dome. (Later in the 17th Century, an additional porch was constructed in front, and this has hindered the overall visual effect).

5. The width of The Hall of Supreme Harmony (Taihedian) is almost three times as great as its height. When one stands at a distance equal to twice its height, the distance is actually only double the width. Applying the above-described visual principle, a conflicting feeling will result because in terms of height, it is a "full view", but in terms of width, it is only a "partial view".

Moreover, as the slope on the roof of the Main Hall is greater than the body of the building, it may not be appropriate to rigidly impose the concept of "vertical elevation".

Instead of calling this principle a theory, it may be better to call it a general accumulation of experience. The visual distances resulting from the kneeling-sitting positions commonly practiced in the Tang Dynasty may very well be the reason for the rules on calligraphic art (one can see the entire sheet of calligraphy if one stands double the distance away) being much stricter than those in the dynasties that followed. However, when we come to stand in front of The Hall of Supreme Harmony (Taihedian) and use this method to "view" the hall, it seems that we cannot get the same visual impression.

The Hall of Supreme Harmony (Taihedian)

The Pavilion of Spreading Righteousness (Hongyige).

The total height of the Main Hall and the platform.

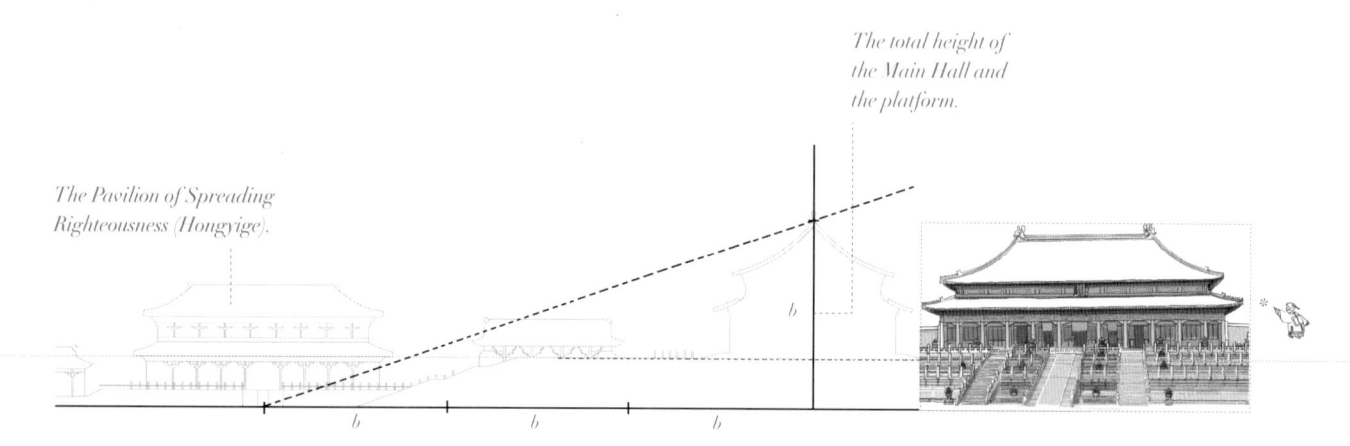

The mid-point between The Hall of Supreme Harmony (Taihedian) and The Gate of Supreme Harmony (Taihemen).

* *Under general circumstances, eaves that are too wide will give the illusion of drooping sides if viewed from too short a distance. Fortunately, traditional Chinese eaves always have the two ends slightly tilted upward, making them appear to be straight and proper.*

The Main Hall With Platform Added

Therefore, we might as well try again to use the Main Hall and the platform as the height unit (b). If we look at the Main Hall from a visual distance of 3:1 (coincidentally, it is the mid-point between The Hall of Supreme Harmony [Taihedian] and The Gate of Supreme Harmony [Taihemen]), the main frame will appear to have been dominated by the platform.

"Beautiful palaces are built on high platforms" is characteristic of traditional Chinese palaces. However one looks at it, the platform is an inseparable part of a palace. Is there something wrong with the so called "analysis of visual points", or are the "situations" just not all the same?

The Main Hall Plus the Sky

Here the same formula is applied in order to carry on "appreciating" the hall. This time the height c (see pg 138) we base on is an inspiration coming from The Hall of Central Harmony (Zhonghedian). Coincidentally, the visual point of 2:1 happens to be exactly the mid-point between the front eaves of The Hall of Supreme Harmony (Taihedian) and The Gate of Supreme Harmony (Taihemen). (The meeting point of the two annex halls The Pavilion of Embodying Benevolence [Tirenge] and The Pavilion of Spreading Righteousness [Hongyige], and The Imperial Boulevard (Yudao), is also the central point of the Square.) Also, the distance of 3:1 is just the spot where one enters the Square through The Gate of Supreme Harmony (Taihemen).

In fact, vision has its own natural choices. Anyone coming to this large Square will naturally appreciate the enormous palaces against the background of the great blue sky and white clouds. However, when you come next time to visit this most important courtyard of The Outer Court (Waichao), you might as well take a full view from The Gate of Supreme Harmony (Taihemen, at a distance of three times of height c) and appreciate the great impact of the magnificent Hall of Supreme Harmony (Taihedian) complemented by the buildings on its two sides.

Based on the saying that "at twice the distance from an object, one can have a full view of it", the overall sense of beauty of The Hall of Supreme Harmony (Taihedian) must include the inseparable platform and the sky that exhibits different hues from season to season. To go one step further, theoretically speaking, will take us into the realms of detailed appreciation.

"The Gate of Great Ming (Damingmen, The Gate of Great Qing [Daqingmen]) is 2.5 kilometers away from the Long Life Hill (Wansuishan or Jingshan) and 1.5045 kilometers from the center of the courtyard of The Hall of Supreme Harmony Square (Taihedian Guangchang). The two figures are in the ratio of 1.5045 : 2.5 = 0.618, which is the same as the ratio of the golden section line! This is sufficient to show how expertly and skilfully mathematics was applied in ancient Chinese architecture." (See Reference 4)

Whether or not the ratio in golden section has any special meaning in a larger spatial blueprint could be a matter for further research. The topographical feature (xing shi) is stressed in fengshui theories (xing represents a hundred feet and shi a thousand feet), which, in modern language, means that an ideal situation is to limit a stand alone building (xing) within 35 meters, and space (shi) within 350 meters. The latter is also considered by modern environmental experts as a strolling distance that would "make your body and soul feel pleasant but not worn out". Both The Meridian Gate (Wumen) (37.95 meters high) which is the tallest building structure on the central axis of The Forbidden City, and The Hall of Supreme Harmony (Taihedian) (35.05 meters), are roughly within the allowance of 100 Chinese feet (xing). The width and depth of the Square is also confined to 1,000 Chinese feet (350 meters). The building structures and corridors on the two sides of the central axis are generally within the 30-meter distance which allows the building (xing) to be visible. After leaving the back door of The Forbidden City (The Gate of Divine Prowess [Shenwumen]), The Imperial Garden and The Prospect Hill (Jingshan) are also 300 meters away where visitors should feel pleasant in body and soul!

The Hall of Supreme Harmony (Taihedian)

The Main Hall + the height of the sky.

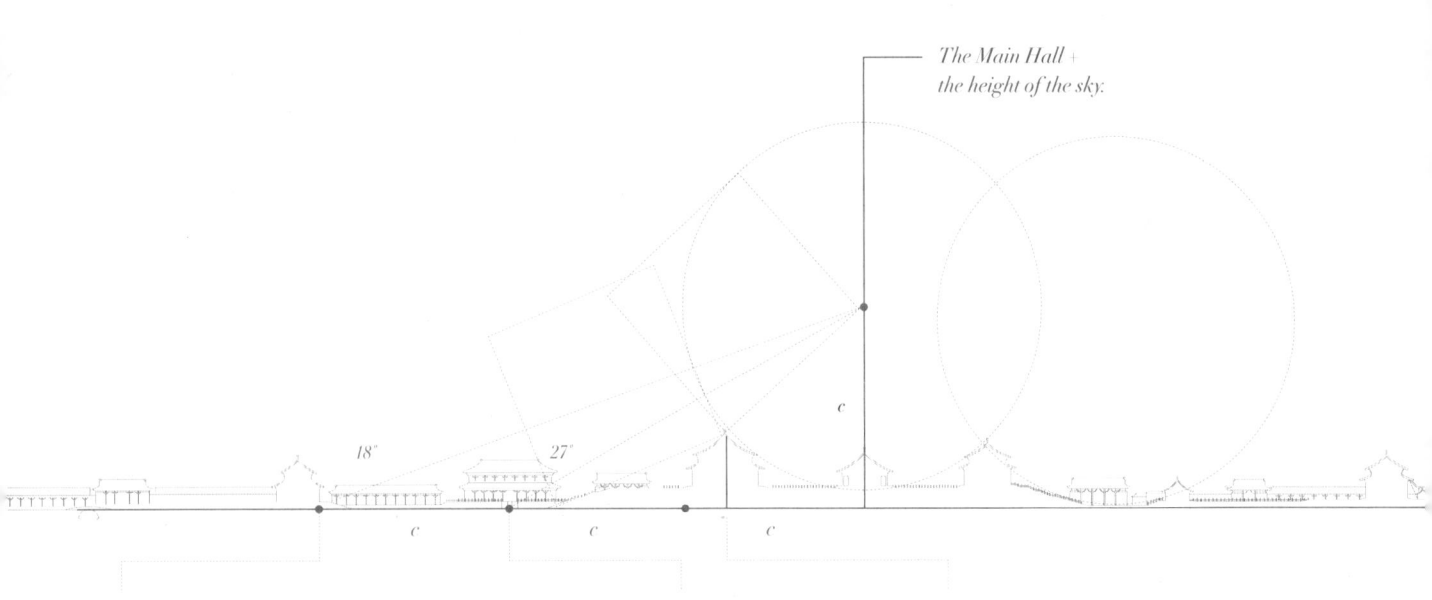

18°   27°

The 3:1 distance is just where one enters the Square from The Gate of Supreme Harmony (Taihemen).
Full view of the splendour of The Hall of Supreme Harmony (Taihedian)

The 2:1 visual point falls right on the front eaves of The Hall of Supreme Harmony (Taihedian).
Appreciating the entirety of the Main Hall.

The central axis of the Main Hall.

Reality Took the Form of Imagination

"A mountain is not high if not hidden". In Chinese painting there is the saying of "planning on the white to determine where the black should be". This is a wonderful aesthetic concept of working on an empty sheet of white paper (space/nature), and determining where to apply the ink (artificial work). When applied to architecture, this may explain why palatial halls were built low in order to show their honorable position.

Whether or not the scenarios above are valid, these few palaces seem to have told us that:

(1) The greatness of nature and its essence may not necessarily be distracted by the intervention of man-made structures. (On the contrary, the boundlessness of the sky could be made more conspicuous by the palaces under it). To cherish nature, it seems that one should start by learning how to cherish the deeper implications of human creativity.

(2) All the "great" cities in the modern world have "great" squares. Their function is to utilize a space with "non-exitstent" artificial structure to exaggerate the "existence" of artificial achievements. (The space without any construction is part of the overall construction blueprint).

The Forbidden City has a few palaces which highlight the extraordinary value of "non-existence"!

The Grand Forbidden City — The Imperial Axis

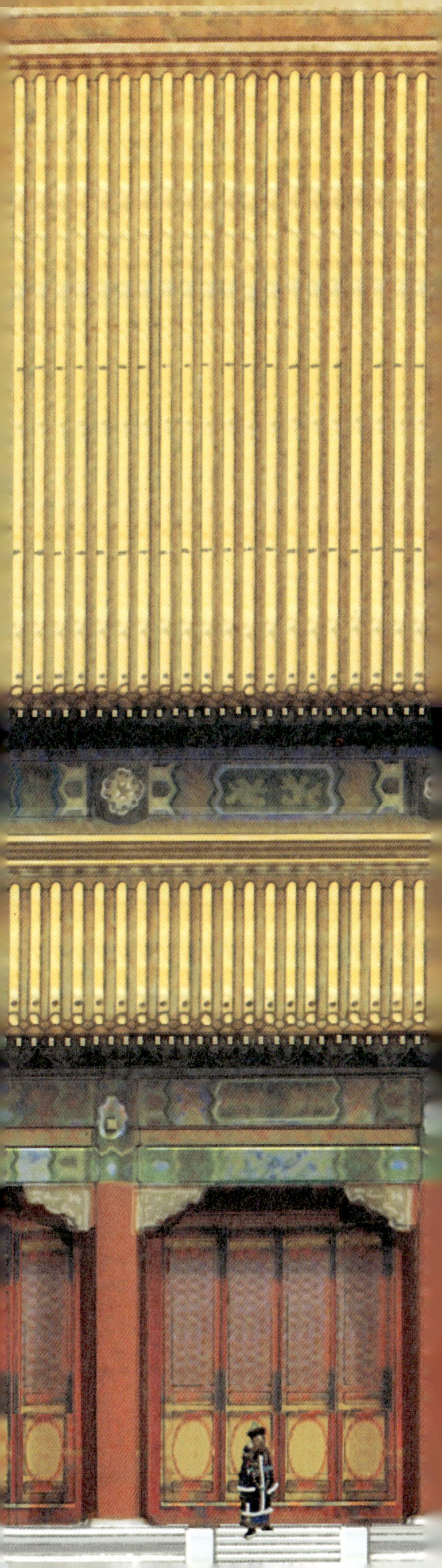

/ Colors

In vision, the outline is important. Color is equally important.

Red (wall), yellow (roof) and blue (sky) are the three primary colors. They can be mixed to create any color (on the paint dish). In photology, they provide colors for a rainbow, and yet can revert to becoming a colorless ray of light.

In the 1920's, modern art started to flourish in the West (including geometric, abstract and even modern basic design), acting as a catalyst for people to research topics regarding the basic elements. Colors were independently studied, and given different properties; e.g., the yellow color, projecting an aggressive visual impression, is more closely related to the triangle in geometry. The vigorous and bright red color is the square. Orange (a trapezoid) is in between. Cooler colors like blue and green are compared with a circle and a flexible curve… This theory has such great impact that until now it is still often applied in 2-dimensional designs. In terms of 3-dimensional designs, there are only some experimental creations, which cannot fully demonstrate the theory. It is certainly a surprise to find this theory being fully applied in the construction of buildings during the Ming and Qing Dynasties. (See Reference 8)

The houses with black tiles and whitewashed walls found in the low-lying region south of The Yangtze River look like a newly finished Chinese painting. The scene touches even without vibrant colours. However, one cannot hide one's excitement when looking at The Imperial Palace with its vivacious and intense colour scheme.

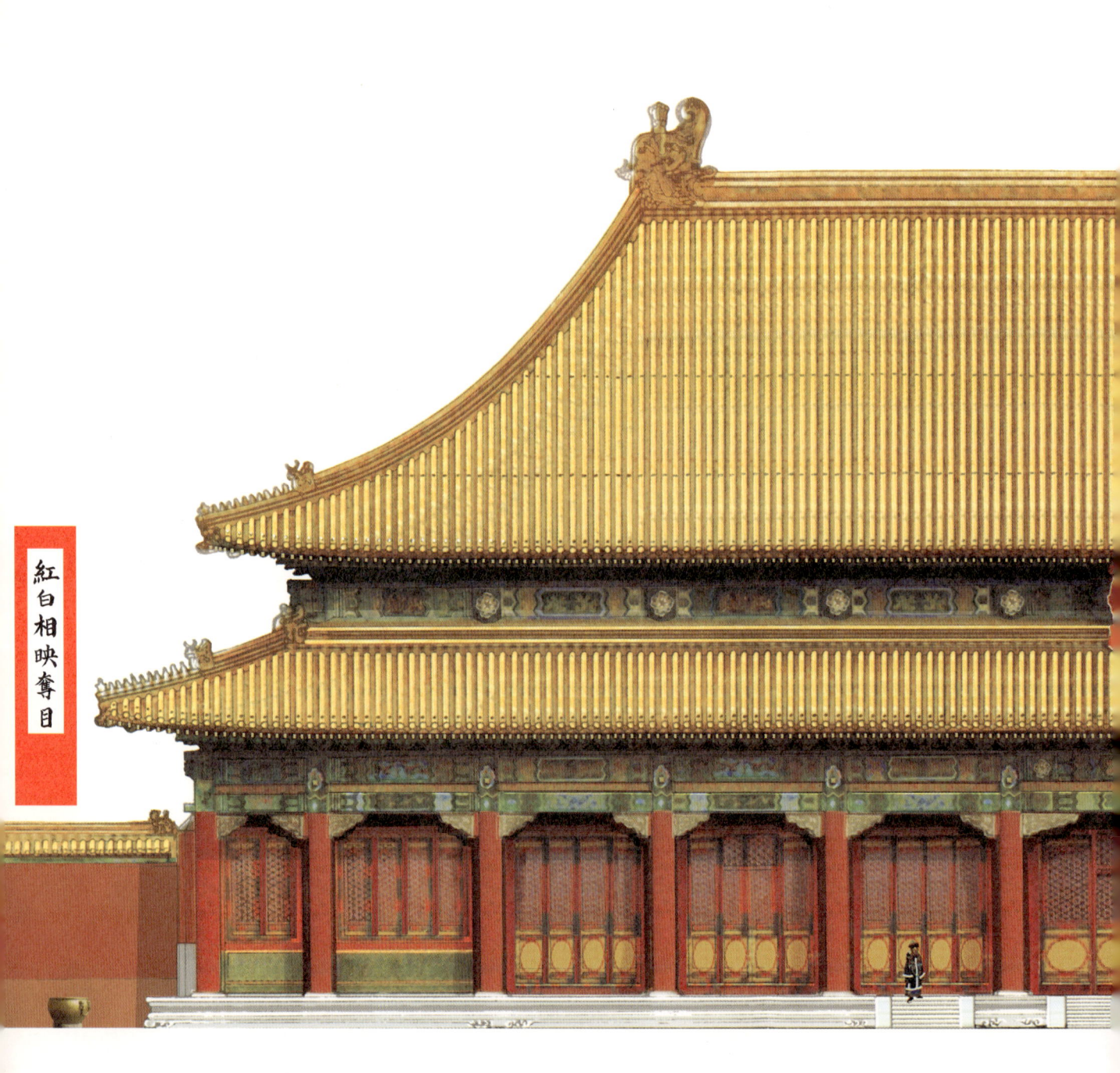

Colors

Blue Sky + Yellow Tiles + Red Walls + Color Painting =

紅白相映奪目

P.140　　The Grand Forbidden City — The Imperial Axis

The three primary colors (The Hall of Supreme Harmony (Taihedian) plus sky) on a 3-dimensional piece of white (the white marble terraces with different shades) in the middle of neutral gray (the Square).

大內聯色尚白

Colors

The roofs of the palaces as seen in different courtyards in The Outer Court (Waichao) almost embrace all major roofing specifications within traditional Chinese architecture.

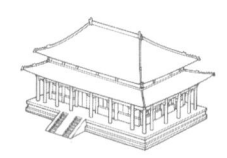

Double-eaved Hip Roof

Hip Roof

Hip Style

Double- and Single-eaved. The single-eaved hip roof has four large slopes and is called Si-a Style. It is also known as Five-Ridge Hall because of the number of roof ridges. It was the highest grade of roof specification in ancient Chinese architecture. The Hall of Supreme Harmony (Taihedian) has the most honorable double-eaved hip roof. Even palaces which were used by the imperial family might not be considered deserving of such design. It was only used when building the most important palaces.

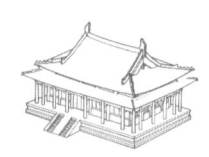

Double-eaved Gable and Hip Roof

Gable and Hip Roof

Gable and Hip Style

Double- or Single-eaved. Single-eaved gable and hip roof was also known as nine-ridge halls (Jiujidian). It was generally used in less important halls, mansions for high officials and noble lords, and buildings constructed with imperial mandates.
The Hall of Preserving Harmony (Baohedian) and The Palace of Heavenly Purity (Qianqinggong) have the double-eaved gable and hip Roof.
The Hall of Supreme Harmony Square (Taihedian Guangchang) was held in high regard as the courtyard of the Son of Heaven. So, as a rare exception, the four corner towers were built with double-eaved gable and hip Roof.

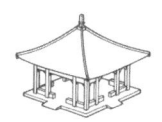

Four-cornered Pyramidal Roof

Four-cornered Pyramidal Roof

The four corners of the drooping ridges rise gradually and meet together. The main ridge disappears and becomes a pyramidal point. This is a popular design for pavilions in gardens. The Hall of Central Harmony (Zhonghedian) uses high-grade partition boards as walls to show that it is more subordinate to the superior class of Main Halls.

Overhanging Gable Roof  *Flush Gable Roof*

Overhanging Gable and the Flush Gable Roof

The overhanging gable roof and the flush gable roof differ in whether or not the eaves stretch out to the sides of the building. They are specifications for ordinary houses of the common people. The flush gable style was prevalent after the Ming Dynasty (14th Century). This simple accommodation, simular to modern public housing was popular after the brick-making industry started to boom.

Ridge Overhanging Gable Roof  *Round Ridge Flush Gable Roof*

The Round Ridge Overhanging Gable Roof and the Flush Gable Roof

The relatively non-rigid round ridge overhanging gable roof and the round ridge flush gable roof, because of their softer contour, were more frequently adopted in decorating structures in scenic gardens, summer houses, and side halls. They were very rarely used for main buildings.

Colors

The mid-day sun on Winter Solstice shines at an angle of 27° in the capital.

Does the mid-day sun on Summer Solstice shine at an angle of 76° in the capital?

The radian of the roof serves to ensure the covering tiles stay more tightly together. At the same time, it makes the rain and snow drain off fast. The roof ridges change their course and they are deposited further away. The roofs have upturned tile ends for longer exposure to sunlight and improvement in ventilation. Visually, they can make the large and heavy roof look delicate and light. This transforms the originally monotonous contour into an exciting skyline.

The design of the eaves will provide shade from the fierce mid-day sun on Summer Solstice. On Winter Solstice, the cat will be able to enjoy the pleasantly warm sunlight if it sits at the same spot.

P.144   *The Grand Forbidden City — The Imperial Axis*

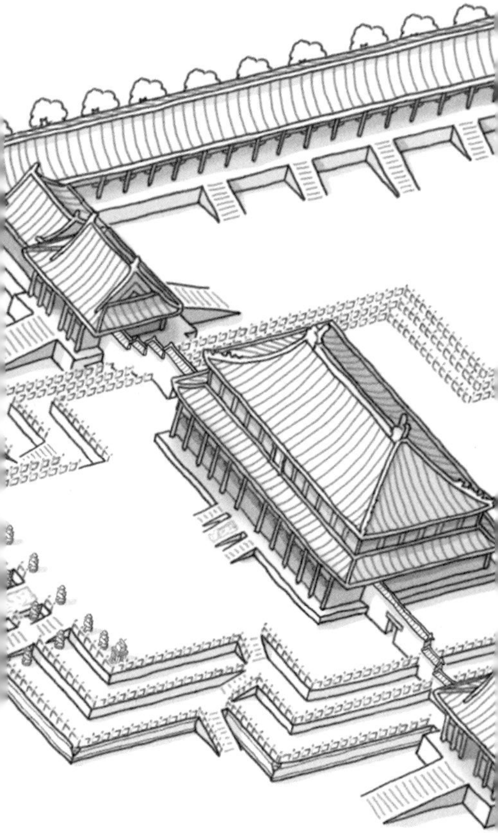

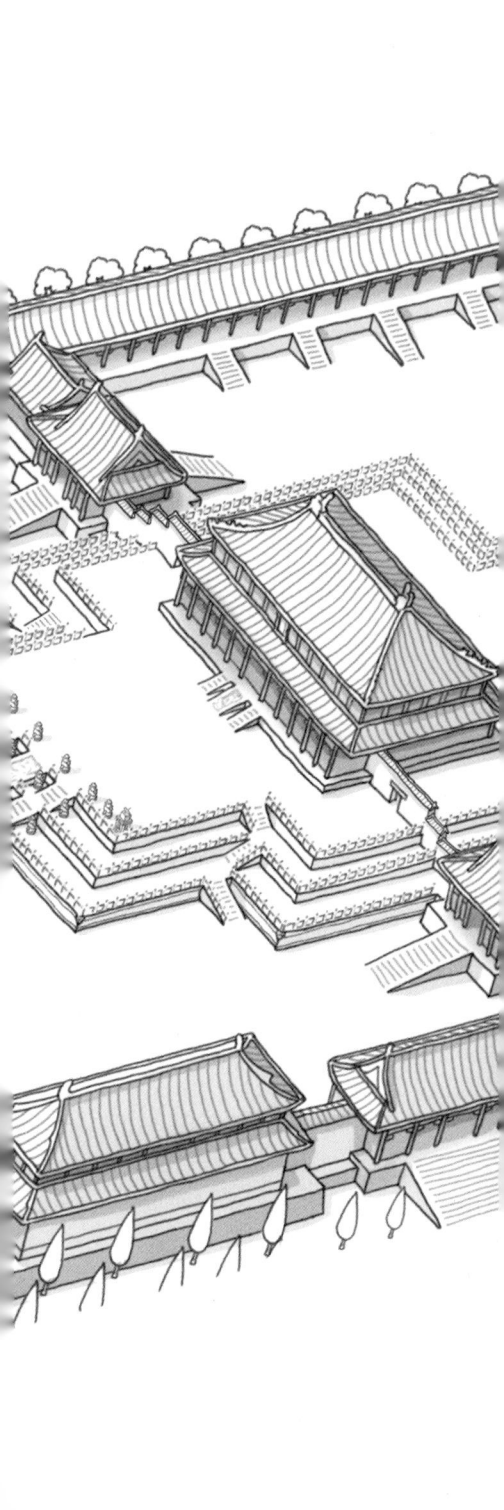

/ The Roofs

During the feudal times the palaces allowed no public access. This ban was lifted long ago. People can now climb up The Prospect Hill (Jingshan) behind The Forbidden City, take a rest at the pavilion and take a bird's eye view of the scenery. As the sun shines, the golden glazed tiles look like waves in the breeze. Visitors often exclaim, "the undulating skyline created by the palaces looks like waves in the sea".

In ancient China, the ceremony to mark a boy reaching manhood consisted of putting an adult hat on his head (Hat-donning). From then on, he would have an inseparable relationship with hats. When he took up different kinds of work or attained different official status, he would wear the appropriate hats accordingly. On more formal occasions, he would make special effort to put them on carefully and properly. People in the West take off their hats to show respect. They may even throw their hats high into the air at graduation ceremonies. For Chinese, the proper etiquette is to make sure the hats stayed firmly on their heads.

The Roofs

Tower Gable and Hip Roof

Overhanging Gable Roof

Gable and Hip Roof

Gable and Hip Roof

Tower Hip Roof

Tower Gable and Hip Roof

Overhanging Gable Roof

Double-Eaved Hip Roof

Gable and Hip Roof

Double-Eaved Gable and Hip Roof

Overhanging Gable Roof

Gable and Hip Roof

Tower Hip Roof

Tower Gable and Hip Roof

Overhanging Gable Roof

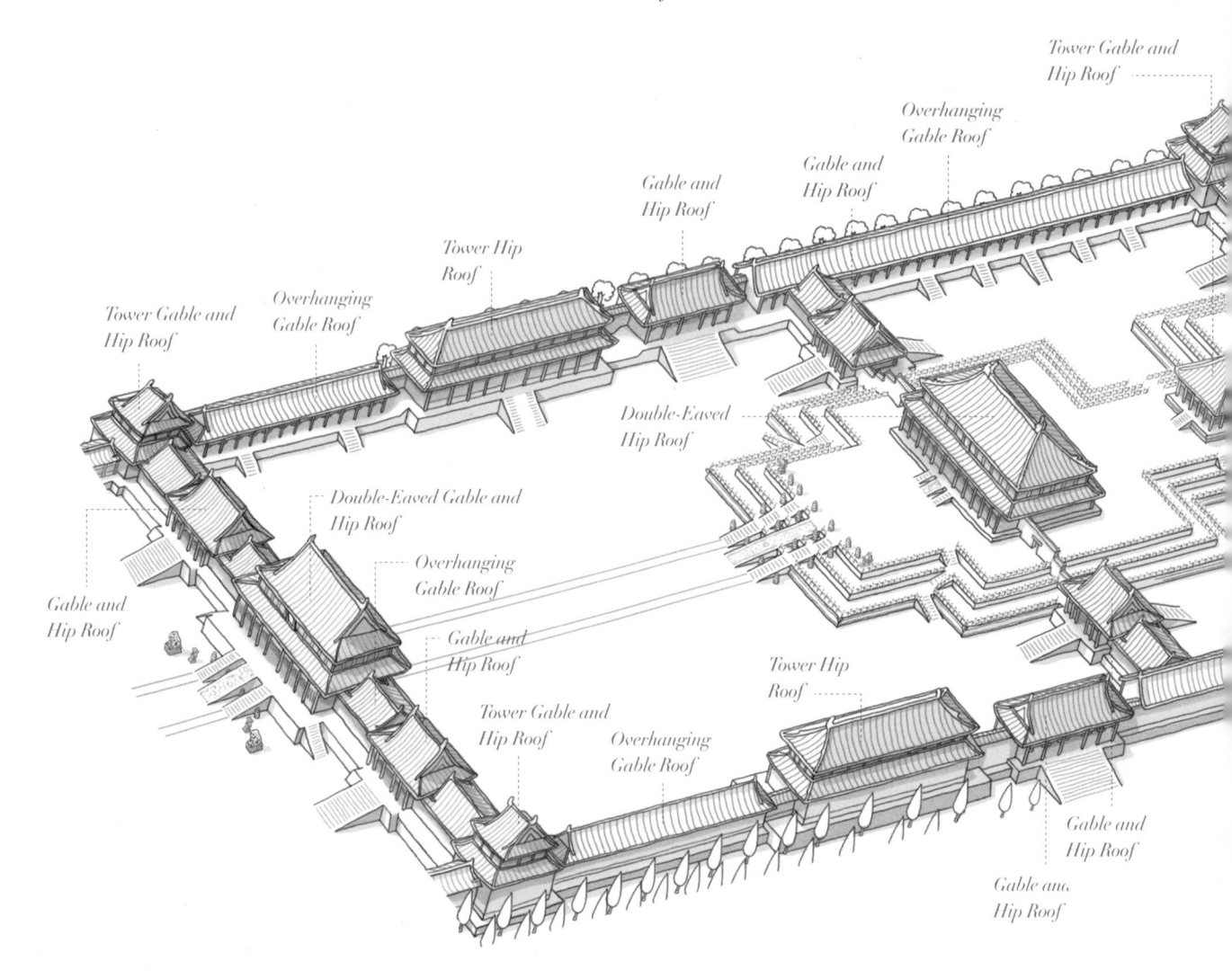

Gable and Hip Roof

Gable and Hip Roof

The concept of having a "dress code" is particularly important in architecture. The two courtyards in the Three Large Halls in The Outer Court (Waichao) along the central axis have different grades of architecture. Among them, The Hall of Supreme Harmony (Taihedian) certainly occupies the core position with its highest grade double-eaved hip style. It has turned the glittering glazed tiles into a golden expanse of waves.

The surrounding palatial buildings were carefully planned and built in accordance with their different functions and positions, thus giving rise to the various grades in roof specifications in traditional Chinese architecture.

If you are interested in the specifications of traditional Chinese architecture, you should take note of the following. From the Three Large Halls on the platform alone, you can find several of the most important original specifications in ancient Chinese architecture. Within the stretch of 437 meters between The Gate of Supreme Harmony (Taihedmen) and The Gate of Heavenly Purity (Qianqingmen), there appear 8 different grades of roofs, each in its rightful position, looking like life-size models straight from the "Encyclopedia of Roofs".

*Gable and
Hip Roof*

*Four-Cornered
Pyramidal Roof*

*Double-Eaved Gable and
Hip Roof*

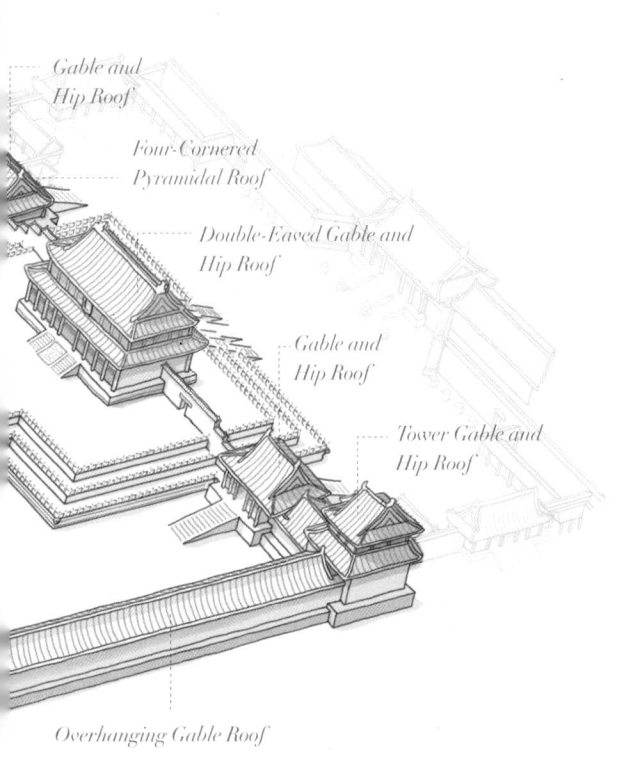

*Gable and
Hip Roof*

*Tower Gable and
Hip Roof*

Overhanging Gable Roof

If we hold the view that "Architecture is the furniture in nature and furniture is the building in architecture" and enter this two-sector super imperial quadrangular court, we can see the strictness of traditional rites and regulations. In fact, to a certain extent, we have already entered its palaces. The square is a sitting room of infinite size. The surrounding corridors, towers, and pavilions are just like furniture on display. Generally at the center of a sitting room, there is always a "Divine Dragon Table" for sacrificial (worship) ceremonies, or Taishi Chairs (so important was the chair that it was named after the senior official title- Taishi) designated for the host and the most important guest.

As in a sitting room, there is one piece of furniture in the center of this Square, which also played a role in sacrificial (worship) ceremonies. What is different is that this one had only the host in the seat, and guests had to kneel on the ground.

The Roofs

The Hall of Supreme Harmony (Taihedian) has an area of 2,377 square meters but only one chair...

- Tall Tower (Chonglou)
- The Storage of The Inner Court (Neiku)
- The Right Gate of The Rear Palaces (Houyoumen)
- The Hall of Supreme Harmony (Taihedian)
- The Hall of Preserving Harmony (Baohedian)
- The Pavilion of Spreading Righteousness (Hongyige)
- The Tea Storage (Chaku)
- The Hall of Central Harmony (Zhonghedian)
- The Left Door of The Rear Palaces (Houzuomen)
- Right Wing Door (Youyimen)
- The Right Door of the Central Court (Zhongyoumen)
- The Gate of Heavenly Purity (Qianqingmen)
- Clothing Storage (Yiku)
- Tall Tower (Chonglou)
- Tall Tower (Chonglou)
- The Gate of Steadfast Virtue (Zhendumen)
- The Storage of The Inner Court (Neiku)
- The Gate of Supreme Harmony (Taihemen)
- The Left Door of the Central Court (Zhongzuomen)
- The Gate of Inspiring Virtues (Zhaodemen)
- The Pavilion of Embodying Benevolence (Tirenge)
- Left Wing Door (Zuoyimen)
- North Saddle Storage (Beianku)
- Tall Tower (Chonglou)
- Armor Storage (Jiaku)

P.150   The Grand Forbidden City — The Imperial Axis

/ Between The Outer Court (Waichao) and The Inner Court (Neichao)

The platform of the Three Large Halls is so enormous that it gives visitors the false sensation of "walking on level ground all the time". When one goes around to the back of The Hall of Preserving Harmony (Baohedian), and looks at The Gate of Heavenly Purity Square (Qianqingmen Guangchang), one can be taken back by the sudden descent to a lower ground level.

*The Outer Court (Waichao)
is recorded history*

*The Imperial Court is both a governmental
structure and a palatial building structure.*

*The Inner Court (Neichao)
is unofficial history.*

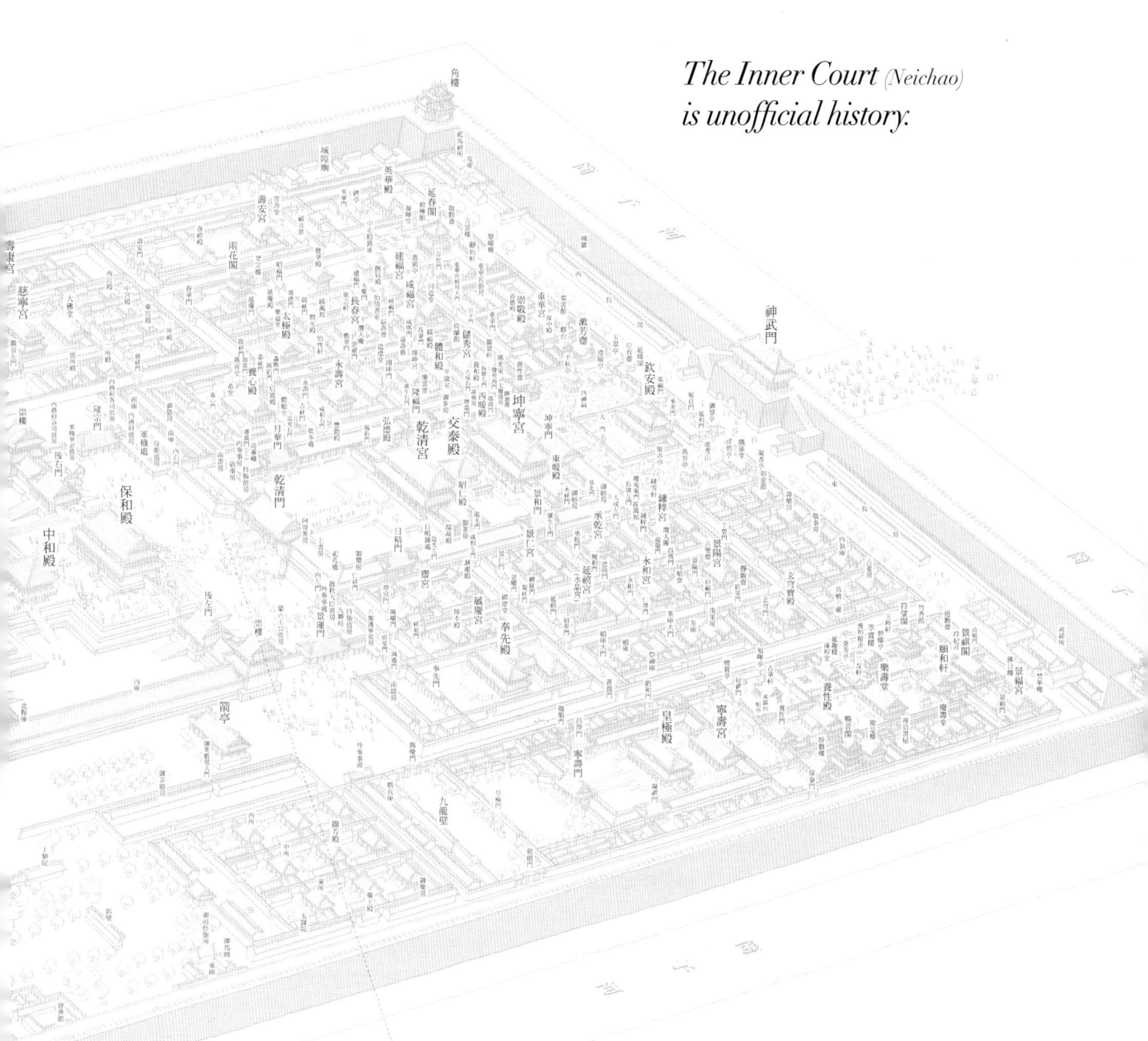

*The Gate of Heavenly Purity Square
(Qianqingmen Guangchang)*

Between The Outer Court (Waichao)
and The Inner Court (Neichao)

The Hall of Supreme Harmony (Taihedian)
35.76 meters high

The Hall of Central Harmony (Zhonghedian)
27.83 meters high

The Hall of Preserving Harmony (Baohedian)
29.47 meters high

The Gate of Heavenly Purity (Qianqingmen)
12.15 meters high

The Palace of Heavenly Purity (Qianqinggong)

The Hall of Union (Jiaotaidian)

The Palace of Earthly Tranquility (Kunninggong)

The platform of the Three Large Halls is so enormous that it gives visitors the false sensation of "walking on level ground all the time". When one goes around to the back of The Hall of Preserving Harmony (Baohedian), and looks at The Gate of Heavenly Purity Square (Qianqingmen Guangchang), one can be taken back by the sudden descent to a lower ground level.

The Grand Forbidden City — The Imperial Axis

Secrets

The Gate of Heavenly Purity (Qianqingmen) is the formal entrance to The Inner Court (Neichao, The Great Interior [Danei] or Imperial Palace) where the emperor lived his daily life. It was also the most mysterious place in the nation during feudal times. In both the Ming and Qing Dynasties, there were rumours of different cases of unsolved "mysteries". Probably only the fading bricks and tiles in The Inner Court (Neichao), would know the truth. In other words, The Gate of Heavenly Purity (Qianqingmen) is also the gate through which officially recorded history becomes unofficial history.

The Gate of Heavenly Purity (Qianqingmen) lies 40% lower than The Hall of Preserving Harmony (Baohedian), which stands up high on the three-tier platform (as much as 8 meters if the drop in elevation is added). Nevertheless, history books had never recorded, throughout the 500 years of the Ming and Qing Dynasties, any one minister being able to get a stealthy "bird's eye view" of any snapshots of life in The Inner Court (Neichao) while discussing state affairs on the platform next to The Hall of Preserving Harmony (Baohedian). This was because the side street between the Inner and Outer Courts (Neichao and Waichao) — The Gate of Heavenly Purity Square (Qianqingmen Guangchang) acted as boundary and barrier.

This is the fourth open space counting from The Gate of Supreme Harmony Square (Taihemen Guangchang), using the same width (about 200 meters) to carve out spaces with different depths. It is even smaller than the courtyard of The Hall of Central Harmony (Zhonghedian) but was able to ingeniously protect the private life of the emperor from the peeping and prying angle of the three platforms.

*Between The Outer Court (Waichao)
and The Inner Court (Neichao)*

When I look at The Gate of Heavenly Purity (Qianqingmen), The Palace of Heavenly Purity (Qianqinggong), The Six Eastern and Western Palaces (Dongxiliugong), and even the The Palace of Tranquility and Longevity (Ningshougong), and The Pavilion of the Rain of Flowers (Yuhuage), I can see them all at a glance, but my vision is limited to their roof ridges.

Appropriateness

In terms of arrangement, this transitional space is important but cannot be too conspicuous. The widest part of The Gate of Heavenly Purity Square (Qianqingmen Guangchang) from north to south does not exceed 50 meters. The narrowest part is only about 30 meters (thus the Square is also called a side street). When compared with other squares on the central axis, it does not only look diminutive, but also, as the reception area of The Great Interior (Danei), it could be a little claustrophobic.

Generally those important officials who were given an audience with the emperor had to enter The Forbidden City through The Eastern and Western Prosperity Gates (Donghuamen and Xihuamen). They had to follow a number of winding paths before reaching and entering The Gate of Thriving Royal House (Longzongmen) or The Gate of Good Fortune (Jingyunmen) on the east and west ends of the Square. Coincidentally, on both sides, their field of vision was 200 meters.

If you observe from The Hall of Central Harmony (Zhonghedian), (this would not have been allowed in the old days), Inner Court (Neichao) all the way to The Prospect Hill (Jingshan) behind the palaces, the field of vision becomes more open. This situation gives rise to the spatial effect of "being able to see deeper from the side and wider from high above".

If you look at The Gate of Heavenly Purity Square (Qianqingmen Guangchang) at eye level from the narrowest spot (the front end of the back stairs of The Hall of Central Harmony [Zhonghedian]), the two glazed tile shadow walls which slant outward in a / \ shape, coincidentally form two sets of slanting lines with elements of plane perspective. This makes the side street, which is only 30 meters wide, into a starting point of perspectivity and eliminates any feeling of narrowness. This design is traditionally described as, "the shadow walls are delicate, exquisite and appropriately arranged". This seemingly casual but ingenious spatial effect cannot be more aptly described than by the word "appropriate".

The shadow walls belong to a high-grade gate specification. The glazed tile shadow walls with the glazed-tile Sumeru throne [pedestal of a Buddha's statue] underneath, bear the highest-grade specifications in The Forbidden City. "Appropriateness" is believed to have come from the accumulated experiences of engineering of many dynasties. Though the construction of the walls might not have drawn on large objective data like modern engineering, the results were always compatible with modern analysis.

The eunuchs and servants of The Inner Court (Neichao), were only allowed to use the Right Gate of The Inner Court (Neiyoumen). The court officials, like the Minister of the Grand Council of State (Junjidachen), members of the South Study of the Imperial Academy (Hanlin), the Minister of The Office of Internal Affairs (Neiwufudachen), were no exception.

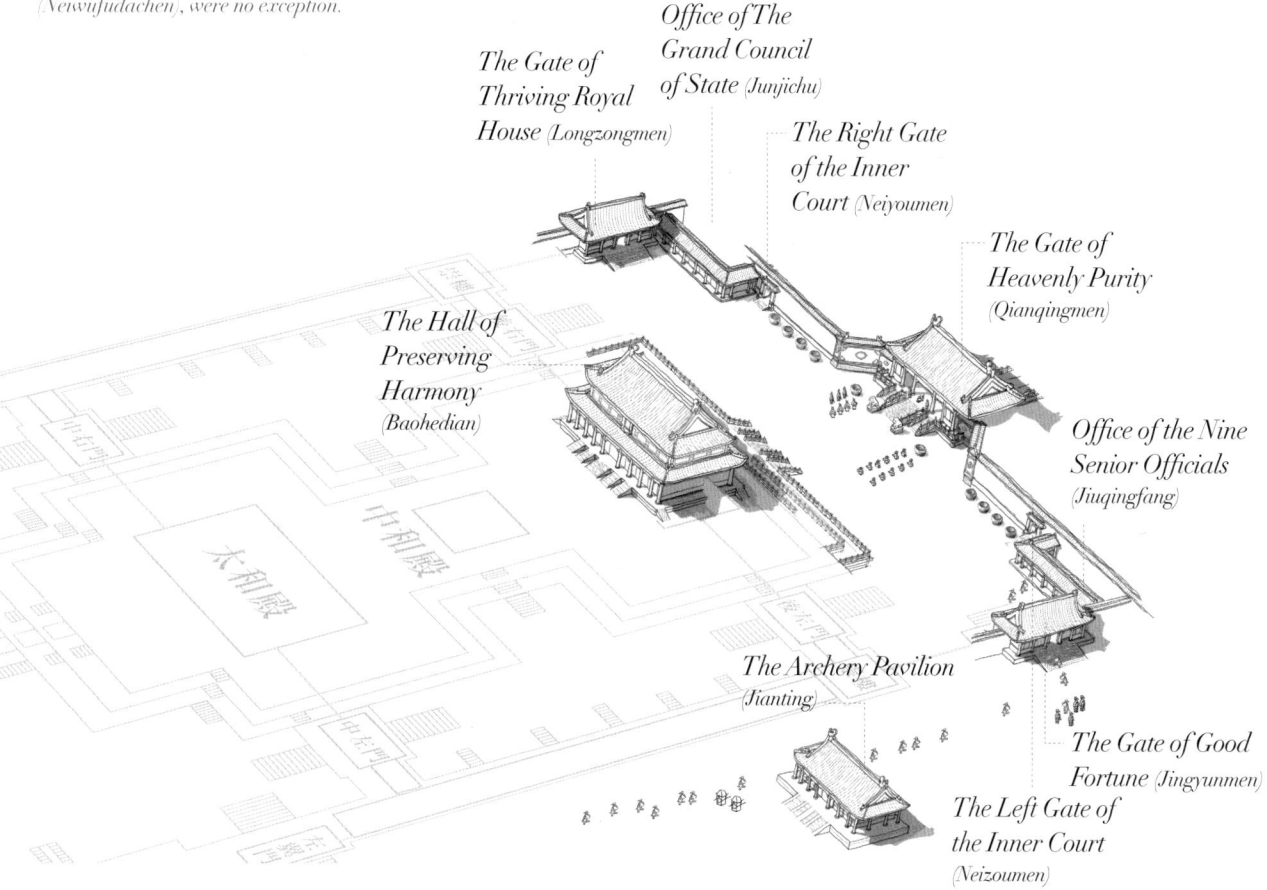

- Office of The Grand Council of State (Junjichu)
- The Gate of Thriving Royal House (Longzongmen)
- The Right Gate of the Inner Court (Neiyoumen)
- The Gate of Heavenly Purity (Qianqingmen)
- The Hall of Preserving Harmony (Baohedian)
- Office of the Nine Senior Officials (Jiuqingfang)
- The Archery Pavilion (Jianting)
- The Gate of Good Fortune (Jingyunmen)
- The Left Gate of the Inner Court (Neizoumen)

The ministers waited at the duty office outside The Gate of Heavenly Purity (Qianqingmen) for the announcement of the emperor's arrival. Minutes before the emperor appeared in court, everyone followed the rules and either knelt or stood in front of The Gate of Heavenly Purity (Qianqingmen), preparing themselves for the commencement of a court session. On rainy or snowy days, the emperor would bestow raincoats upon them or permit them to enter The Gate of Heavenly Purity (Qianqingmen).

After the reigns of Xianfeng and Tongzhi (the Empress Dowager administered state affairs behind a curtain), the system of administering state affairs at the imperial gate came to an end.

The Nine Senior Officials

Censorate (Duchayuan), Edict Office (Tongzhensi), Judicial Office (Dalisi), Rites and Ceremony Office (Taichangsi), Office for Agriculture and Raising Livestock (Taipusi), Office for Banquets (Guanglusi), Office for Management of the Capital City (Shuntianfuyin), Office for Sacrifices and Worship (Zhongrenfucheng), and Office for Management of Vassal State (Lifanyuan).

Between The Outer Court (Waichao)
and The Inner Court (Neichao)

In the 21st Year of Kangxi (1682), the elderly and weak member of the South Study of the Imperial Academy (hanlin), Zhu Yizun, was the first minister permitted to ride inside the palace.

The ministers dismounted from their horses when they reached The Archery Pavilion (Jianting) after entering The Eastern Prosperity Gate (Donghuamen), whereas those who entered through The Western Prosperity Gate (Xihuamen) dismounted when they reached the front of the Head Office of The Office of Internal Affairs (Neiwufu).

Ministers who were elderly would be granted special favor by the emperor to be carried on sedan chair to attend court. The place for them to get down was still The Archery Pavilion (Jianting). After the 36th Year of Qianlong (1771), the regulations were relaxed and court officials at Grades One and Two or above, and aged 60 or over, could take the sedan chair and enter the The Eastern Prosperity Gate (Donghuamen), The Archery Pavilion (Jianting) was closer to The Gate of Good Fortune (Jingyunmen). Then, the ministers entered The Gate of Good Fortune (Jingyunmen). Their attendants would stand and wait twenty steps away from The Gate of Good Fortune (Jingyunmen). In the later years of Qianlong, Heshen, who was the emperor's favourite eunuch, answered to no one except the Emperor himself. He exploited the relationship and even dared to be carried on his sedan chair through The Gate of Good Fortune (Jingyunmen).

In the middle and late phases of the Qing Dynasty, the special permission granted by the emperor to ride on horseback inside The Forbidden City was known as "Award to Ride Horses in Court" (Shangchauma).

Throughout the Ming Dynasty, the ministers were never permitted to ride or use any means of transport in The Forbidden City.

After Emperor Qianlong had enjoyed the dynasty's last prosperous era, the national power of the Manchurian Qing Dynasty began to deteriorate. Mismanagement in political and economic affairs led to protests and unrest among the people. The hostility between the Manchu and the Han ethnic groups was reignited in the absence of a strong government. When Emperor Jiaqing first ascended to the throne, he tried to reform the government by immediately punishing Heshen, the favourite eunuch of Qianlong, and injected all the 8 trillion taels of silver that had been confiscated (equivalent to the total national treasury income for 20 years) from him into rescuing the economy. Even so, the glorious period of the early years of the Qing Dynasty could never be revived. For about a hundred years since the beginning of the reign of Jiaqing, social unrest never subsided. Finally, the Qing government, beset with internal and external problems, collapsed.

Arrow head

The Gate of Thriving Royal House (Longzongmen)

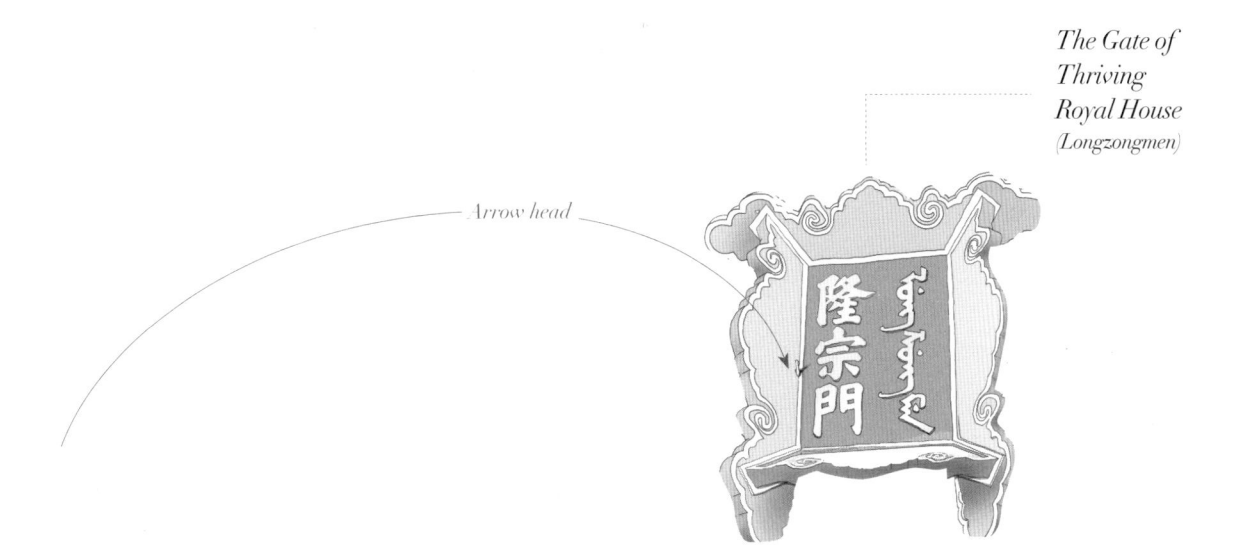

18th Year of Jiaqing (1813) "The Rebellion of Lin Qing"

Lin Qing, a rioter belonging to the Heavenly Doctrine Sect (Tianlijiao), plotted with the eunuchs in the palace and led his followers into The Forbidden City through The Eastern Prosperity Gate (Donghuamen) and The Western Prosperity Gate (Xihuamen). They intended to pass through The Gate of Good Fortune (Jingyunmen) and The Gate of Thriving Royal House (Longzongmen), and go straight into The Great Interior (Danei).

When the uprising happened, Minning (later Emperor Daoguang), the second son of the emperor, was studying in the upper study inside the The Gate of Heavenly Purity (Qianqingmen). He immediately picked up an air gun and prepared confrontaion. By that time, some Heavenly Doctrine believers had already climbed up to the top of the walls on the west side of The Hall of Mental Cultivation (Yangxindian). Minning raised his gun and shot one intruder dead (thanks to all these useful riding and shooting lessons).

In the scuffle, a metal arrowhead was left in the horizontal inscribed plaque of The Gate of Thriving Royal House (Longzongmen). Afterwards, Emperor Jiaqing issued an edict that the arrowhead should remain where it was to remind everyone to be mindful and alert. The arrowhead is still on the plaque to this date. As the arrowhead was shot from down below, this could have been an arrow shot by one of the guards at the Heavenly Doctrine Sect rioters who had already climbed up The Gate of Thriving Royal House (Longzongmen).

There were no street lights in The Outer Court (Waichao) of The Forbidden City. When the emperor went to The Outer Court (Waichao) before sunrise, his attendants would hold a ram's horn lantern to light the way. In the Yongxiang Lane in The Inner Court (Neichao), however, there was one delicate stone based bronze lamp every several tens of meters.

Before Jianqing the entire stretch of land outside The Gate of Good Fortune (Jingyunmen) and The Gate of Thriving Royal House (Longzongmen) had no street lights. After Jiaqing had executed Heshen, he gave Heshen's mansion to Prince Yonglin. The 36 bronze street lamps inside The Mansion of Heshen (Heshenfu) were relocated to the outside of The Gate of Good Fortune (Jingyunmen) and The Gate of Thriving Royal House (Longzongmen).

Concrete Balance

The rise and fall of various dynasties in China were mainly caused by external officials (including feudal lords) and internal attendants (including close relatives and distant relatives). When the external forces became too powerful, the nation disunited. When there was internal disorder, court discipline became dishevelled. Historically, those emperors who could keep these two parties in a relatively reasonable state of balance were considered good emperors. When the internal and external forces were in competition, an ineffective emperor would be plunged into turmoil.

The front section of this roughly kilometer-long central axis which runs through The Forbidden City, is The Hall of Supreme Harmony (Taihedian). It was a center for holding ceremonies and performing rites. From the rules of Nature to the rules of law, everything was carried out in accordance with the national laws (rites). Even the emperor had no free reign in this regard.

Historians have never used the grandeur displayed at important ceremonies at The Hall of Supreme Harmony to judge the achievement of an emperor, but rather they based their judgment on how he administered and managed daily state affairs. The Gate of Heavenly Purity Square (Qianqingmen Guangchang) in The Inner Court (Neichao) is equivalent to the Yan Court (The Outer Court [Waichao] of the residential palace. In the Ming Dynasty, the administration of state affairs was done personally by the emperor at The Gate of Supreme Harmony [Taihemen], which was even further than The Outer Court [Waichao].) in the "Five-Gates-Three-Courts". The Square comparatively bears a stronger flavor of practicality.

Until the reign of Emperor Yongzheng, all three parties involved in the balance of power appeared every day in this inconspicuous side street. Located between the Outer and The Inner Courts (Waichao and Neichao), The Gate of Heavenly Purity (Qianqingmen) became the focal point of this relentless power struggle. The emperor had to keep a balance in this potential storm centre, or else the two forces would mutually infiltrate, counteract, and at the end this could lead to the downfall of the dynasty.

Every publication introducing this palace in The Forbidden City will tell its readers how logical and open the design of The Outer Court (Waichao) was, and how human sentiments were taken into account when decorating in The Inner Court (Neichao), as well as how The Outer Court (Waichao) and the palaces at the back, in a ratio of 6:4, produce a very clever and first class amalgamation of public and private space. "Balance" in politics is not easy. In architecture, this ideal can be embodied within the design positively.

Between The Outer Court (Waichao)
and The Inner Court (Neichao)

- In the Ming Dynasty, the emperor personally administered state affairs at The Gate of Heaven Worship (Fengtianmen, known as The Gate of Supreme Harmony [Taihemen] in the Qing Dynasty). Emperor Taizu of the Ming Dynasty abolished the position of the Prime Minister. The important tasks of delivering edicts, as well as coordinating communication between the Inner and Outer Courts (Neichao and Waichao), were assigned to the eunuchs. During the later half of the Dynasty, most of the emperors were hedonistic. They relied heavily on the eunuchs, and were not interested in state affairs. They shunned the practice of daily attendance at the court, and their idleness developed into non-attendance for years. The worst of them all was Emperor Wanli who ignored state affairs continuously for as many as 24 years. The Ming Dynasty gradually deteriorated and faced eventual downfall.

-In the Ming Dynasty there were as many as 100,000 eunuchs (some of them lived along the river in the west of The Forbidden City. Most of them lived in The Imperial City). In the early phase of the Qing Dynasty there were only 400-plus eunuchs. (Towards the end of the Qing Dynasty, the number increased to more than 3,000).

-In the Qing Dynasty, the venue for administering state affairs was changed to The Gate of Heavenly Purity (Qianqingmen), greatly reducing the distance between where the emperor resided and where he presided. An Office of Internal Affairs was also set up and headed by a prince of the imperial clan, canceling all management responsibilities of the eunuchs in The Imperial Palace. Thus the chances of " insurgence " caused by eunuchs handling communication were reduced to minimum. (Until the end of the Qing

Dynasty, the most abominable eunuch could only mesmerize his master but could not intervene in court affairs.)

-It was recorded (see Reference 11) that in the early years of Qianlong, the emperor assigned three surnames — Qin, Zhao, and Gao — to his close attendants in the palace to remind himself that the harm done by the eunuch Zhao Gao of the Qin Dynasty was not forgotten. (Despite this, Emperor Qianlong favoured the eunuch Heshen, who ruined the economy of the entire nation.)

-After the first three reigns in the Qing Dynasty, their authority and power outside of the court began to decline, followed by inappropriate interference with The Outer Court (Waichao) by Inner Court (Neichao) powers (with situations like the emperor being weak or the empress dowager dictating). Simple traditional Outer Court (Waichao) affairs had developed to include new cultural thinking and foreign powers which previous feudal dynasties never had to face before. There was a continuous infiltration of an external power. Finally the Qing Dynasty had to silently succumb. The internal circle then confined itself within The Inner Court (Neichao) to stay on as a "small imperial court", which was at best a farce.

By the time most of the thresholds of The Inner Court (Neichao) were sawed off to enable the young last emperor to ride his bicycle freely, the external power had usurped the last remaining inner circle, leaving behind nothing but the once complete representation of political ideals — this palatial city.

Between The Outer Court (Waichao) and The Inner Court (Neichao)

Emperor Shunzhi strictly forbade the eunuchs from interfering with state affairs. He had written the prohibition orders on an iron plaque and erected it inside The Hall of Union (Jiaotaidian).

At the end of the Qing Dynasty, most of the thresholds of The Inner Court (Neichao) were sawed off to make it easier for the young emperor Puyi to cycle!

P.166　　The Grand Forbidden City — The Imperial Axis

/ Office of The Grand Council of State (Junjichu)

The two circles are just figurative metaphors. The actual situation was of course more complex; particularly when administration of state affairs at the imperial gate evolved into a practice whereby the emperor could discuss national issues with his trusted ministers anytime he chose. Hence, in between the two circles appeared a cliquey, exclusive small circle of power. This became the pinnacle of the two-thousand-year old feudal imperial political system. (In the end, to everyone's surprise, it also turned out to be a trigger of the downfall of the dynasty.)

Office of The Grand Council of State (Junjichu)

In the early days of the Qing Dynasty, the Garerdan of the Zhungarer Tribe in Xinjiang Province colluded with the Tsarist Russians and rebelled. The rebellion lingered on until the 7th Year of Yongzheng (1729). It was believed that if the cabinet was set up outside The Gate of Supreme Harmony (Taihemen), too many people would be involved, creating an environment conducive to the leaking of national secrets. A duty office was set up outside the south wall of The Hall of Mental Cultivation (Yangxindian, inside The Gate of Thriving Royal House [Longzongmen]) for the discussion of military affairs. It was formally named Office of The Grand Council of State (Junjichu) in the 10th Year of Yongzheng (1732).

Its name was changed once to "Office for Overall Administration" when Qianlong succeeded Yongzheng, but was soon reinstated until the 3rd year of Xuantong (1911) when the system of responsible cabinet was established. For 182 years (1729 to 1911), this row of small duty offices remained the most important nerve centre of the nation. Most of the edicts were issued here. However, it might sound grand to be the Minister of the Grand Council of State (Junjidachen), the nature of this position did not surpass that of the private secretary of the emperor. The position itself did not carry any real decision-making power.

On the west side of The Gate of Heavenly Purity (Qiaqingmen), there is a row of simple and unassuming houses. This is the famous Office of The Grand Council of State (Junjichu) of the Qing Dynasty. It handled important national issues and was heavily guarded. Not only were the eunuchs strictly forbidden to approach the winding corridors of The Office of The Grand Council of State (Junjichu), even the senior officials in the duty offices in the east end of the side street were not allowed to come close. The emperor appointed a prince as Principal Minister of The Grand Council of State (Shouxijunjidachen) to head up the Office. Below him, there were posts like Minister of The Grand Council of State (Junjidachen), Undesignated Minister of the Grand Council of State, Minister Intern of The Grand Council of State, and Assistant Minister of The Grand Council of State (particularly responsible for handling official communications, also known as Mini-Minister of Grand Council of State). Every day each section had to submit a memorial by the second hour of yinmao (3 to 7 am). The Assistant Minister of The Grand Council of State would resubmit the memorials to the various Ministers of The Grand Council of State for their review. The memorials were sent from The Office of The Grand Council of State (Junjichu), through The Right Gate of The Inner Court, to The Hall for Mental Cultivation

(Yangxindian) in The Inner Court (Neichao), and returned with verbal instructions from the emperor. The memorials would then be drafted, reviewed, and amended before promulgated as edicts. The entire process was carried out most efficiently and did not take more than an hour.
When the emperor left the palace, the Minister of the Grand Council of State (Junjidachen) on duty would accompany him, to prevent any dangerous delay in dealing with state affairs.

The horizontal inscribed plaque with the words "House of Harmony (Yitangheqi)" in the handwriting of Emperor Yongzheng was once hung inside The Office of The Grand Council of State (Junjichu).
During the reign of Emperor Xianfeng, the plaque read, "Good Tidings of Victory (Xibaohongjing)".
In the 34th Year of Guangxu (1908), the same plaque read: "In Preparation for the Formulation of Constitution (Choubeilixian)".

"Harmony" because in the reign of Yongzheng, the Ministers of the Grand Council of State (Junjidachen), Eertai and Zhang Tingyu, were at odds with each other. "Good Tidings" was a hope cherished by Emperor Xianfeng, because during his reign he did not fare well in wars. Yet for Guangxu, "In Preparation for the Formulation of Constitution" remained an ideal because nothing went beyond the preparation stage and no constitution was established. The horizontal inscribed plaques are witnesses of history.

The Office of The Grand Council of State (Junjichu) had yet another function that was not common knowledge; that is, "to increase imperial income".

Generally, fines imposed by The Imperial Court were decided by The Board of Civil Service (Libu) and collected by The Ministry of Revenue (Hubu). However, for convicted officials who negotiated the amounts of fine, their cases were followed up and fines collected by The Office of The Grand Council of State (Junjichu). (The income from this source, instead of going into the national coffer, went to The Office of Internal Affairs [Neiwufu] to be used as income for the palaces in The Inner Court [Neichao]). Some of the income came from officials who exploited the common people. They made false accusations so that when victims were convicted and fined, they could raise extra money to "please" the emperor. Sometimes these payments could be negotiated and even paid by instalments.

Office of The Grand Council of State (Junjichu)

The Gate of Supreme Harmony *(Taihemen)*

In the Ming Dynasty, administration of state affairs at the imperial gate was carried out at The Gate of Heaven Worship (Fengtianmen, known as The Gate of Supreme Harmony [Taihemen] in the Qing Dynasty). Here was the office for the senior aides who worked closely with the emperor (The Cabinet). However, because it was far from the palaces in The Inner Court (Neichao), it indirectly led to the disruptions of state affairs by the internal attendants (the eunuchs) who ran errands between the Cabinet and the Inner Court.

The Gate of Blending Harmony *(Xiehemen)*

(Known as The Left Gate of Obedience [Zuoshunmen] in the Ming Dynasty).

Office for the Senior Confidential Officials.
(Office for Overseeing Matters Related to Imperial Edicts and Room for the Imperial Mandates of the Cabinet).

The Cabinet

The Cabinet was the central privy council institution established by Emperor Taizu (Zhu Yuanzhang) of the Ming Dynasty after he abolished the position of prime minister. It was replaced by The Office of The Grand Council of State (Junjichu) in the Qing Dynasty. The Cabinet minister job had become a noble but idle position, or a promotional official position that was in fact a demotion.

P.172 The Grand Forbidden City — The Imperial Axis

Office of The Grand Council of State (Junjichu)
Snacks were always served along the corridors of the Duty Houses of The Office of The Grand Council of State (Junjichu), ready for hungry ministers anytime.

The Gate of Mental Cultivation (Yangxinmen)
It only takes 73 steps to go from the Gate of Observing Righteousness (Zunyimen) to the Gate of Mental Cultivation (Yangxinmen).

Leads to The Palace of Maternal Love and Peace (Cininggong) on The West Route.

The Gate of Thriving Royal House (Longzongmen)
A total of 97 paces from The Office of The Grand Council of State (Junjichu) to The Gate of Observing Righteousness (Zunyimen).

The Gate of Lunar Essence (Yuehuamen)

The Hall of Mental Cultivation (Yangxindian)
The Qing emperor simply needed to walk from The Hall of Mental Cultivation (Yangxindian) to The Gate of Observing Righteousness (Zunyimen), walk along the 7 metre wide First Western Corridor (Xiyichangjie), and then walk along the corridors of The Gate of Lunar Essence (Yuehuamen), to come to The Gate of Heavenly Purity (Qianqingmen) to administer state affairs.

The Right Gate of The Inner Court (Neiyoumen)

The Gate of Observing Righteousness (Zunyimen)

The Gate of Heavenly Purity (Qianqingmen)

Reception Rooms

To The Palace of Tranquility and Longevity (Ningshougong) on The East Route.

The Gate of Good Fortune (Jingyunmen)
The princes and ministers based in the capital came through The Gate of Good Fortune (Jingyunmen) or The Gate of Thriving Royal House (Longzongmen) and waited at the Reception Rooms on the east side, in front of the The Gate of Heavenly Purity (Qianqingmen). They proceeded in order and passed through The Gate of Heavenly Purity (Qianqingmen), The Gate of Lunar Essence (Yuehuamen), and entered The Hall of Mental Cultivation (Yangxindian) to have an audience with the emperor.

The Left Gate of The Inner Court (Neizuomen)

P.173

Office of The Grand Council of State (Junjichu)

The Gate of Heavenly Purity Square (Qianqingmen Guangchang) was the most important convergence point for traffic within The Forbidden City. It defined the boundary between the Inner and Outer Courts (Neichao and Waichao). The Gate of Good Fortune (Jingyunmen) was linked with The East Route which led to the architectural complex of The Palace of Tranquility and Longevity (Ningshougong), that Qianlong had constructed for his retirement. The Gate of Thriving Royal House (Longzongmen) was linked with The West Route which led to The Palace of Maternal Love and Peace (Cininggong) where the empress dowager and the imperial concubines of the late emperor lived.

The architectural complex of The Palace of Tranquility and Longevity (Ningshougong) is extensive. The arrangement is similar to the Main Hall on the central axis. For a long time, it had been called an imperial palace within an imperial palace. The Hall of Mental Cultivation (Yangxindian) was even smaller than an ordinary mansion of a nobleman. Nonetheless, eight emperors of Qing Dynasty, starting from Yongzheng, lived and administered state affairs here. It was therefore also looked upon as an imperial court within an imperial court. It was situated on the west side of the grand central axis.

/ The Hall of Mental Cultivation (Yangxindian)

The first two characters "Yang-xin" were taken from a saying of the scholar Mengzi, "Yangxin [cultivation of the mind] is best achieved by limiting one's desires".

Emperor Kangxi passed away on November 13 in the 61st Year of Kangxi (1722). Prince Yong Yinzhen succeeded him as Emperor Yongzheng and moved from The Palace of Heavenly Purity (Qianqinggong) to stay in The Hall of Mental Cultivation (Yangxindian). The Palace of Heavenly Purity (Qianqinggong) was changed into a palace used specially for holding court meetings, administering state affairs, and secretly selecting crown princes. After the establishment of The Office of The Grand Council of State (Junjichu), administration of state affairs was no longer held at The Gate of Heavenly Purity (Qianqingmen).

Qianlong spent 64 years in The Hall of Mental Cultivation (Yangxindian) and founded the last prosperous period in the last dynasty.

The Hall of Mental Cultivation (Yangxindian)

The Gate of Mental Cultivation
(Yangxinmen)

The gate tower was constructed in the gable and hip style with wood effect glazed tile. The base is a white marble pedestal called Sumeru throne [pedestal of a Buddha's statue]. The exterior walls were covered with glazed tiles, obviously of a higher grade than other palaces in The Inner Court (Neichao).

The Hall of Mental Cultivation (Yangxindian)

The Gate of Mental Cultivation (Yangxinmen)

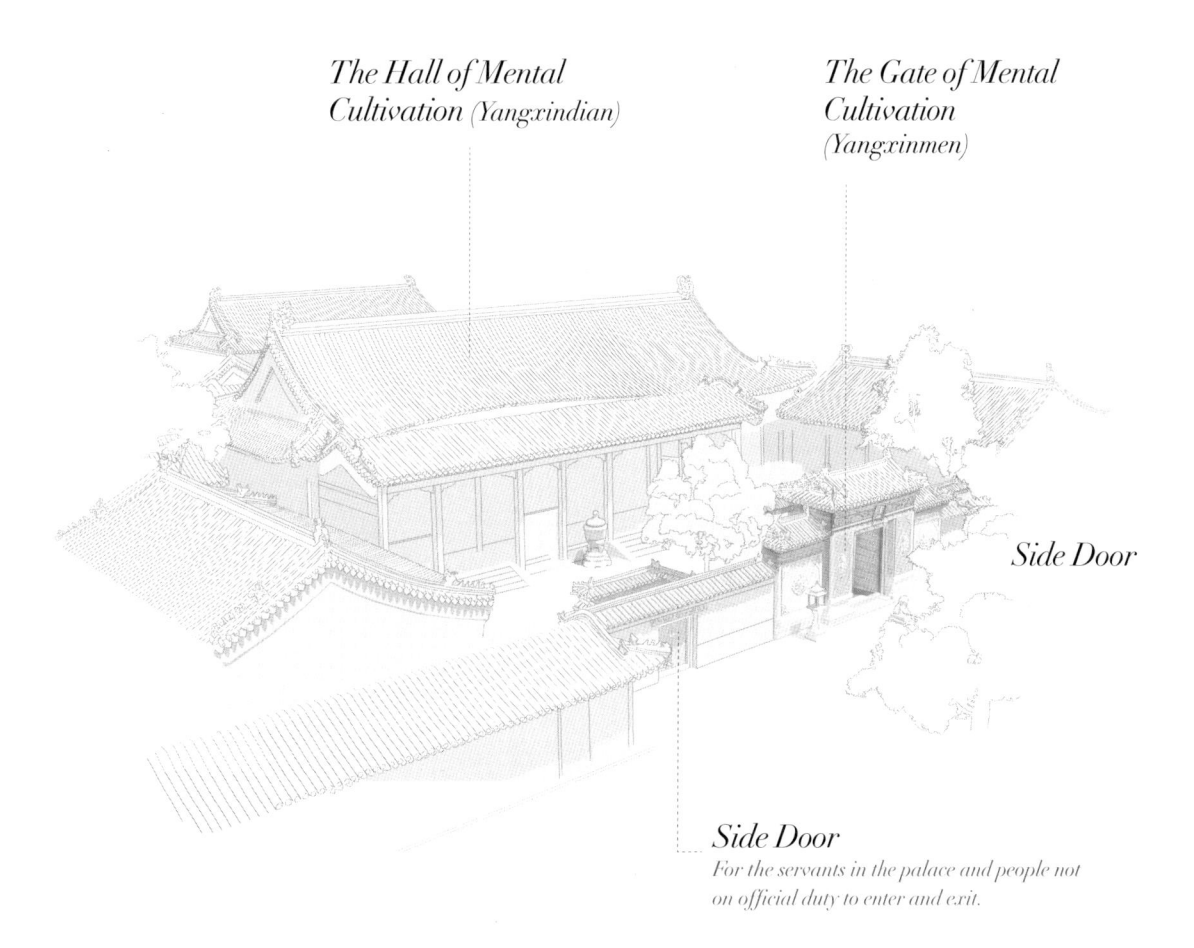

Side Door

Side Door
For the servants in the palace and people not on official duty to enter and exit.

A Day in the Emperor's Life

The emperor, living in the chambers behind The Hall of Mental Cultivation (Yangxindian), wakes up every day at 5 am (Mao Hour). After having a wash and getting dressed, he first takes a nourishing snack, like a bowl of 'birdsnest' stewed with rock sugar. Then he will read, in The West Chamber of Warmth (Xinuange), a chapter about the history on the past dynasties or decrees from former emperors. At 7 am in spring and winter (6 am in summer and fall), he will formally take breakfast. At the same time, he will pick from a plate already prepared by the eunuchs the name cards (known as "meal cards", as they are presented when the emperor is having meals) of officials he would like to receive, thus starting his administrative work for the day.

After breakfast, if it is not a day for an early court, he will greet empress dowager at her palace. He then give, audience to the reporting officials, and discuss administrative matters with the Minister-on-Duty of The Office of Grand Council of State (Dangzhi Junjidachen), or instruct an imperial scholar make a presentation on ancient classics and/or endorse memorials, etc.

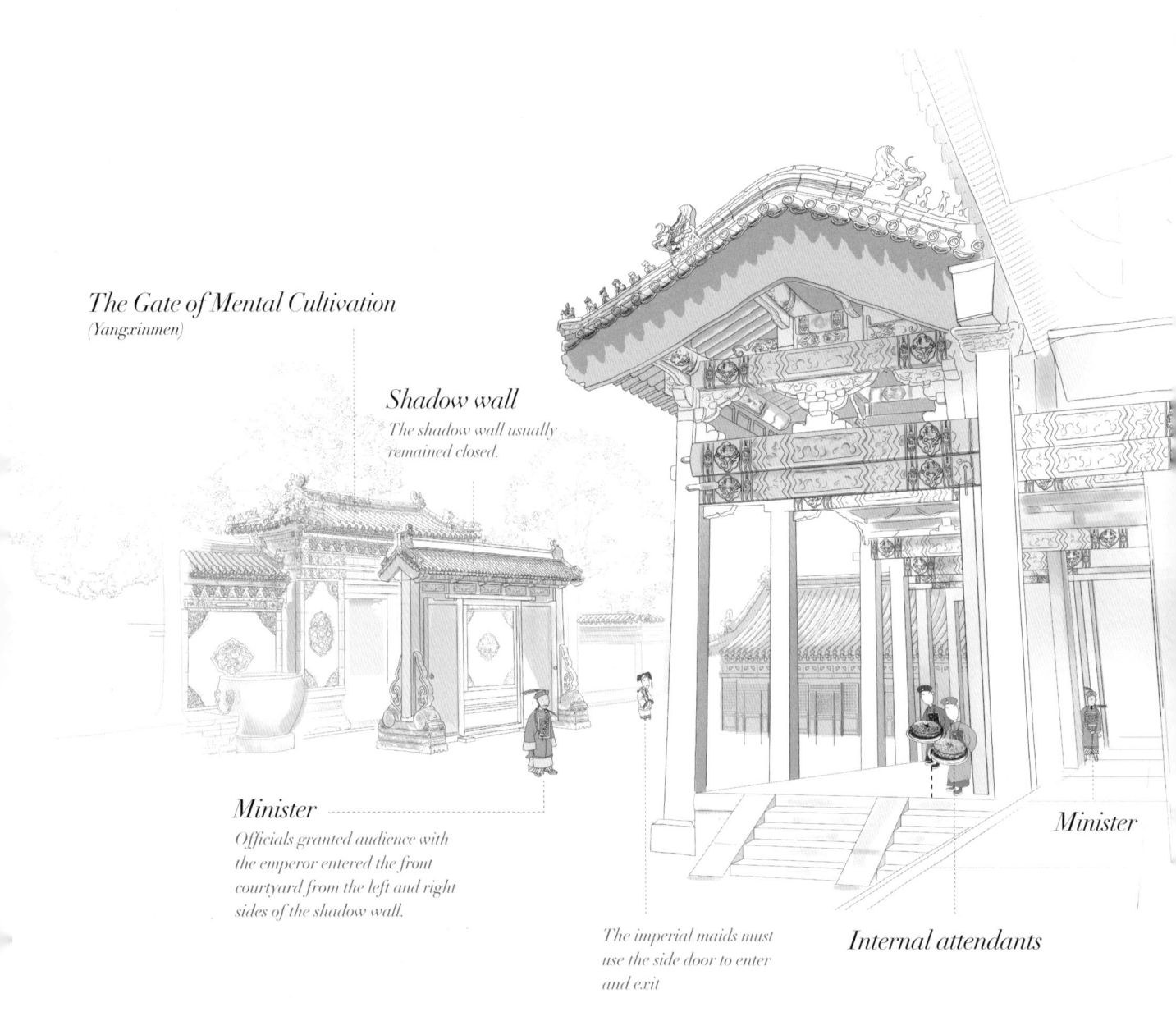

The Hall of Mental Cultivation (Yangxindian)

The Gate of Mental Cultivation
(Yangxinmen)

Shadow wall
The shadow wall usually remained closed.

Minister
Officials granted audience with the emperor entered the front courtyard from the left and right sides of the shadow wall.

The imperial maids must use the side door to enter and exit

Internal attendants

Minister

At the Wei Hour (1 to 3 pm), he will have dinner. Then it is time for relaxation, composing poems or amusing himself in the garden. Later in the evening, he will have some light supper. Basically the day comes to end. The ratio between work and rest was of course very different for an emperor like Kangxi, who was the most diligent emperor in history. He always worked late into the night on national affairs. On the other hand, while Qianlong might not have been as diligent as his father (Yongzheng) and his grandfather (Kangxi), he had, in particular, a lot of hobbies and pastimes. He lived long and in his old age he slept late and woke up early. All the people serving him; from imperial maids and internal attendants to Ministers of The Grand Council of State (Junjidachen), had to stay alert and be on call round the clock.

The Grand Forbidden City — The Imperial Axis

The Room of Three Rarities (Sanxitang)

Situated on the west side, there is the possibility of longer exposure to natural light. When the emperor writes, he will also not have his back to the light.

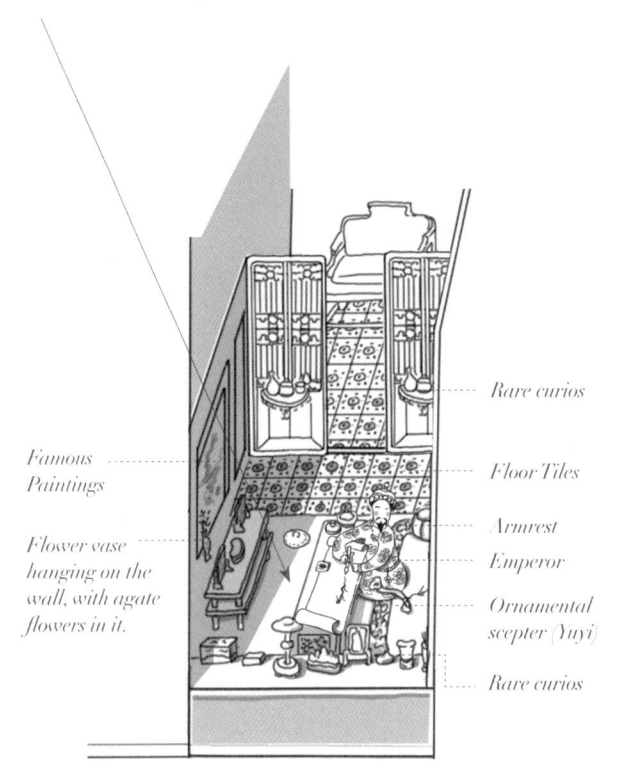

The Room of Three Rarities *(Sanxitang)*

It was a small, quiet room set up for Emperor Qianlong to pursue his interests and hobbies. It was only a little over 8 square meters and was devided into one inner and one outer room.

It was so named because inside were kept three rare and precious manuscripts of three very famous calligraphers: "Snow, Sunny Script" by Wang Xizhi, "Mid-Autumn Script" by Wang Xianzhi, and "Baiyuan Script" by Wang Xun.

The Hall of Mental Cultivation (Yangxindian) was one of the first group of palaces that were redecorated with large glass panes (imported from Guangzhou).
The Room of Three Rarities (Sanxitang), like the Clear Window (Mingchuang) on the East Side; is delicate and exquisite. When the emperor, who owned the entire nation and everything under Heaven, wanted to relax, he only had this space of about 4 square meters (the outer room). The decors of this room made one feel cosy and it reflected the refined taste of the emperor. This is a prime example for demonstration of interior design favoured by Qing Dynasty noblemen.

Famous Paintings

Flower vase hanging on the wall, with agate flowers in it.

Rare curios

Floor Tiles

Armrest

Emperor

Ornamental scepter (Yuyi)

Rare curios

P.181

The Hall of Mental Cultivation (Yangxindian)

Under Heaven there should be only one person with absolute power to rule

This authority to reign is not to be shared with anyone

The palaces in The Inner Court (Neichao) were designed for the convenience of day to day living and administration of state affairs. The rules on strict symmetry were not rigidly followed like the other palaces along the central axis in The Outer Court (Waichao).

Partitions

The West Chamber of Warmth (Xinuange): Here is where the emperor administered daily state affairs and gave individual audiences to ministers.

Hall Tiles to be Knocked by the Head

Underneath the hall tiles are rows of overturned earthen jars. Stepping on them will produce some echoing sounds. When ministers were granted an audience, it was considered a great honor. When their grandfathers were mentioned, they were required to knock their heads hard (kowtow) on the floor, and the thumping noise should reach the emperor to show the greatest respect. Therefore, a huge bribe had to be given to the eunuchs of The Inner Court (Neichao), to get an indication of where to knock to give the most effective sound. Otherwise, one could achieve no sound but could acquire a very bruised forehead. (See Reference 11)

The Grand Forbidden City — The Imperial Axis

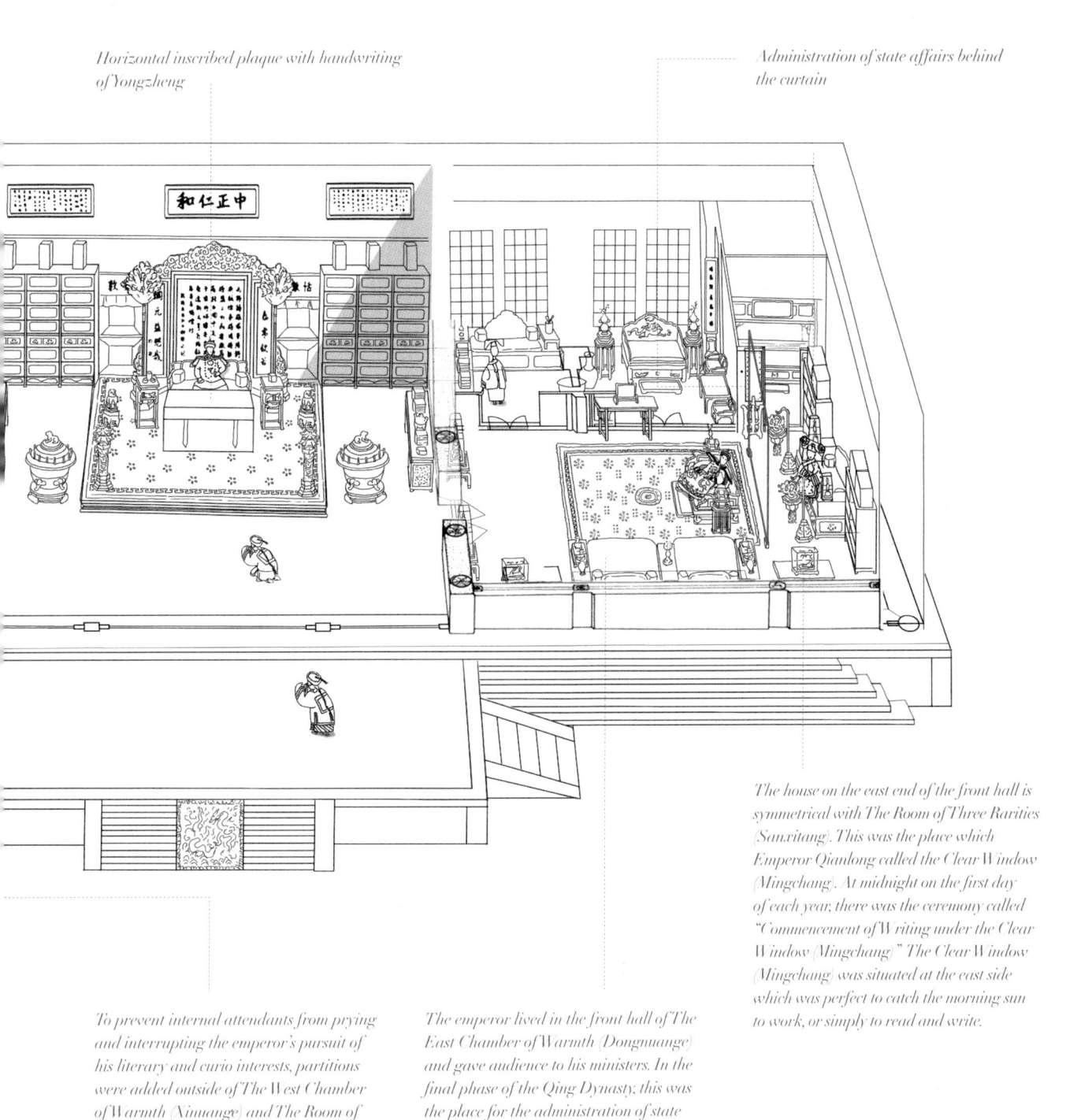

Horizontal inscribed plaque with handwriting of Yongzheng

Administration of state affairs behind the curtain

To prevent internal attendants from prying and interrupting the emperor's pursuit of his literary and curio interests, partitions were added outside of The West Chamber of Warmth (Xinuange) and The Room of Three Rarities (Sanxitang).

The emperor lived in the front hall of The East Chamber of Warmth (Dongnuange) and gave audience to his ministers. In the final phase of the Qing Dynasty, this was the place for the administration of state affairs behind the curtain.

The house on the east end of the front hall is symmetrical with The Room of Three Rarities (Sanxitang). This was the place which Emperor Qianlong called the Clear Window (Mingchang). At midnight on the first day of each year, there was the ceremony called "Commencement of Writing under the Clear Window (Mingchang)." The Clear Window (Mingchang) was situated at the east side which was perfect to catch the morning sun to work, or simply to read and write.

The Hall of Mental Cultivation (Yangxindian)

Administration of state affairs behind the curtain

At the end of the Qing Dynasty, The East Chamber of Warmth (Dongnuange) of The Hall of Mental Cultivation (Yangxindian) was the place where the empress dowagers of the reigns of Tongzhi and Guangxu (Cixi and Cian. In fact, all decisions were made by Cixi.) administered state affairs behind a curtain for twenty-seven years. The emperor's imperial seat was placed in the middle of The Chamber of Warmth (Nuange), facing west. Behind it was the imperial seat for the empress dowager, which was rectangular in shape, measuring about 2 meters long and 1 meter wide. It had a yellow silk cushion. In front of the seat was hung a gauze curtain.

After Emperor Guangxu failed in the "Reform Movement of 1898" (Wuxu Bianfa), Empress Dowager Cixi removed the curtain, sat right next to Guangxu, and proceeded with what was known as "administration intern". Cixi sat on the throne and Emperor Guangxu sat on a much smaller seat on her left. All the ministers knelt facing the empress dowager.

On December 25 (lunar calendar) of the 3rd Year of Xuantong; i.e, February 12, 1912 AD; Empress Dowager Longyu escorted Emperor Xuantong to formally promulgate, at The Hall of Mental Cultivation (Yangxindian), the Edict of Abdication of the Throne in the Qing Dynasty.

On November 5, 1924, the last emperor Puyi and the members of the imperial family were evicted from The Forbidden City.

/ The Three Palaces of The Inner Court (Neichao)

Area: north-south 220 meters long; east –west 120 meters wide.
Accompanied by the sun and the moon and uniting heaven (qian) and earth (kun). The main hall is built on a ±-shaped 2.86-meter platform, correlating with the three palaces in The Outer Court (Waichao).

The red walls on the left and right sides of The Gate of Heavenly Purity (Qianqingmen) stretched for 1.6 kilometers and embraced the independent courtyard of the Three Palaces of The Inner Court (Neichao). The moods and atmosphere of The Outer Court (Waichao) and The Inner Court (Neichao) are distinctly different. In front of The Gate of Heavenly Purity (Qianqingmen), there are two shadow walls with detailed and exquisite engraved glazed glass, displaying the contrast between the Inner and Outer Courts in relation to the tempo of life (Neichao and Waichao). The life of an imperial family was anything but ordinary.

The Three Palaces of The Inner Court (Neichao)

It was believed that the scratch marks on the "Gold-plated Vats" (Dujinhai) were made by greedy looters among the Allied Armies when they entered the palaces and were in a hurry to collect some gold.

Vats

They are also called "Propitious Vat" (Jixiang Gang), "Peace Vat" (Taiping Gang), or "Sea at the Door"(Menhai) . Water was stored in them in case it was needed to extinquish fire.

In The Forbidden City, there are 308 bronze and iron vats. Among them are 18 gilded bronze vats, placed on the left and right sides of The Hall of Supreme Harmony (Taihedian), The Hall of Preserving Harmony (Baohedian) and The Gate of Heavenly Purity (Qianqingmen). Every year at the festival of Slight Snow (Xiaoxue, [the beginning of the 20th of the 24 solar terms in the Chinese calendar, or November 22 or 23]), the vats would be covered with lids. Each lid came with an iron compartment with hot charcoals inside, to prevent the water in the vat from freezing. In midwinter, when the water began to freeze, the Fire Warming Office (Shouhuochu) would assign eunuchs to heat the vats to prevent the water from freezing, until The Waking of the Insects (Jingzhe, [the beginning of the 3rd of the 24 solar terms in the Chinese calendar, or March 5, 6, or 7]) in the following year.

In the Ming Dynasty, the vats were mainly iron or bronze. They were "luxurious" (wide) on the top and "stingy"(narrow)

In the past, it was important to make sure that it would not leak but now, it is vital to ensure that it will not collect water!

at the bottom. Each vat had one iron ring on each side. They were not as smooth and well-made as the vats in the Qing Dynasty and the design was also less sophisticated.

The Propitious Vats made in the Qing Dynasty were gilded, and very decorative, with rings and ornamental beast faces. Each of the several "Gold-plated Vats" (Dujinhai) placed in front of the door of the main hall, and bearing the inscription "Made in the Reign of Qianlong of the Qing Dynasty", was about 1.2 meters tall, 1.6 meters in diameter and reached 3,392 kilograms in weight. They added on extra dimension to the palaces and gave them a majestic look.

There were other devices for putting out fires, called "Water Jets "(Jitong). They were more conscious about fire prevention in the Qing Dynasty than in the Ming Dynasty. In the Water Jets Office (Jitongchu) in The Outer Court (Waichao), apart from a system of accountability (like having Sula [handymen in the palace] held responsible for filling up the tanks), there were two large scale fire drills every year. During the reign of Kangxi, smoking was even once prohibited.

The Three Palaces of The Inner Court (Neichao)

The Emperor lived in The Palace of Heavenly Purity *(Qianqinggong)*

It is 9 bays (48 meters) wide, 5 bays deep (26 meters), and 31.36 meters high. From Yongle of the Ming Dynasty to Kangxi of the Qing Dynasty, a total of 16 emperors lived here. Whenever there was a grand ceremony, the emperor left the palace from here. When the emperor passed away, his casket would be placed here before burial, to show that he had "come to the end of his years and gone to an eternal sleep with dignity" (shouzhong-zhengqin). And behind the horizontal plaque with inscribed words "Just and Honest" (Zhengda Guangming), was hidden the box containing the secret designation of the crown prince.

The Gate of Heavenly Purity *(Qianqingmen)*

The Gate of Lunar Essence (Yuehuamen)

The Right Gate of The Inner Court (Neiyoumen)

Inner Room for Memorials to the Emperor (Neizoushifang)

When eunuchs and other service staff of the palace entered or left the palace, they had to use the The Right Gate of The Inner Court (Neiyoumen). The court officials, like The Ministers of The Grand Council of State (Junjidachen), members of the South Study (Nanshufang) of the Imperial Academy (Hanlin), and the Ministers of The Office of Internal Affairs (Neiwufudachen) also had to use this door to enter and exit.

Gilt Bronze Lion

The gilt bronze lions stand in front of The Imperial Terrace (Danbi). The distance between the lions is less than that between the pair in front of The Gate of Heavenly Purity (Qianqingmen).

Gilt Bronze Vat

The empresses lived in The Palace of Earthly Tranquility (Kunninggong)

The Palace of Earthly Tranquility (Kunninggong) was the main palace of the empresses in the Ming and Qing Dynasties. Starting from the reign of Yongzheng, the empresses in the Qing Dynasty no longer resided in The Palace of Earthly Tranquility (Kunninggong). During imperial weddings, The East Chamber of Warmth (Dongnuange) was used as the chamber for the newly weds to spend their first night. After marriage, one of The Six Eastern or Western Palaces (Dongxiliugong) would be chosen as a place of residence. The Palace of Earthly Tranquility (Kunninggong) then became the venue for making sacrifices according to the Manchurian traditional religion (Shenjiao), there was a chimney at the back of the Palace.

In late Qing, the grand wedding ceremonies of Tongzhi and Guangxu were both controlled and organized by the Empress Dowager Cixi. The wedding of Emperor Guangxu was the grandest in the Qing Dynasty, and the most typical imperial wedding ceremony in the history of imperialism of China. The total cost of the wedding was 5 million taels of silver.

The Hall of Union (Jiaotaidian)

It was one of the residences of the empresses in the Ming Dynasty. In the Qing Dynasty, it stored 25 jade imperial seals (25 being the summation of 1, 3, 5, 7, and 9, and a number connected with destiny [Tianshu]. The East Zhou, the longest dynasty in China, lasted for 25 reigns.).
On their birthdays, the empresses received salutations from the imperial concubines and the princes.
An ancient timer, copper clepsydra (water-clock), was placed in the east and a chiming clock in the west.
The bell in The Gate of Divine Prowess (Shenwumen) rang and announced the time to the entire city.

The Left Gate of The Inner Court (Neizuomen)

Outer Office for Memorials to the Emperor (Waizoushichu)

In front of The Palace of Heavenly Purity (Qianqinggong), there was a gedao (plank road built on wooden brackets) left behind by the old system. It was 10 meters wide and 50 meters long. The Ministers went in and out from the doors on the left and right. They proceeded along the plank road stairs until they reached The Imperial Terrace (Danbi) in front of the palace to have audience with the emperor. The eunuchs could only pass through the "tiger holes" (laohudong [tunnels]) under The Imperial Terrace (Danbi) in order to cross The Imperial Boulevard (Yudao).

The Three Palaces of The Inner Court (Neichao)

The Inner Room for Memorials to the Emperor (Neizoushifang)

Before midnight, the staff from different ministries and offices responsible for submitting the memorials (in note form) would assemble and wait outside The Gate of Eastern Prosperity (Donghuamen). When The Gate of Eastern Prosperity (Donghuamen) opened at midnight, they would follow the palatial officials in charge of the memorials and enter The Gate of Good Fortune (Jingyunmen). At the Outer Office for Memorials to the Emperor (Waizoushichu), they submitted the memorials to officials there. At 2 am, The Gate of Heavenly Purity (Qianqingmen) opened and the officials of the Outer Office for Memorials to the Emperor (Waizoushichu) would hand the memorials to the responsible eunuch at The Inner Room for Memorials to the Emperor (Neizoushifang), who would then submit the memorials to the emperor. The entire routine was conducted in darkness.

The Outer Office for Memorials to the Emperor (Waizoushichu) was in the duty office on the east wing outside The Gate of Heavenly Purity (Qianqingmen).

The Hall of Diligence (Maoqindian)

Used to store books and historical documents. Every year, starting from winter solstice, a scroll called "Chart of Dissipating the Coldness 99" (Jiujiuxiaohantu) would be hung on the wall. On the scroll, there were nine characters in Chinese, meaning "In front of the pavilion, the hanging willows wait eagerly for the spring breeze". Each character had 9 strokes. The outline of each stroke traced. The duty minister of the Imperial Academy filled out one stroke each day. It took 81 days to complete the chart and its completion proclaimed the beginning of Spring.

Customary Use of Sedan Chair

The eunuchs carried the emperor everywhere on a sedan chair within palatial grounds.

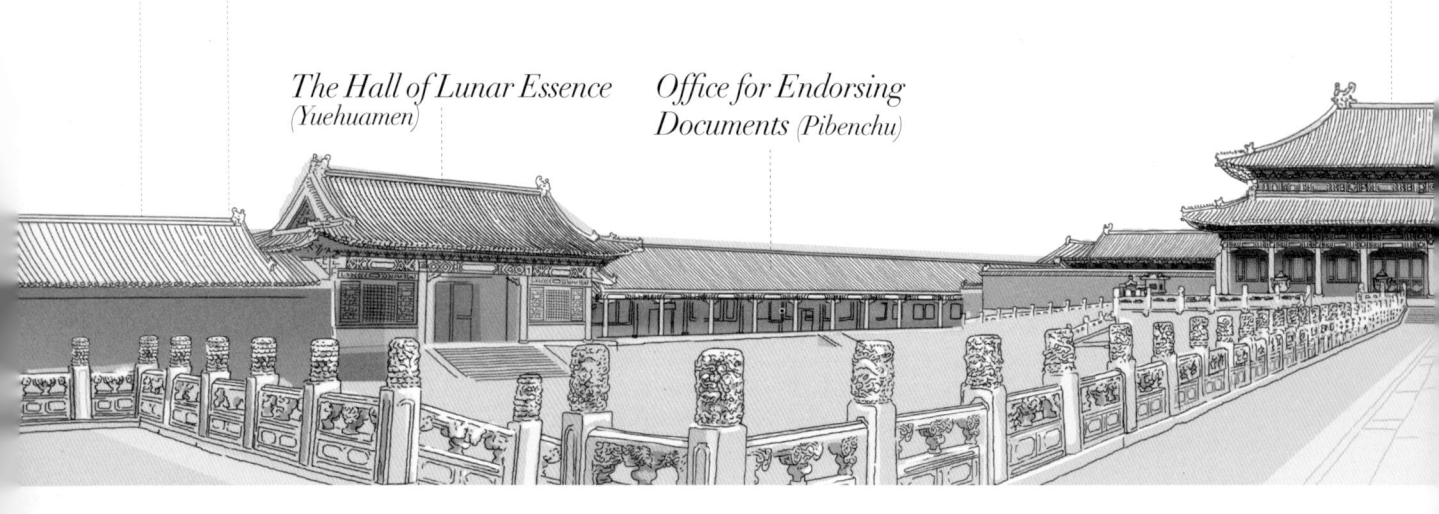

The emperor lived in The Palace of Heavenly Purity (Qianqinggong)

The Hall of Lunar Essence (Yuehuamen)

Office for Endorsing Documents (Pibenchu)

The Imperial Tearoom
(Yuchafang)

It was responsible for providing the emperor with tea, water, snacks and fruits, as well as supplies for other parts of the palaces. It also played a role in the banquets held during various festivals.

Chiming Clock Office

This Office started in the Ming Dynasty and continued in the Qing Dynasty. The emperor's daily personal needs in bathrooms and lavatories were important but they were private matters that should not be given too much publicity. Hence, the elegant name of Chiming Clock Office was adopted so that the officers could carry out their tasks discreetly.

The Imperial Pharmacy

This is the head office of the imperial physicians on duty in the palace. There were five other duty stations (Zhibandian), including The Palaces of Tranquility and Longevity (Ningshougong), of Maternal Love and Peace (Cininggong), of Accumulated Purity (Zhongcuigong), of Longevity and Health (Shoukanggong), and of Longevity and Peace (Shouangong). The overall name was Six Duties (Liuzhi).

The Hall of Proper Demeanor
(Duanningdian)

Its name implied, "proper way of putting on hats and tassels". It was used to store crowns and hats.

The Gate of Solar Essence
(Rijingmen)

The Three Palaces of The Inner Court (Neichao)

The Thousand-Senior Banquet at The Palace of Heavenly Purity *(Qianqinggong)*

In the spring of the 61st Year of Kangxi (1722), Emperor Kangxi reached the age of 69. To celebrate his 70th birthday early, 70 ministers at the age of 60 and over, and 660 aged seniors in the capital (altogether 730 seniors) were present at the Thousand-Senior Banquet hosted by the Emperor.

As many as three thousand people attended the Thousand-Senior Banquet held in the 50th Year of Qianlong (1785). There were 800 tables set up in The Outer and Inner Courts (Waichao and Neichao). Among these, 50 were inside the Hall, 244 on the terraces, 124 in the passageways, and 382 were on the left and right of The Imperial Terrace (Danbi).

The Imperial Maids in the Qing Dynasty The imperial maids in the Ming Dynasty had to stay in the palace for life. If they flouted any rules, the offenders were punished by having to ring warning bells at night. They had to follow a designated route of walking from the front of The Palace of Heavenly Purity (Qianqinggong) to The Gate of Solar Essence (Rijingmen), then to The Gate of Lunar Essence (Yuehuamen), and back to the front of The Palace of Heavenly Purity (Qianqinggong). They had to do this circuit till dawn. The imperial maids in the Qing Dynasty were relatively luckier than those in the Ming Dynasty. They had a fixed term of service, and when the term ended, there was the possibility for them to be released and get married.

The Imperial Maids in the Qing Dynasty

The Six Eastern and Western Palaces (Dongxiliugong) and The Imperial Garden (Yuhuayuan)

The palaces in The Inner Court (Neichao) of The Forbidden City consist of three routes:

On the Outer East Route was the courtyard for the emperor's father — The Palace of Tranquility and Longevity (Ningshougong), (built between the 36th and 41st Year of Qianlong). On the Outer West Route was the empress dowager palatial complex, first built during the Jiajing years in the Ming Dynasty — The Palace of Maternal Love and Peace (Cininggong).

In between the two routes was the area [Middle Route] where the emperor and empress lived.

The Six Eastern and Western Palaces (Dongxiliugong)
and The Imperial Garden (Yuhuayuan)

This cart is similar in style to the one Cixi took when she fled to Xian upon the entry of the Eight-Country Joint Forces to the capital. It is on display in the exhibition hall in the tower of The Proper Gate (Duanmen). The cart looks basic and uncomfortable, Cixi had no choice as she left in haste.

The three palaces in the Middle Route use the Heaven (Qian) and Earth (Kun) Palaces as the core and the Sun (Ri) and Moon (Yue) Gates as complements. The Six Eastern and Western Palaces (Dongxiliugong) are evenly distributed on their left and right. At the back, there are The Five Eastern and Western Abodes (Dongwusuo and Xiwusuo). This pattern is symbolic of the number of the 12-star constellation (Shierxingsu) and the numbers of the Heavenly Stems (Tiangang [10]) and Earthly Branches (Dizhi [12]).

A poet in the Tang Dynasty used the words, "the three thousand beauties in the palaces in The Inner Court (Neichao)" to describe the numerous of concubines that the emperor had. In the Ming Dynasty, the number of beauties in those palaces was a staggering 9,000! Considering the area ratio between the Outer and Inner Courts (Waichao and Neichao) was 6:4, then in the Ming Dynasty the 9,000 concubines and imperial maids spent their entire lives in a space of 289,453.2 square meters.

The residential space in The Inner Court (Neichao, i.e., the three palaces plus The Six Eastern and Western Palaces [Dongxiliugong]) alone covers an area of 139,500 square meters, being 450 meters wide from the east to the west, and 310 meters long from the north to the south.

The Six Eastern and Western Palaces (Dongxiliugong) spread on the left and right sides of the three palaces in The Inner Court (Neichao). They look like the middle column of six squaes in the squared paper for practicing Chinese calligraphy (Jiugonge). Each of them measures 50 meters on each side.

The Six Eastern and Western Palaces (Dongxiliugong) adhered to the basic standard with "one main hall and two wingrooms". Each palace covered an area of 2,500 square meters. The owner of each palace (a concubine) would have had beaten 8,988 competitors before becoming rightful owner. Those women who lost, if lucky, could serve in these palaces. One would not want to imagine the destiny of the remaining competitors.

The distance between the palaces in the East and West Routes is about 150 meters. Only a narrow lane of a few meters wide separates every couple of palaces on the same route. However, two neighboring imperial maids might not have a chance to meet one another in their lifetime. Because of this, a statement made earlier needs to be amended: a lucky imperial maid may spend her entire life within a space of 2,500 square meters.

A rule was laid down in the 12th Year of Shunzhi: at The Palace of Heavenly Purity (Qianqinggong) concubines installed should include: one furen, one shuren, 6 wanshi, 30 each of rouwan and fangwan. Apart from the empress, there were a total of 68 concubines and also a variable number of serving maids of different ranks.

The palace for the empress dowager had 12 senior imperial maids, and following a strict hierarchy, the empress had 10, the imperial honorable concubine (huangguifei) had 8, an imperial concubine (guifei) had 8 and other concubines (fei) had 6 each, an honorable lady (guiren) had 4, a lady-in-waiting (changzai) had 3 and a responder (daying) had 2.

*The Six Eastern and Western Palaces (Dongxiliugong)
and The Imperial Garden (Yuhuayuan)*

The Outer West Route is the Empress Dowager palace complex — the district of The Palace of Maternal Love and Peace (Cininggong).

The Middle Route is the residential area for the emperor and the empress.

The Palace of Great Benevolence (Jingrengong)

The Palace of Prolonging Happiness (Yanxigong)

The Outer East Route was the palatial court for the father of the emperor — The Palace of Tranquility and Longerity (Ningshougong).

There are 7 ranks of concubines of the emperor: namely imperial honorable concubine (huangguifei), imperial concubine (guifei), concubine (fei), concubine in ordinary (bin), honorable lady (guiren), lady-in-waiting (changzai), and responder (daying).

Emperor Qianlong enjoyed both longevity and good fortune. Altogether, he had 3 empresses, 5 imperial honorable concubines (huangguifei), 5 imperial concubines (guifei), 6 concubines (fei), 6 concubines in ordinary (bin), 12 honorable ladies (guiren), 4 ladies-in-waiting (changzai), a total of 41. The other women in the palace were not within any classification.

The guard of honor and attendants of Empress Xiaoqin (Cixi) when she attended the court.

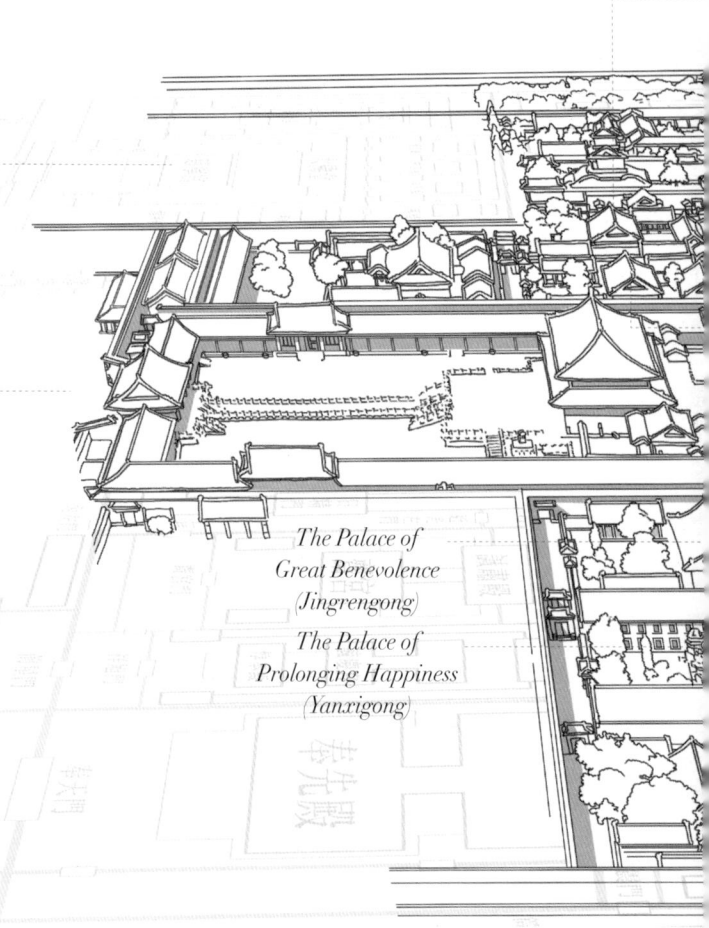

The Hall of the Supreme Pole (Taijidian)

The Palace of Eternal Spring (Changchungong)

The Palace of Universal Happiness (Xianfugong)

The Palace of Eternal Longevity (Yongshougong)

The Palace of Earthly Honor (Yikungong)

The Palace of Preserved Elegance (Chuxiugong)

The Palace of Celestial Favor (Chengqiangong)

The Palace of Accumulated Purity (Zhongcuigong)

The Palace of Eternal Harmony (Yonghegong)

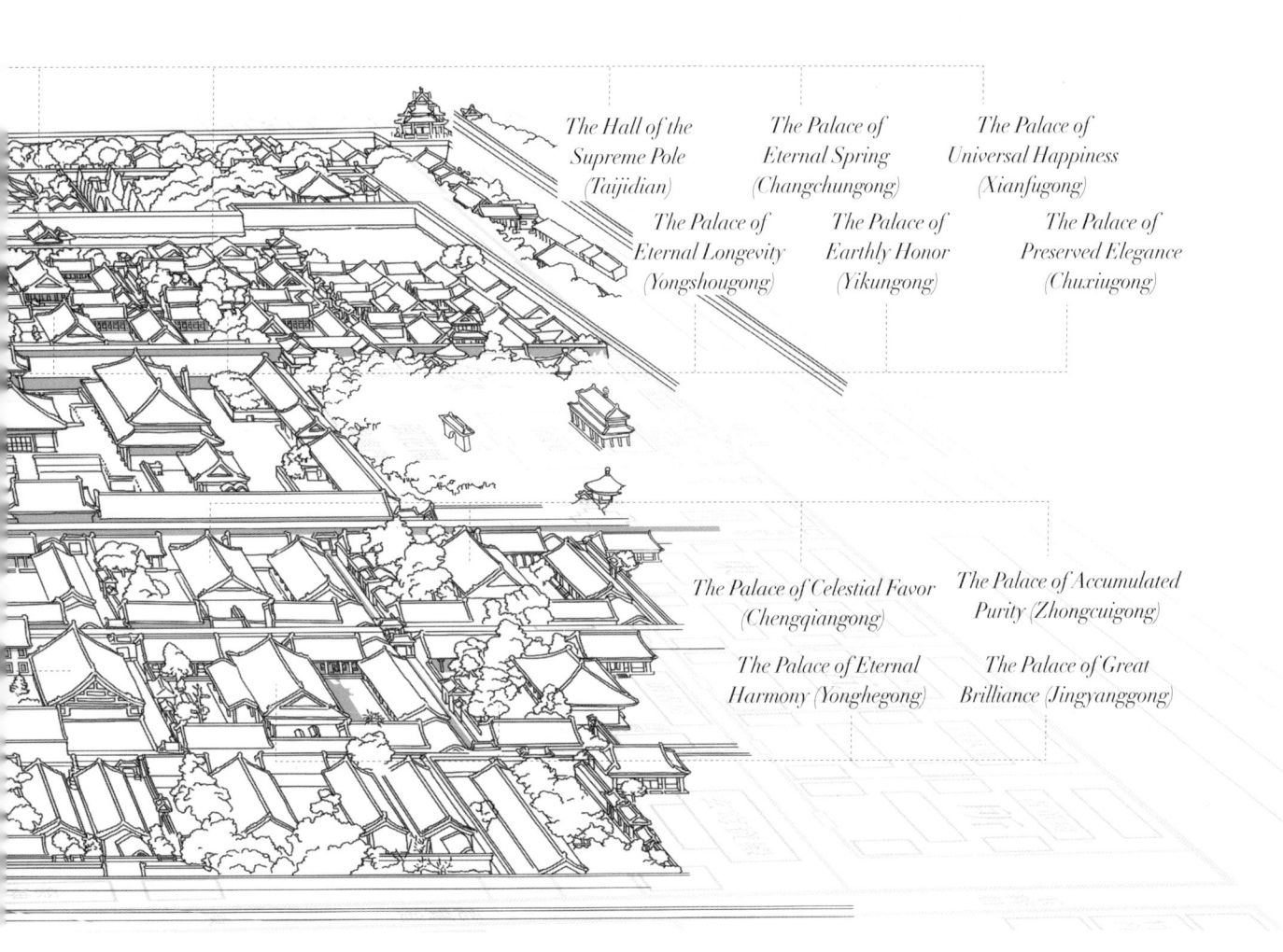

The Palace of Great Brilliance (Jingyanggong)

When Empress Xiaoqin left her palatial residence to attend court, she would usually sit on an open sedan chair carried by 8 eunuchs of The Inner Court (Neichao), dressed in ceremonial dress. Li Lianying [eunuch] was on her left, supporting the sedan chair, and another one or two eunuchs of The Inner Court (Neichao) on her right. In front of the sedan chair there were four 5th-grade eunuchs, and at the back twelve 6th-grade eunuchs. Each of them carried things like clothes, shoes, towels, combs, brushes, fragrant powder, incense burner, silver, cinnabar, brushes, ink, yellow paper, tobacco, shredded tobacco, and various types of mirrors. The last one held a yellow satin chair. There were also 2 amahs, and 4 imperial family members, also carrying various articles. Dezong (Emperor Guangxu) walked on the right side of the sedan chair, and the empress, amahs, and imperial family members all walked on the left side of the sedan chair. (See Reference 11).

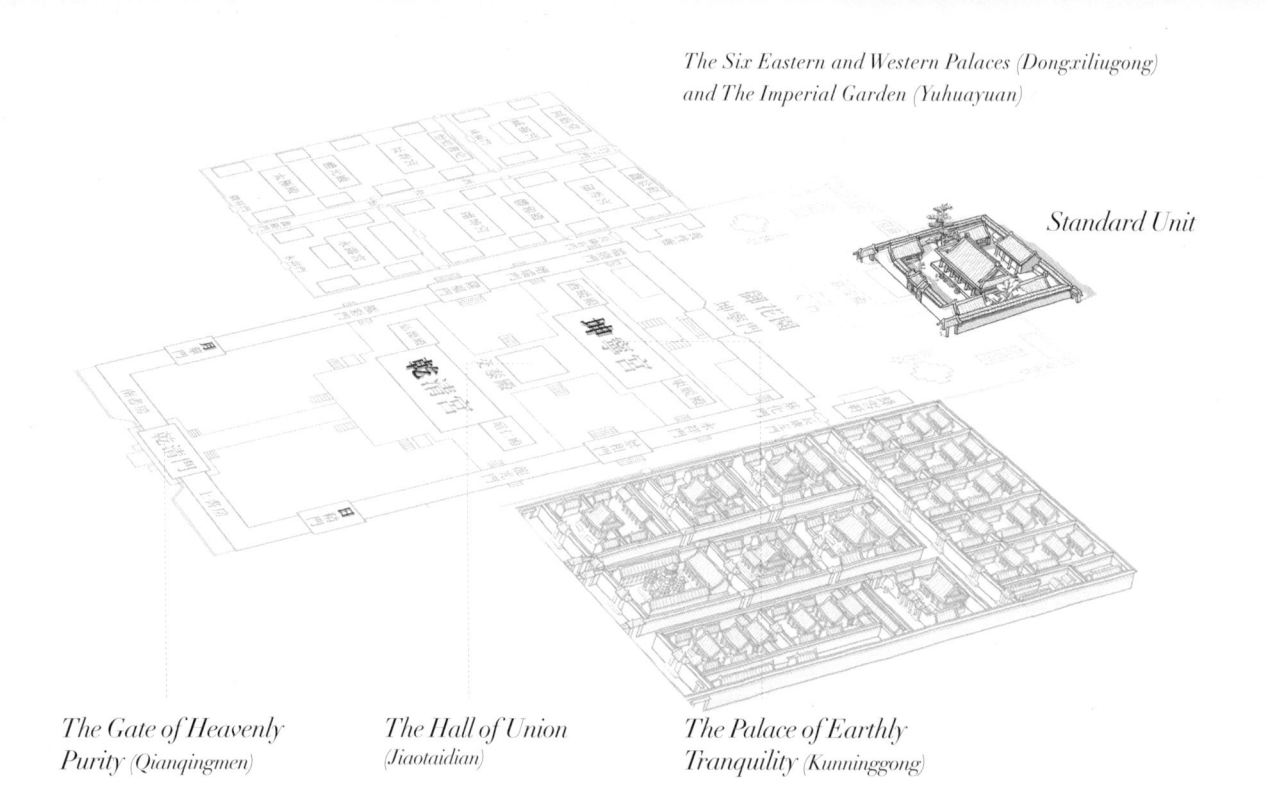

*The Six Eastern and Western Palaces (Dongxiliugong)
and The Imperial Garden (Yuhuayuan)*

Standard Unit

The Gate of Heavenly Purity (Qianqingmen)

The Hall of Union (Jiaotaidian)

The Palace of Earthly Tranquility (Kunninggong)

Emperor Guangxu, the empress, and eunuchs, etc., up to 30 to 40 people usually accompanied and made themselves available to serve Empress Dowager Cixi when she went around in the palace. It was a grand display of exhibitionism. An imperial maid once gave a first hand account on the life within the palaces. And in the eyes of the imperial maids, Empress Dowager Cixi was apparently a very different person from how she was normally portrayed. She was a kind empress dowager who took a hands-on approach on national affairs and was very considerate towards her servants. (See Reference 17)

With the downfall of the Qing Dynasty, hundreds and thousands of eunuchs and imperial maids were released. These eunuchs and imperial maids were of course not recognized nor highly regarded inside the palaces. Sadly, their fate after leaving the palaces did not justify an entry in the history books either.

In the early years of the Qing Dynasty, The Great Interior (Danei) was rather quiet. There were only 400 imperial maids. At a later stage, the number grew and matched the decription of "There were 3,000 beauties in The Inner Court (Neichao)".

The occupants of different palaces received vastly different treatments depending on whether the concubines in residence were the emperor's favourite. It was recorded (see Reference 11) that when Empress Xiaoqin (Cixi) slept, apart from having senior eunuchs on the look-out, there were close to a hundred junior eunuchs quietly on sentry duty. This description deviates slightly from another publication, which records that no one was allowed access to the sleeping chambers other than the imperial maids who were assigned to wait on the empress while she slept. Senior or junior eunuchs were probably only instructed to stand guard outside the chambers. (See Reference 17).

What is certain is that some of the lady residents in the palaces where out of favour empresses or concubines were housed had to subsidise their allowance by sending eunuchs out of the palace to sell their embroidery. Television drama series always carry the provocative message that none of the wells in the palaces provided drinkable water because so many imperial maids ended their lives by throwing themselves into them. An exaggeration this might be, but in the Ming Dynasty, there were real, heart-rending stories about imperial maids dying of starvation because of unfair distribution of food.

In the Ming Dynasty the number of eunuchs reached 100,000. Apart from some of them living in the narrow strip between the riverside in the west of The Forbidden City, and the city wall (The Golden Water River again played the role here of separating the inside from the outside), a great majority of them lived outside of the palaces but within The Imperial City compound. This was because when The Forbidden City was completed in early Ming Dynasty, it had 9,999 bays. (Four columns make up a bay. Recently The Forbidden City has been under renovation. About 8,700 bays still exist, with a total of 980 halls and houses.) the number 100,000 would have meant that within each set of four columns there were 10 eunuchs. Since the eunuchs were only allowed to be on duty within The Inner Court (Neichao), the number of occupiers in The Inner Court (Neichao) would be doubled. Even if they had worked on shifts, it would have been unbearably overcrowded.

The concubines who belonged to the former reigns and had retreated to other palaces were entitled to very meagre monthly allowances. They frequently had to provide for themselves by sending their embroidery with the eunuchs of The Inner Court (Neichao) to sell in the markets.

All the twelve palaces in The Inner Court (Neichao) built in the early years of the Ming Dynasty followed one model with standardized specifications. Later on, whether one deserved to stay in one or several palaces depended on the status and power of individuals concerned. In some cases walls were torn down to form larger units. (In the Qing Dynasty, the Six Western Palaces (Xiliugong) had already become a large palatial courtyard with three compounds, each with 4 sections).

It is impossible for anyone in the past to have seen the palaces from the viewpoint of the illustrations in this book. The female imperial family members living in any of the palatial courtyards did not have any idea where their exact location was within The Imperial Palace. Intruders who trespassed in The Great Interior (Danei) would easily get lost among the palatial alleys in between these standard units.

*The Six Eastern and Western Palaces (Dongxiliugong)
and The Imperial Garden (Yuhuayuan)*

*The Gate of Obedience
and Loyalty
(Shunzhenmen)*

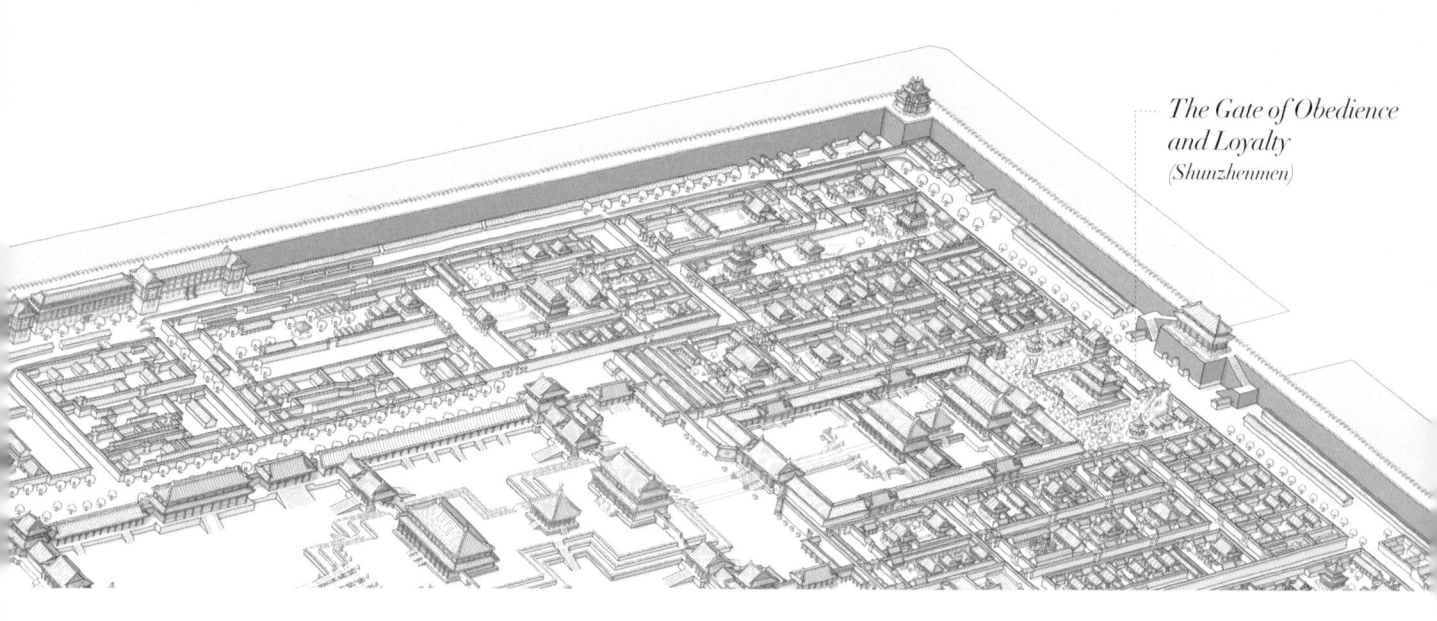

Selected the Beaties (Xiunu)

The Gate of Obedience and Loyalty (Shunzhenmen) in The Inner Court (Neichao) was the place where the Qing palaces selected the Beauties (xiunu). In the Qing palaces, the selection of the Beauties (xiunu) from the Eight Banners groups (to become senior imperial maids who waited on the emperor and the concubines, with a possibility of promotion) took place once every three years. However, the selection of the Beauties (xiunu) from the Three Banners groups of The Office of Internal Affairs (Neiwufu; as low-ranking servants, without hope of promotion) had to take place annually. Every year each Banner group had to submit a register of girls aged 14-16.

During the latter half of the Qing Dynasty, the female residents inside the palace often met their relatives here outside The Gate of Obedience and Loyalty (Shunzhenmen). In contrast, the imperial maids in the Ming Dynasty would not have been allowed to leave the palace alive.

It was recorded that, " [During the Qi Dynasty of the Five Dynasties about a thousand years ago, a nobleman Hun ordered that] pieces of gold to be carved into the shape of water lilies and stuck on the ground. He ordered Concubine Pan to walk on them, saying, 'This means your every step will produce a charming lily. '". (See Reference 18). Later a woman's small bound feet were called "golden lilies" because of this story.

One thousand years later, when Gaozhong (Qianlong) was selecting the Beauties (xiunu), he suddenly saw on the ground powdery prints that resembled water lilies, and wanted to investigate. It was actually a woman who carved on the soles of her shoes the design of a lily and compressed powder into the carved out grooves. Thus, as if water lilies appeared along where she walked.

This Beauty (xiunu) who stepped out of line might have read the stories of the Five Dynasties, but did not realize the difference between a quaint idea put into practice by an emperor and "one that was created with her own initiative". Furthermore, how could she compare the "Qi nobleman Hun" [during the period of the Five Dynasties] with the glorious emperor currently on the throne! As a result, she received a serious rebuff. Emperor Qianlong became very angry and "immediately ordered the eunuchs of The Inner Court (Neichao) to expel her".

Two reigns later, in the winter of the 9th Year of Xianfeng (1859), Emperor Wenzong personally selected the Beauties (xiunu). The candidates were respectfully waiting early in the morning by the steps in front of the palace. However, after a long time there was still no sign of the emperor. All the girls were shivering in the cold winds. One of them could not endure any more and wanted to leave. With a loud shout, the eunuch from The Inner Court (Neichao) who was in charge prohibited her from leaving. They started arguing and the girl said loudly, "I thought all matters in The Imperial Court were prioritized and managed accordingly. Now that wars are everywhere, food supplies in the capital are diminishing day by day, and the residents in the city could only live on congee. Most of them do not know where the next meal is going to come from. Parents and their children can no longer protect each other. Yet The Imperial Court does not select and make good use of the generals and ministers or seek advice from virtuous people. Instead, efforts are put into selecting concubines today and Beauties (xiunu) tomorrow. I've always heard about the tyrannical and hedonistic emperors in ancient times. How is our emperor on the throne different?"

At that time, Emperor Xianfeng was coming out from behind the screens at the back of the hall. He asked what all that commotion was about. All the girls were "scared to death and failed to respond". This girl came forward, knelt down and repeated word for word of what she had said. She demonstrated amazing courage by "accepting responsibility for what she herself had done". The emperor was speechless and the selection process was abandoned. The girl's daring speech made her famous throughout the capital. It seemed apt for the written record to state that "A person with noble character is one who dares to speak his/her mind".

Since this incident was strictly a one-off episode, there was no cause for celebration really. The fearlessness of the girl might be more than adequate to earn her the title of a "chivalrous lady". However, according to the records she was merely a "girl". The story was called "A Biography of an Outspoken Girl" (in Chinese, See Reference 19), written by

*The Six Eastern and Western Palaces (Dongxiliugong)
and The Imperial Garden (Yuhuayuan)*

P.206　　　*The Grand Forbidden City — The Imperial Axis*

Wang Kaiyun at the end of the Qing Dynasty. The author recorded, "Later the Emperor furnished a reason to demote the girl's father. There was another record saying that after the abandonment of the selection process, it so happened that a court official lost his spouse. "The girl was then assigned to marry him". The ending of the story was hardly encouraging nor celebratory.

Inside The Imperial City in Beijing, there is one hall called Abode of Fortune and Peace (Jiansuo). It was reserved specially for low status women in The Inner Court (Neichao), like ladies-in-waiting and responders, and concubines who were no longer the emperor's favourite. When they had fatal illnesses, or died a sudden death, they were not allowed to stay in the palace and had to be moved immediately to this Abode of Fortune and Peace (Jiansuo). This hall still exists and is located on the Jingshan East Street. (In the Ming Dynasty, there was The Hall of Comfort and Joy [Anletang], but now only the name of the place remains). When palace attendants died, they were buried outside The Gate of the City of Abundance (Fuchengmen). In the old days scholars visited the site to pay their respects. They called this place Palace Attendants Ramp (Gongrenxie). (See Reference 12).

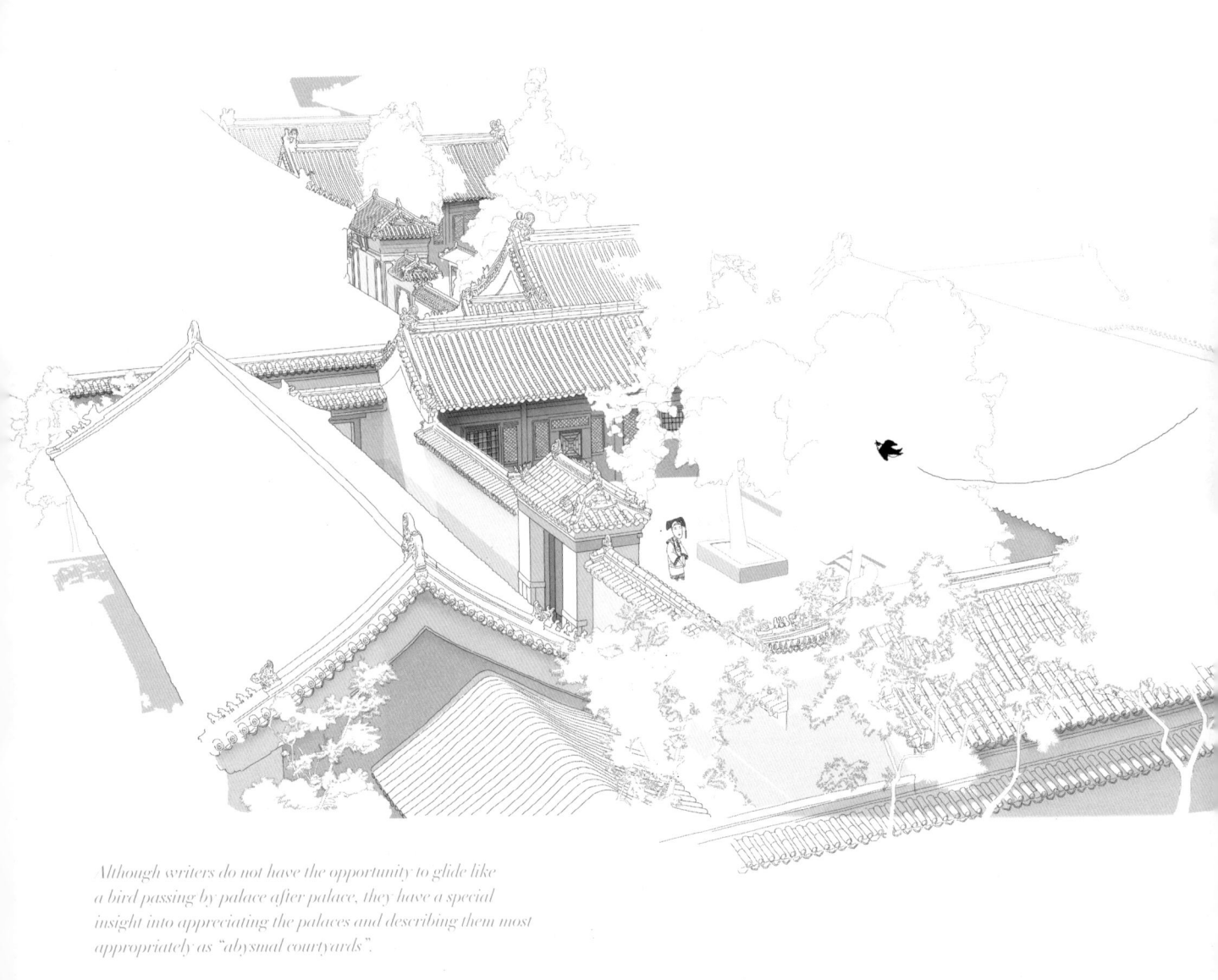

*The Six Eastern and Western Palaces (Dongxiliugong)
and The Imperial Garden (Yuhuayuan)*

*Although writers do not have the opportunity to glide like
a bird passing by palace after palace, they have a special
insight into appreciating the palaces and describing them most
appropriately as "abysmal courtyards".*

P.208   The Grand Forbidden City — The Imperial Axis

/ The Imperial Garden (Yuhuayuan)

Outside of The Gate of Earthly Tranquility (Kunningmen) is the last section of the Central Axis of The Forbidden City.

There are four imperial gardens in the entire palatial city. The other three include: The Qianlong Garden (Qianlonghuayuan) in The Palace of Tranquility and Longevity (Ningshougong) on The East Route, The Garden of Maternal Love and Peace (Cininghuayuan) in The Palace of Maternal Love and Peace (Cininggonghuayuan) on The West Route, and the Garden of The Palace of Established Happiness (Jianfugonghuayuan) in the northwest. Among them, The Garden of Maternal Love and Peace is unattended and neglected. The Garden of The Palace of Established Happiness (Jianfugonghuayuan) is being reinstated to its former glory and the first phase of reconstruction has just been completed (to be discussed later). The Qianlong Garden is known for being tasteful and exquisite. The largest of them all is the imperial garden behind the Three Palaces of The Inner Court, which is commonly called The Imperial Garden (Yuhuayuan).

The Imperial Garden (Yuhuayuan)

The Shrine of the Four Deities
(Sichenci)

In the Ming Dynasty, The Imperial Garden (Yuhuayuan) was also called Rear Garden of the Palace (Gonghouyuan). Maybe this is a more appropriate name. The true imperial gardens should have included The Old Summer Palace (Yuanmingyuan), better known as "The Garden of All Gardens", The Summer Palace (The Garden of Well Nourished Harmony [Yiheyuan]) of Empress Dowager Cixi, The West Garden (Xiyuan) that is near the western end of The Forbidden City, and The Chengde Summer Resort (Chende Bishu Shanzhuang) which is some distance away.

The wealthy families in ancient times valued the concept of "taking vacation" or living leisurely after retirement in a "second home". The landscape designs in these enclosed courtyards would have certainly provided retreats from daily pressures but they were not in the same league as real gardens. Of course, large-scale second homes would have impressive gardens that topped the league.

These gardens inside The Forbidden City, were not very big considering the size of the whole place. Hence, the design's emphasis was on being tasteful and exquisite; making sure that the emperor, after administering state affairs, could have a sanctuary akin to nature which gave him pleasure. Inside the garden, there were beautiful plants and rockeries, pavilions and deckings. The walkways were all decorated with mosaic, all arranged in great detail. Compared with the geometric gardens in the palaces in the Western world, which almost stand still in time, The Imperial Garden (Yuhuayuan) manages to preserve the rhythm of nature, embracing everything that the four seasons bring along with them. It is definitely not just a supersized flowerpot.

Outside of The Imperial Garden (Yuhuayuan) is the magnificent Gate of Divine Prowess (Shenwumen). Leaving the Gate will mark the end of a chapter for the axis of The Forbidden City. One has to continue imagining the line in order to come up with a layout of the city. If possible, it is best to climb up to The Prospect Hill (Jingshan) and see how the axis extends to The Bell and Drum Tower (Zhonggulou) in the north. Along the Imperial Axis that we just walked past, all the trees and plants flourished in the sunshine.

Taking a bird's eye view from the highest point of this Axis, The Forbidden City, which should originally be rectangular, always appears to be a magnificent square palatial city .

P.212 *The Grand Forbidden City — The Imperial Axis*

The Pavilion of a Thousand Autumns (Qianqiuting)

The Jade Pavilion (Yucuiting)

The Hall of Imperial Palace (Qinandian)

The Gate of Divine Prowess (Shenwumen)

The Auspicious Water-Cleansed Pavilion (Chengruiting)

The Studio of Establishing Teachings (Weiyuzhai)

The Pavilion of Prolonging Splendor (Yanhuige)

The Lodge for Cultivating One's Character (Yangxingzhai)

The Gate of Heavenly Unity (Tianyimen)

The Gate of Obedience and Loyalty (Shunzhenmen)

The Imperial Prospect Pavilion (Yujingting)

The Shrine of the Four Deities (Sichenci)

The Belvedere of Crimson Snow (Jiangxuexuan)

The West Imperial Garden Gate (Qiongyuanximen)

The Mountain of Accumulated Elegance (Duixiushan)

The Pavilion of Floating Jade (Fubiting)

The Gate of Earthly Tranquility (Kunningmen)

The East Imperial Garden Gate (Qiongyuandongmen)

The Pavilion of Myriad Springtimes (Wanchunting)

The Pavilion of Concentrated Fragrance (Ningxiangting)

The Hall of Ornate Writing (Chizaotang)

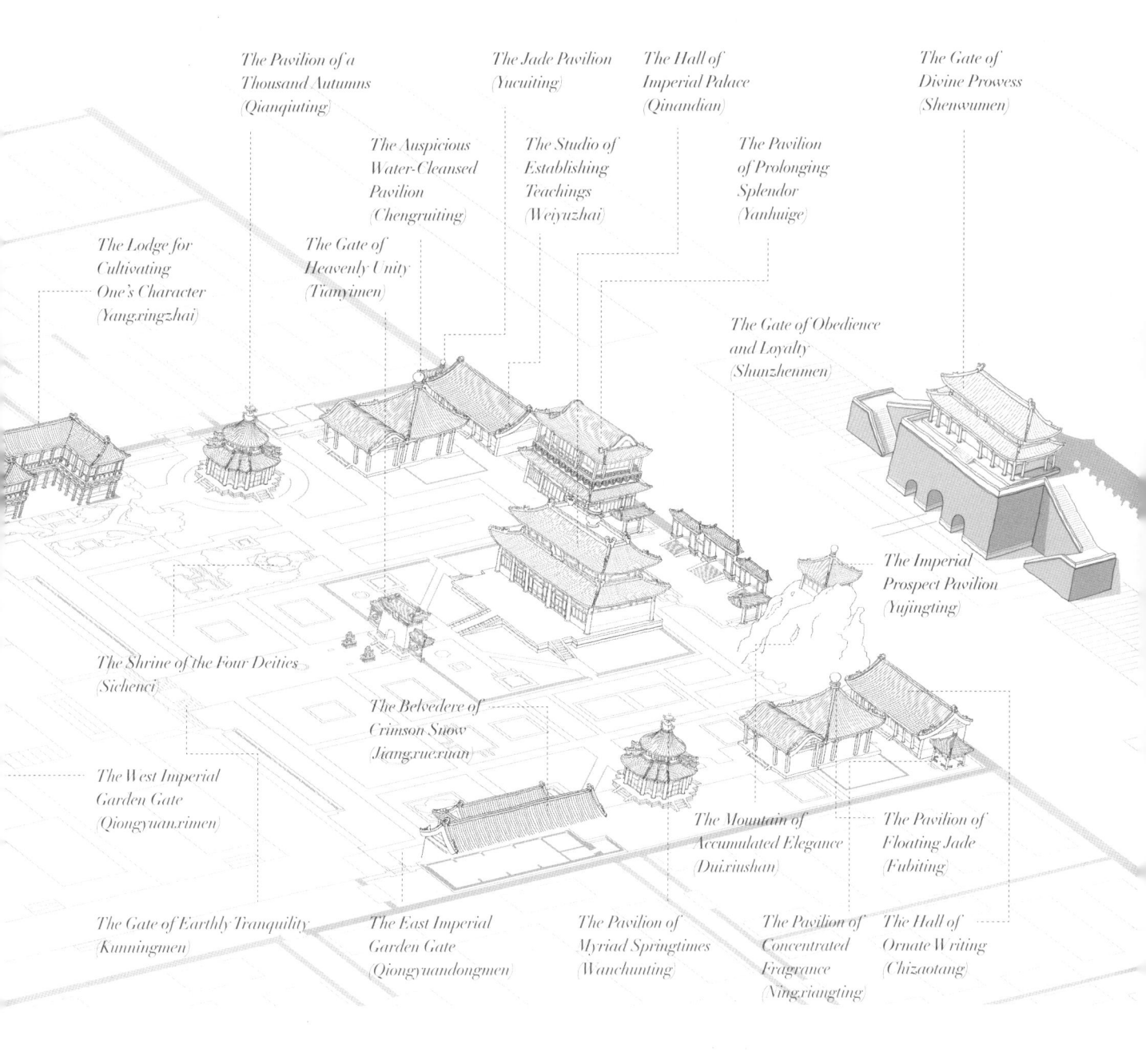

P.213

The Imperial Garden (Yuhuayuan)

The East and West Routes of The Inner Court *(Neichao)* and The Six Eastern and Western Palaces *(Dongxiliugong)*

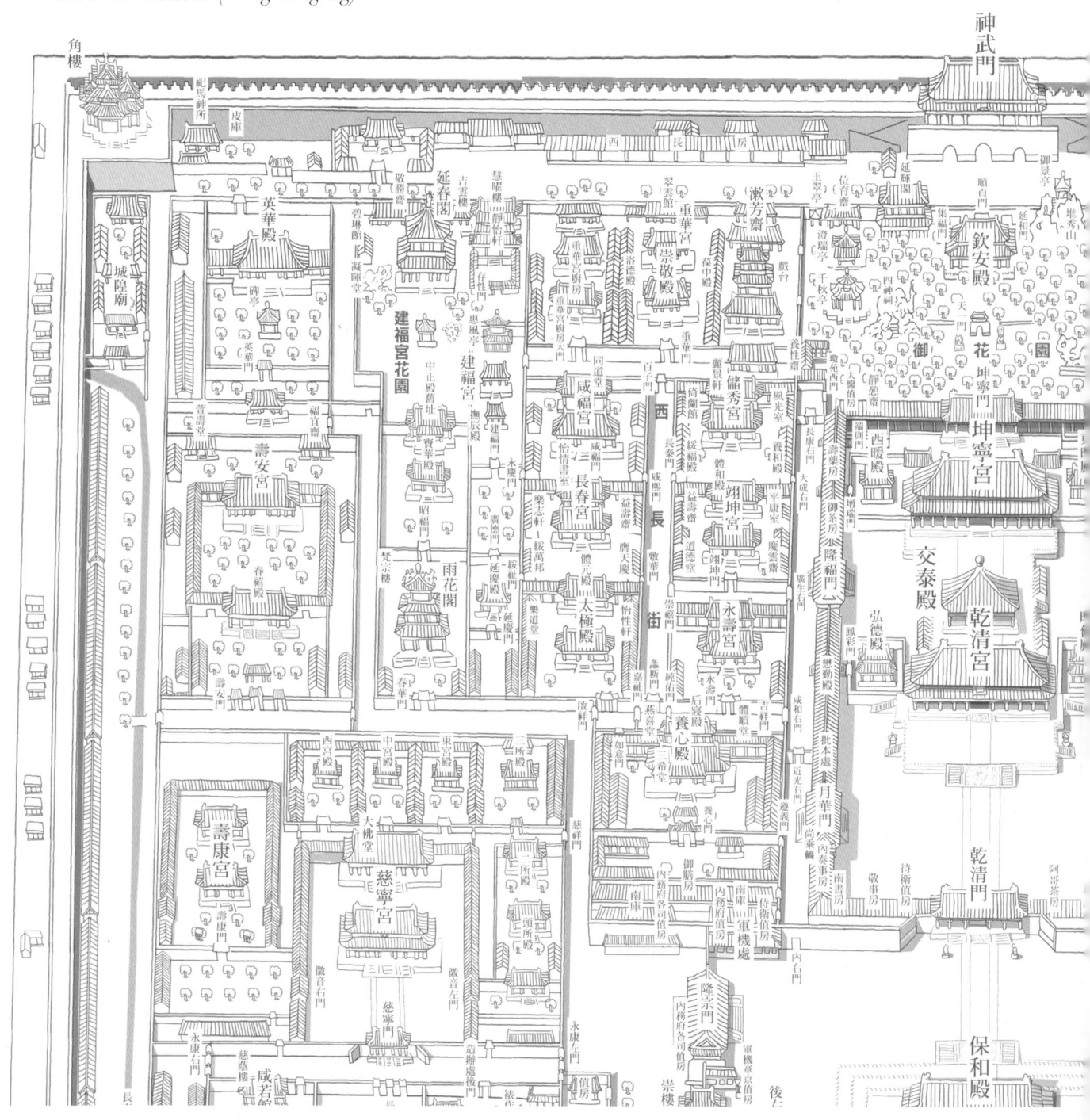

紫禁城平面图（东部）

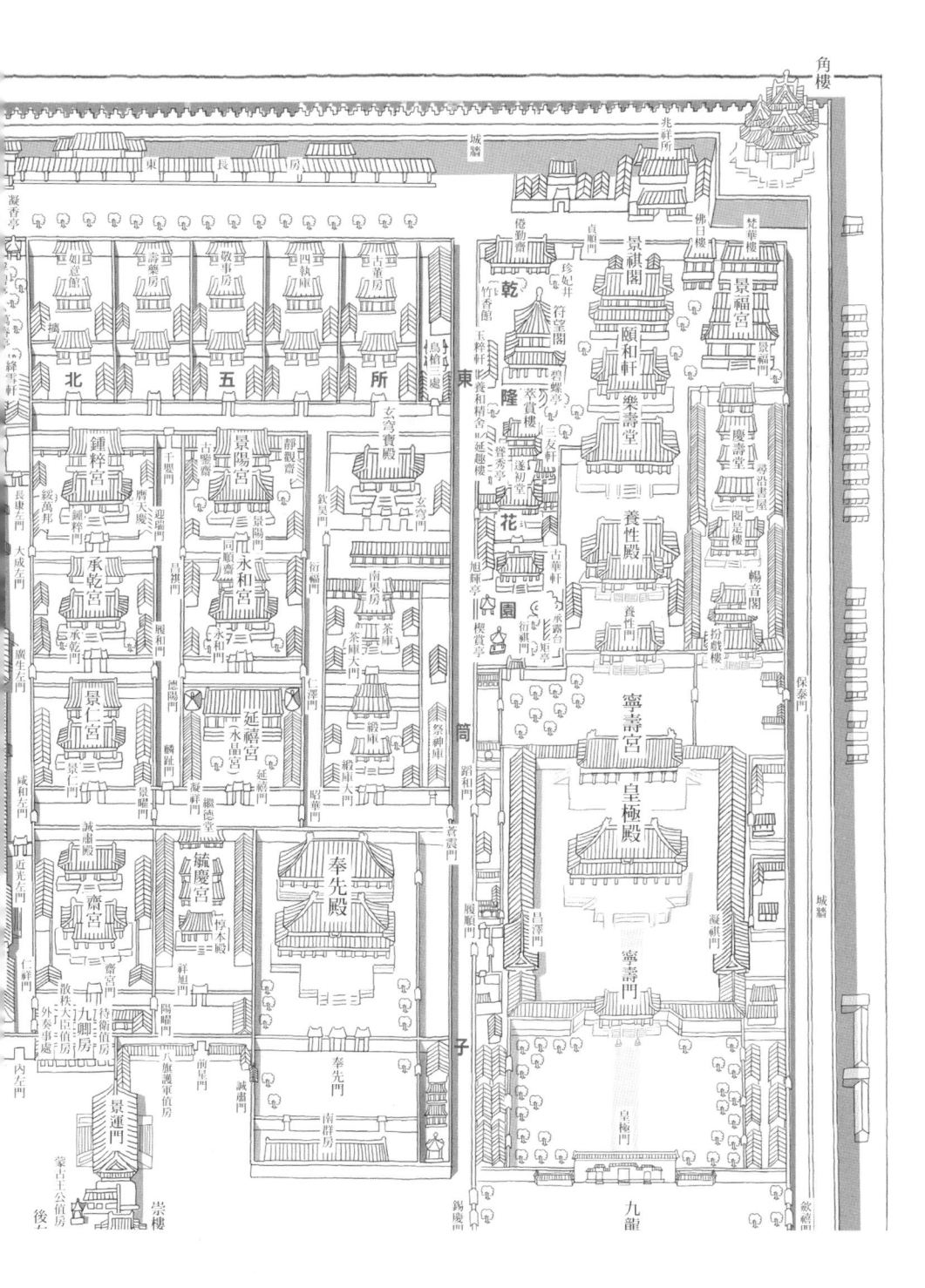

角楼

城牆
兆祥所
佛日樓
梵華樓
景祺閣
景福閣
景福門
慶壽堂
尋沿書屋
閣足樓
暢音閣
扮戲樓

凝香亭
東長房
凝祥亭 如意館 壽藥房 敬事房 四執庫 古董房
北五所
烏槍處
倦勤齋 貞順門
竹香館 珍妃井 符望閣
玉粹軒 萃賞樓 頤和軒
碧螺亭 三友軒 樂壽堂
遂初堂
養和精舍 延趣樓
乾隆花園
古華軒
旭輝亭
櫻賞亭
承露台
養性殿
養性門

鍾粹宮 靜怡齋
千嬰門 唐天慶
綏萬邦 鍾粹門 迎禧門 景陽門
承乾宮 承乾門
昌祺門
頤和門
景陽宮 永和宮 玄穹寶殿
同順齋
鍾粹宮 延禧宮（水晶宮）
景仁宮
毓慶宮
誠肅殿
齋宮 惇本殿
祥旭門

玄穹門
南果房
茶庫
茶庫大門 仁澤門
緞庫
緞庫大門
祭神庫

東筒子

行福門
行慶門
昭華門

靈壽宮
皇極殿
昌澤門
凝祺門

奉先殿
奉先門

寧壽門

長康左門
大成左門
麗生左門

咸和左門
近光左門

景運門

蒙古王公值房
崇樓

待衛值房 齋宮門
散秩大臣值房
外奏事處
九卿房
八旗護軍值房
南星門
南群房

錫慶門
九卿
皇極門
欽禧門

保泰門
城牆

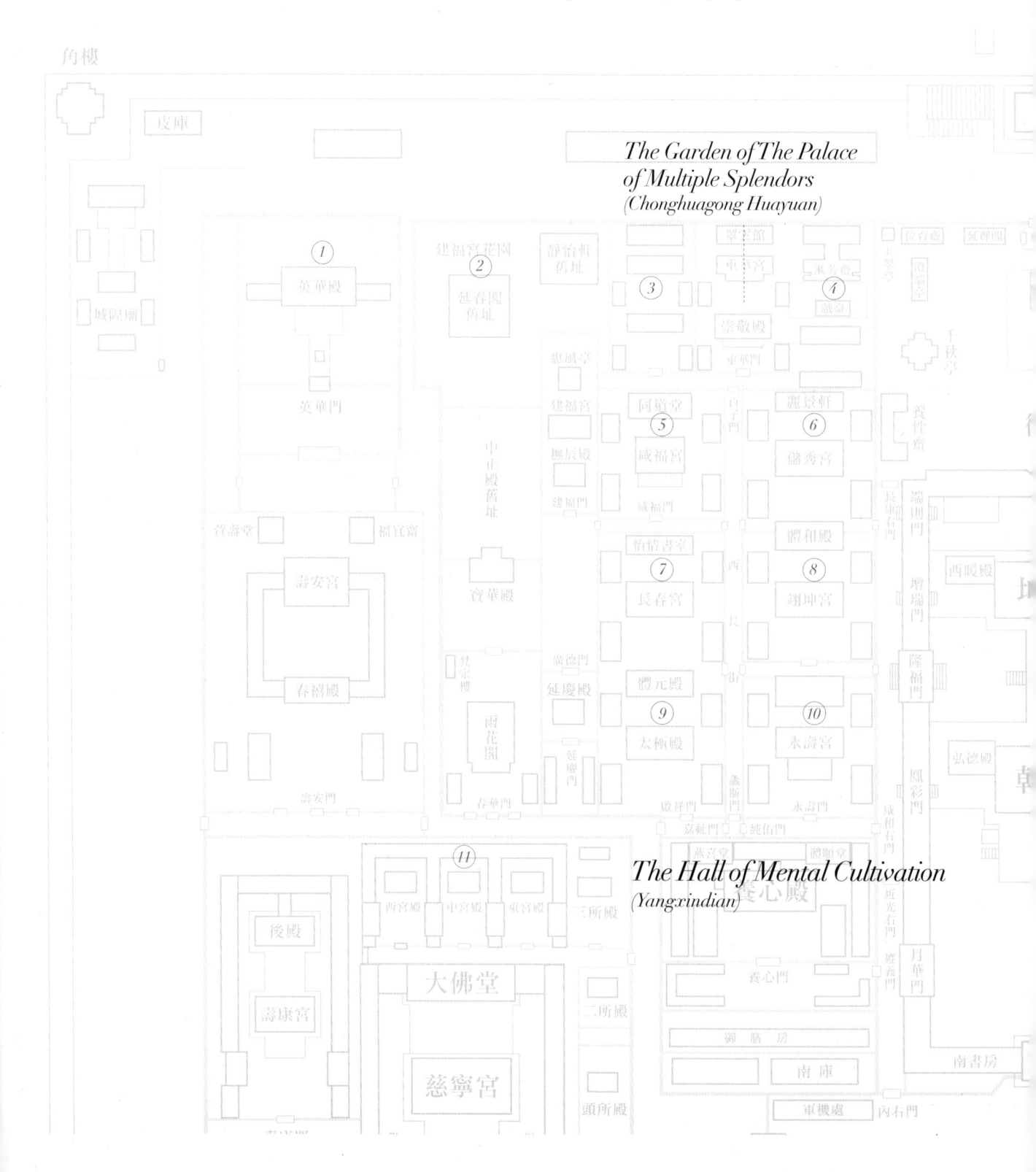

The Imperial Garden (Yuhuayuan)

角樓
皮庫
① 英華殿
英華門
城隍廟

The Garden of The Palace of Multiple Splendors (Chonghuagong Huayuan)

建福宮花園
② 延春閣舊址
靜怡軒舊址
③ 翠雲館 重華宮 ④ 崇敬殿
慧曜樓
摛藻堂
建福宮
撫辰殿
⑤ 同道堂 咸福宮
⑥ 麗景軒 儲秀宮
建福門 咸福門
中止殿舊址
⑦ 福倩書室 長春宮
⑧ 體和殿 翊坤宮
萱壽堂 福宜齋
壽安宮
春禧殿
寶華殿
雨花閣
揖峯亭
咸安門
⑨ 延慶殿 太極殿
⑩ 體元殿 永壽宮
啟祥門 純佑門
長康右門
端則門
西暖殿
增瑞門
隆福門
鳳彩門
弘德殿

The Hall of Mental Cultivation (Yangxindian)

⑪ 西宮殿 中宮殿 東宮殿 三所殿
後殿
壽康宮
大佛堂
慈寧宮
二所殿
頭所殿
燕喜堂 體順堂 養心殿
養心門
御膳房
南庫
軍機處 內右門
咸和右門
近光右門
遵義門
月華門
南書房

P.216　　The Grand Forbidden City ― The Imperial Axis

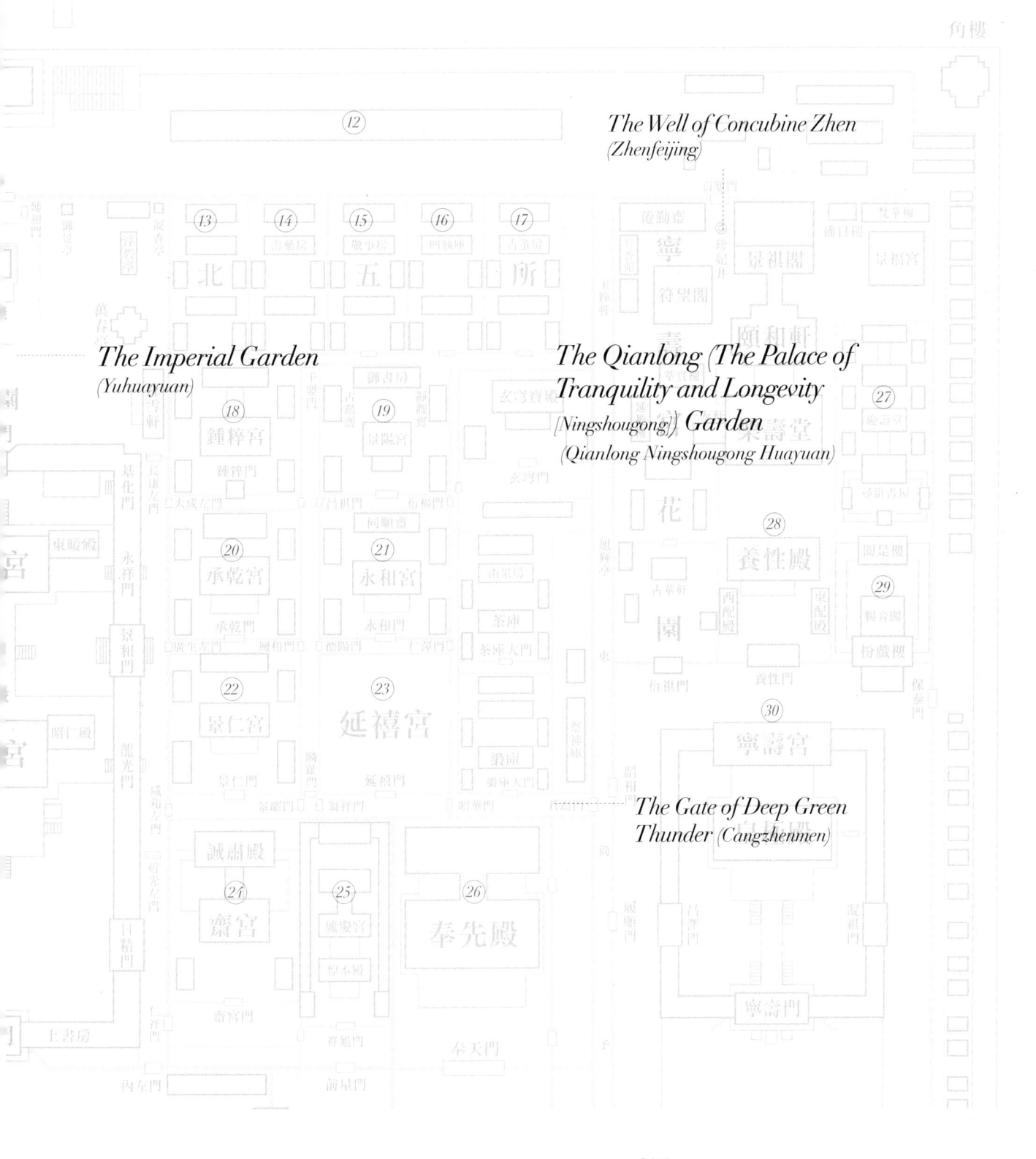

The Well of Concubine Zhen (Zhenfeijing)

The Imperial Garden (Yuhuayuan)

The Qianlong (The Palace of Tranquility and Longevity [Ningshougong]) Garden (Qianlong Ningshougong Huayuan)

The Gate of Deep Green Thunder (Cangzhenmen)

The Imperial Garden (Yuhuayuan)

(1) The Hall of Exuberance (Yinghuadian).
The Hall was where the Empress Dowager and the imperial concubines of the former emperor worshipped the Buddha.

(2) The Garden of The Palace of Established Happiness (Jianfugonghuayuan).
Old site of The Garden of The Palace of Established Happiness (Jianfugonghuayuan).
It was built in the 7th Year of Qianlong (1742), and destroyed by fire in 1923. It is now being rebuilt in phases since 2001 (See P.162-163).

(3) Qianlong West Five Abodes (Qianxiwusuo)
Qianlong lived here when he was young. It was later upgraded to become The Palace of Multiple Splendors (Chonghuagong), Towards the end of the Qing Dynasty, it was gradually being neglected. The west side is commonly called "Old Garden" (Laoyuan). Concubine Zhen was once under house arrest here.

(4) The Hall of Cleansing Fragrance (Shufangzhai).
The stage was most frequently used for shows in the latter part of the Qing Dynasty.

(5) The Palace of Universal Happiness (Xianfugong)
In the 4th Year of Jiaqing (1799), the retired emperor Qianlong passed away. Jiaqing moved here to make funeral arrangements. When Jiaqing passed away, his son (Daoguang) also lived here to oversee funeral arrangements.

(6) The Palace of Preserved Elegance (Chuxiugong)
(Known as The Palace of Legevity and Prosperity [Shouchanggong]) in the Ming Dynasty). In the 18th Year of Jiaqing (1813), the son Minning (later Emperor Daoguang) of the second Empress of Emperor Jiaqing (Empress Xiaohe, also known as Madam Niuhulu), showed his cool-headed courage during the Riots of Lin Qing and the Heavenly Doctrine Sect (Tianlijiao). He shot dead an intruder who broke into the palace in The Inner Court (Neichao).
In the 1st Year of Xianfeng (1851), a young girl called Yehenala Laner was conferred the title of honorable lady (guiren). She moved into The Palace of Preserved Elegance (Chuxiugong). Within 10 years, she was promoted from honorable lady to virtuous concubine (yibin), then to virtuous imperial concubine (yifei), and after that, imperial honorable concubine (yiguifei), and finally she achieved the status of empress dowager (taihou, Cixi).
The wife of Puyi, Wanyong, changed The West Chamber of Warmth (Xinuange) of The Palace of Preserved Elegance (Chuxiugong) into a Western style bathroom, and Belvedere of Scenic View (Lijingxuan) into a Western style restaurant. On November 5, 1924, Puyi and Wanyong left The Palace of Preserved Elegance (Chuxiugong), and their departure marked the end of the Qing Dynasty.

(7) The Palace of Eternal Spring (Changchungong)
Qianlong's Empress lived here once.
During the reign of Guangxu, Concubine Zhen and Concubine Jin suggested decorating the walls with a mural about the story of The Dreams of the Red Chambers (Hongliumeng).
At the end of the Qing Dynasty, Empress Dowager Cixi was successful in launching the "Revolution of Xinyou in 1861" (Xinyou Zhengbian). She co-administered state affairs with Empress Dowager Cian. Both empress dowagers lived here

together in The Palace of Eternal Spring (Changchungong). The rear hall of The Palace of Initiating Auspiciousness (Qixianggong) and the gate of The Palace of Eternal Spring (Changchungong) were rebuilt and became The Hall of Following the Nature (Tiyuandian). A theatrical stage was built behind the Hall for birthday banquets and entertainment. In the 10th Year of Tongzhi (1871), Empress Dowager Cian moved to the Palace of Accumulated Purity (Zhongcuigong, in the Six Eastern Palaces [Dong liugong]). In the 10th Year of Guangxu (1884), Cixi moved to The Palace of Preserved Elegance (Chuxiugong). Concubine Wenxiu of Emperor Puyi was its last resident from the imperial household.

⑧ The Palace of Earthly Honor (Yikungong)
(Known as The Palace of Eternal Peace [Wanangong] or The Palace of Earthly Honor [Yikungong] in the Ming Dynasty). Whistling pigeons were reared here in the Ming Dynasty. Cixi lived here once. Guangxu selected Empress Longyu, Concubine Zhen and Concubine Jin here at The Hall of Harmonious Conduct (Tihedian).
At the end of the Qing Dynasty, The Palace of Earthly Honor (Yikungong) and The Palace of Preserved Elegance (Chuxiugong) were combined into one.

⑨ The Hall of the Supreme Pole (Taijidian)
(Known as The Ongoing Palace [Weiyangong] or The Palace of Initiating Auspiciousness [Qixianggong] in the Ming Dynasty). It was rebuilt during the reign of Jiajing.
During the reign of Empress Dowager Cixi, The Palace of Initiating Auspiciousness (Qixianggong) and The Palace of Eternal Spring (Changchungong) were combined into one. The front hall of The Palace of Initiating Auspiciousness (Qixianggong) was renamed The Hall of the Supreme Pole (Taijidian). Longyu (Empress of Guangxu), the mother of Xuantong, moved in when she became empress dowager.

⑩ The Palace of Eternal Longevity (Yongshougong)
(Known as The Palace of Eternal Happiness [Changlegong] or The Palace of Nurturing Virtue [Yudegong] or The Palace of Eternal Longevity [Yongshougong] in the Ming Dynasty). Emperor Wanli had to move here when The Palace of Heavenly Purity (Qianqinggong) had a big fire in the 24th Year of Wanli (1596).
It was rebuilt in the 13th Year (1656) of Shunzhi in the Qing Dynasty.

⑪ The Palace of Tranquility and Longevity (Ningshougong) district.
The palatial complex where the empress dowagers and concubines of the former emperor spent their final years. The emperors in the Qing Dynasty came to greet and honour the respected ladies once or twice every day. Sometimes, it was even twice a day, in the morning and in the evening.
The emperors in the Ming Dynasty came once every few days.

⑫ The Eastern Five Abodes of Qianlong (Qiandongwusuo)
Initially, they were residences for the princes. In the latter period of the Qing Dynasty, they became offices inside the palaces.

⑬ Lodge of Fulfilled Wishes (Ruyiguan)

The Imperial Garden (Yuhuayuan)

(14) Longevity Medicinal Workroom (Shouyaofang)

(15) Administrative Offices (Jingshifang)

(16) Formal Attire Storage (Sizhiku)
Management of imperial hats, robes, belts, and shoes.

(17) The Room for Curios (Gudongfang)

(18) The Palace of Accumulated Purity (Zhongcuigong)
(Known as Xianyang Palace [Xianyanggong] in the Ming Dynasty)
Emperor Xianfeng lived here when he was a prince.
Xianfeng's Empress Dowager Cian lived here.
Guangxu's Empress Longyu lived here.

(19) The Palace of Great Brilliance (Jingyanggong)
(Known as The Palace of Eternal Brilliance [Changyanggong] or
The Palace of Great Brilliance [Jingyanggong] in the Ming Dynasty).
This was a bleak and desolate place. It was used for book
storage (The Imperial Study [Yushufang]) in the Qing Dynasty.

(20) The Palace of Celestial Favor (Chengqiangong)
(Known as The Palace of Eternal Peace [Yongninggong] in
the Ming Dynasty).

(21) The Palace of Eternal Harmony (Yonghegong)
Yongzhen was born here.
Concubine Jin of Guangxu lived here.

(22) The Palace of Great Benevolence (Jingrengong)
In the 11th Year of Shunzhi (1654), Kangxi was born here.
At the end of the Qing Dynasty, Concubine Zhen lived here.

(23) The Palace of Prolonging Happiness (Yanxigong)
(Being in a desolate and unpopular spot, it was the residence for
concubines who were no longer the emperor's favourite.)
The Gate of Deep Green Thunder (Cangzhenmen) was the only
gate for eunuchs and servants to go in and out of The Inner
Court (Neichao). Disasters caused by fire happened frequently.
The gate had been rebuilt many times in the Qing Dynasty.
In the 1st Year of Xuantong, Empress Dowager Longyu spent
millions on building a crystal palace to "suppress" the fire in the
fengshui sense, but soon after the Qing Dynasty collapsed.

(24) The Hall for Abstinence (Zhaigong)
It was built in the 9th Year of Yongzhen (1731). The emperor
had to abstain from eating meat and stay here for three days
before making sacrifices to and asking blessing from Heaven.
He would stay in The Hall of Mental Cultivation (Yangxindian)
followed a vegetarian diet when he wanted to make sacrifices
at the Altar of Good Harvest (Shejitan) and Imperial Ancestral
Temple (Taimiao).

P.220 *The Grand Forbidden City — The Imperial Axis*

㉕ The Palace for Nurturing Joy (Yuqinggong).
   It was built in the 18th Year of Kangxi (1679) as residence for the crown prince. Later it became a place where the princes both lived and studied. Qianlong lived here once and later moved to The Western Five Abodes of Qianlong (Qian.xiwusuo). Jiaqing spent his childhood here and then moved to The Western Five Abodes of Qianlong (Qian.xiwusuo). Guang.xu also studied here.

㉖ The Hall for Ancestral Worship (Fengxiandian)
   This was for Ancestral worship and also for paying respect to the memorial tablets for past emperors and empresses.

㉗ The Hall for Celebrating Birthdays (Qingshoutang)
   It was the temporary residence for visiting nobles and their female family members.

㉘ The Hall of Cultivating One's Character (Yang.xingdian).
   Its model is similar to The Hall of Mental Cultivation (Yang.xindian). Empress Dowager Ci.xi once lived in The Palace of Tranquility and Longevity (Ningshougong) for two years. Her sleeping quarter was The Hall of Joyful Longevity (Leshoutang, where she gave audience to envoys and The Ministers of the Grand Council of State (Junjidachen)). She dined in The Hall of Cultivating One's Character (Yang.xingdian).

㉙ The Pavilion of Pleasant Sounds (Changyinge).
   It was the largest stage in the palace.

㉚ The Palace of Tranquility and Longevity (Ningshougong).
   It was the palatial district for empress dowagers in the Ming Dynasty. It was built in the 28th Year of Kangxi (1689) for the empress dowager. In the 37th Year of Qianlong (1772), Qianlong extended it for himself in preparation for his retirement.
   A hundred years after Qianlong passed away, Empress Dowager Ci.xi moved in.
   The Palace of Tranquility and Longevity (Ningshougong) and The Palace of Maternal Love and Peace (Cininggong) were both built for the retired emperor and empress dowagers. Their structures were different. The Palace of Tranquility and Longevity (Ningshougong), in particular, was built during a period when the national power of the Qing Dynasty was at its peak. It formed an axis by itself. In terms of building structure, decoration, and landscape garden design, they were all extremely unique and outstanding.

The Imperial Garden (Yuhuayuan)

Additional Notes: The Garden of The Palace of Established Happiness *(Jianfugonghuayuan)*

The Pavilion of Prolonged Spring *(Yanchunge)* inside The Garden of The Palace of Established Happiness *(Jianfugonghuayuan)*

P.222   The Grand Forbidden City — The Imperial Axis

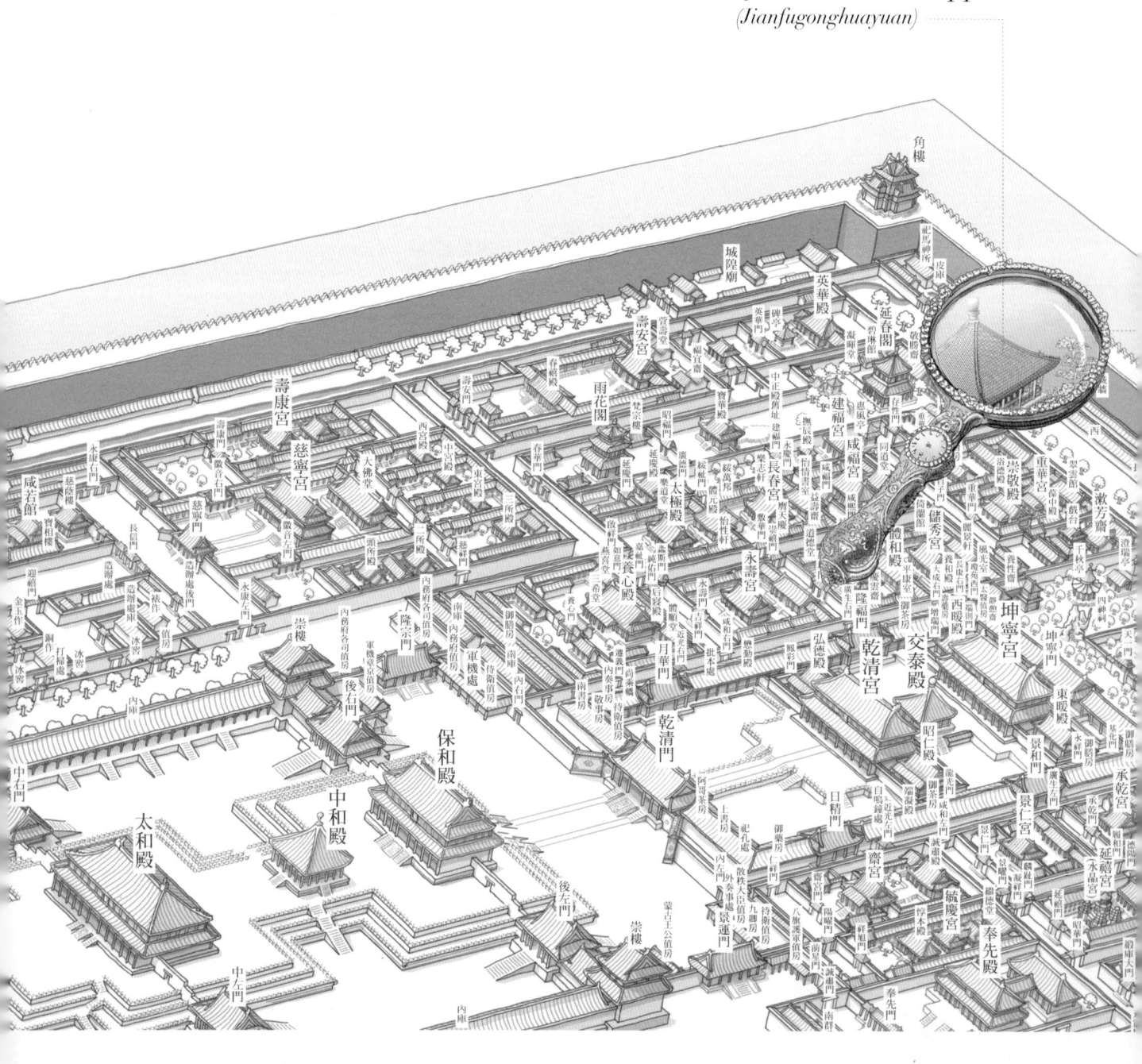

A Handheld Enamel Mirror with a Watch

An exquisite mirror which was used by the concubines. There was a small watch on it. It was made in England in the 18th Century.

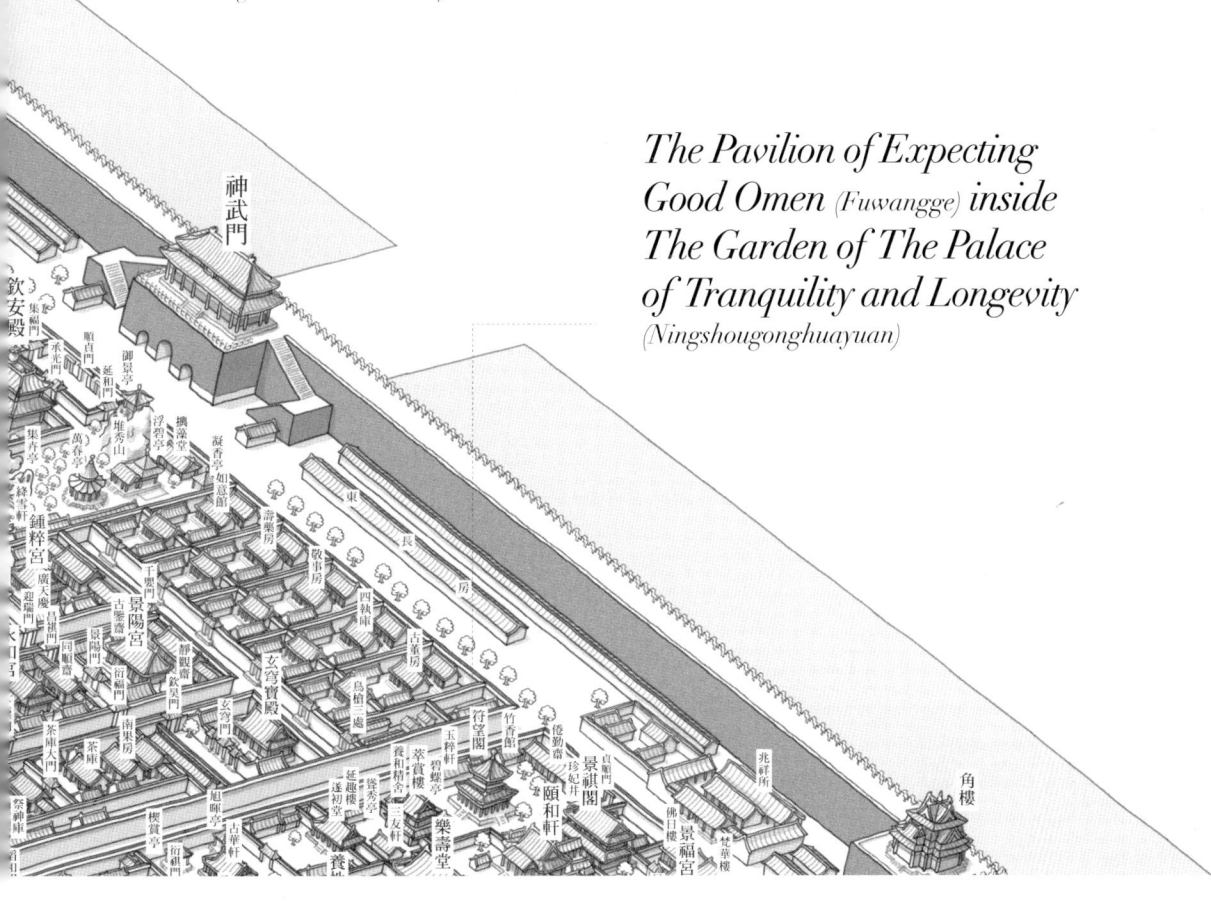

The Pavilion of Expecting Good Omen (Fuwangge) inside The Garden of The Palace of Tranquility and Longevity (Ningshougonghuayuan)

The Imperial Garden (Yuhuayuan)

The Pavilion of Prolonged Spring
(Yanchunge)

* *The exquisite stone pedestal inside the Qianlong Garden of The Palace of Tranquility and Longevity (Ningshougong Qianlong Huayuan)*

The Palace of Established Happiness (Jianfugong) was built in the 7th Year of Qianlong (1742). Apart from serving as a place of rest for the emperor, at one time it provided the largest storage space for treasures in The Imperial Palace. It was burned down in 1923 during the small imperial court period of the last emperor of China, Puyi. Some said that burning candles of the hall for worshipping Buddha caused the fire. Some said that the fire was caused by a fault in the electrical wiring system. The most dramatic reason given was that the eunuchs were the arsonists who wanted to destroy evidence because they feared an updated inventory of the treasures might reveal their misdemeanour and impropriety. No matter what the true reason was, this palatial courtyard with an area only second to The Imperial Garden (Yuhuayuan), was then deserted for more than eighty years, until in 2000, the China Culture Relics Protection Foundation raised enough funds for its reconstruction.

Imperial constructions had always depended upon the efforts of the common people. The Forbidden City was no exception. The remodeling plan started formally in 2001. The first phase was completed in 2005, 263 years after the initial construction. Now, from The Pavilion of Expecting Good Omen (Fuwangge) inside The Garden of The Palace of Tranquility and Longevity (Ningshougonghuayuan) in The East Route we no longer need to see the sad views of a deserted plot of land on The West Route. The making of The Forbidden City, its prosperity and downfall, all determined by the will of the common people.

Should we, after all, reconstruct on the ancient ruins? 500 years have passed, and 500 years have yet to come. Whether newly built or already existing, it is all part of The Grand Forbidden City.

/ Epilogue

- After the Tang Dynasty, the Ming Dynasty was the dynasty in which the Han ethnic group unified all of China. In terms of cultural history, it was not the most outstanding. However, in terms of industrial and engineering technology, it was the third golden period in Chinese architecture after the Tang and Song Dynasties.

- Up to the early years of the Ming Dynasty, City planning in China had always been ahead of other countries.

- During this era of grand standards, from the eight-part essay (baguwen—[a rigid literary form advocated by the imperial examination in the Ming and Qing Dynasties]) to the design of a single piece of brick, all had standard specifications. It was recorded that when The Great Wall was built in the Ming Dynasty, all the materials were fully utilised with one brick to spare when the entire construction ended at Shanhai Pass [a strategic pass at the eastern terminus of The Great Wall]. The fact that one, and only one, brick was left over is actually typical of the Chinese philosophy of waste not want not.

- The Great Wall project in the Ming Dynasty involved scaling mountains and hills. Zheng He led the largest ocean-going fleet on earth and explored new worlds. The 13 tombs of the Ming Dynasty reached the pinnacle in underground construction. The Forbidden City is a comprehensive demonstration of architecture and engineering design of wooden structures which were gradually perfected throughout the dynasties.

- The Central Axis of The Forbidden City goes from north to south. It is the meridian that divides the city and time zones. All the tallest and most important palatial buildings had been built along this axis. All the largest and most important ceremonies were also held along this axis.

- Although Beijing was the base of Emperor Yongle, to move the national capital to the front line (so-called "the Son of Heaven guarding the border") was a very bold and daring move. When the Qing Dynasty took over China, the ethnic group with a farming background (Ming) and the ethnic group with a normad background (Qing) worked together. The Great Wall then became the national "Court Wall" covering a much wider geographical area. It was rare that the rulers of the Qing Dynasty did not rush into destroying the palatial buildings and construction of the former dynasty in order to from a new governing body and build everything from scratch.

- The first emperor of the Ming Dynasty was from the grass roots, and the emperors in the Qing Dynasty came from outside and became the hosts. They were keen to show convincingly that their ruling power "came from Heaven". The most concrete demonstration was the adoption of the highest traditional imperial standards as stated in (The Rites of Zhou--Zhouli) when building palaces. This last palatial city of the feudal dynasties in China also allows us to have a glimpse of the original designs of the most ancient palaces.

This small book has only actually covered about 1/7 of "The Imperial Axis", a distance of about a kilometer from The Meridian Gate (Wumen) to The Gate of Divine Prowess Shenwumen). The miscellaneous thoughts presented are association of ideas and reflections which came to my mind while traveling along this kilometer. For a tourist, the most unforgettable image, apart from palace after palace, must be window after window*. Permanently locked within these windows are dullness and dreariness of history of several centuries. Forever kept out by these windows are probably our emotions and feelings.

CHIU KWONG CHIU
July 2005

* In Chinese, there is a distinction between windows on the wall (you) and windows on the roof (chuang). Here it refers to windows on the wall (you).

Acknowledgement

Special thanks are due to

*Senior Engineer (Professorial Grade) Luo Zhewen, Chief of the Experts Group on
Historical Buildings, State Cultural Relics Bureau. Mr Luo gave me guidance throughout and
took time from his very busy schedule to write the Preface of this book.
Ms. Zhang Zhiping, Senior Engineer, China National Institute of Cultural Property.*

*Mr. Zhai Defang, Editor in Chief, Hong Kong Chung Hwa Book Company, Limited
Mr. Li Xin, Asst. Editor in Chief, Joint Publishing (Beijing) Company Limited
Miss Chen Chui Ling, Executive Editor in Chief, Joint Publishing (Hong Kong) Company Limited
Ms. Dong Xiuyu, Consultant; Ms Ma Kin Chuen, Editor in Chief ; Mr. Luk Chi Choeng, Design Supervisor ;
Yishi Cultural Workshop, Beijing.*

*Mr. Hui Chui, Director of Information Department, The Palace Museum
Mr. Shi Zhimin, Director of Historical Architecture Conservation Department , The Palace Museum
Mr. Yuan Honggi, Deputy Director of Palace Department , The Palace Museum
Mr. Li Yongge, Director of Historical Architecture Conservation Centre, The Palace Museum
Mr. Wu Shengmao, Engineer of Historical Architecture Conservation Centre, The Palace Museum*

*Associate Research Fellow Luo Suizu, and Ms Zhao Lihong, The Palace Museum
Project Director Miss Happy Harun, Consultant Zhang Shengtong , Miss Teo Lay Pheng, China Culture Relics Protection Foundation*

*My colleagues at The Hong Kong Polytechnic University when I taught there: Dr. Wah Lup Keung, Dr. Kwok Yun Chi
Mr. Kwok Chiu Wai, Miss Lam Lai Yee (Conception and Final Phase Production)*

*All members of the Workshop on Design and Cultural Studies:
Au Cheuk Sun, Lee Yu Hin, Chan Lap Hang (Information Management)
Tsang Hok Shing, Kwok Suk Ling (Production and Design)
Chan Hon Wai, Ngai Chung Han, Cheung Chi Yan, Ma Kin Chung (Drawing and Computer Technology)
Apart from Drawing and Production, Mr Ma Kin Chung has given me great help in composition.*

*Kwong Lung, my second elder brother, and Kwong Fai, my third elder brother,
for their encouragement and support in every respect.*

*Deputy Director Mr. Wang Yamin, Editor Miss Jiang Ying and
Mr. Zhang Nan of The Palace Museum is great support in English edition.*

References:

1. *Zhong Guo Da Bai Ke Cong Shu*, mei shu juan yi, juan er, xiu ding ben, Zhong guo da bai ke quan shu chu ban she, 2003.
2. *Luo Zhewen Gu Jian Zhu Wen Ji*, Luo Zhewen, Wen wu chu ban she, 1998.
3. *Fu Xinian Jian Zhu Shi Lun Wen Ji*, Fu Xi Nian, Wen wu chu ban she, 1998.
4. *Zhong Guo Gong Dian Jian Zhu Lun Wen Ji*, Gu gong bo wu guan xue shu wen ku, Yu Zhuoyun, Zi jin cheng chu ban she, 2002.
5. *Zi Jin Cheng Gong Dian*, Yu Zhuoyun, Xiang gang shang wu yin shu guan, 1982.
6. *Zhong Guo Zi Jin Cheng Xue Hui Lun Wen Ji Di Yi Ji*, Shan Shiyuan, Yu Zhuoyun, Zi jin cheng chu ban she, 1997.
7. *Zhong Guo Zi Jin Cheng Xue Hui Lun Wen Ji Di Er Ji*, Yu Zhuoyun, Zhu Chengra, Zi jin cheng chu ban she, 2002.
8. *Zhong Guo Zi Jin Cheng Xue Hui Lun Wen Ji Di San Ji*, Yu Zhuoyun, Zhu Chengra, Zi jin cheng chu ban she, 2004.
9. *Zhong Guo Gong Dian Jian Zhu*, Lou Qingxi, Yi shu jia chu ban she, 1994.
10. *Jiu Du Wen Wu Lue*, Tai wan guo li gu gong bo wu guan, 1974.
11. *Qing Bai Lei Chao*, Xu ke (Qing), Bei jing zhong hua shu ju, 1984.
12. *Wo Zai Gu Gong Qi Shi Nian*, Shan Shiyuan, Bei jing shi fan da xue chu ban she, 1997.
13. *Bu Zhi Zhong Guo Mu Jian Zhu*, Chiu Kwong Chiu, Xiang gang san lian shu dian, 2000.
14. *Zhou Yi Xi Ci Shang.*
15. *Fu Xinian Jian Zhu Shi Lun Wen Ji : Guan Yu Ming Dai Gong Dian Tan Miao Deng Da Jian Zhu Qun Zong Ti Gui Hua Shou Fa De Chu Bu Tan Tao*, Fu Xinian, Wen wu chu ban she.
16. *Zhong Hua Wen Ming Chuan Zhen : Ming, Xing Yu Shuai De Qi Ji*, Liu Wei, Wang Li, Xiang Gang Shang Wu Yin Shu Guan.
17. *Gong Nv Tang Wang Lu*, Jin Yi, Shen Yiling.
18. *Nan Shi Qi Dong Hun Hou Ji.*
19. *Zhi Ci Nv Tong Zhuan.*
20. *Zi Jin Cheng Gong Dian : Jian Zhu He Sheng Huo De Yi Shu*, Yu Zhuoyun, Xiang Gang Shang Wu Yin Shu Guan.

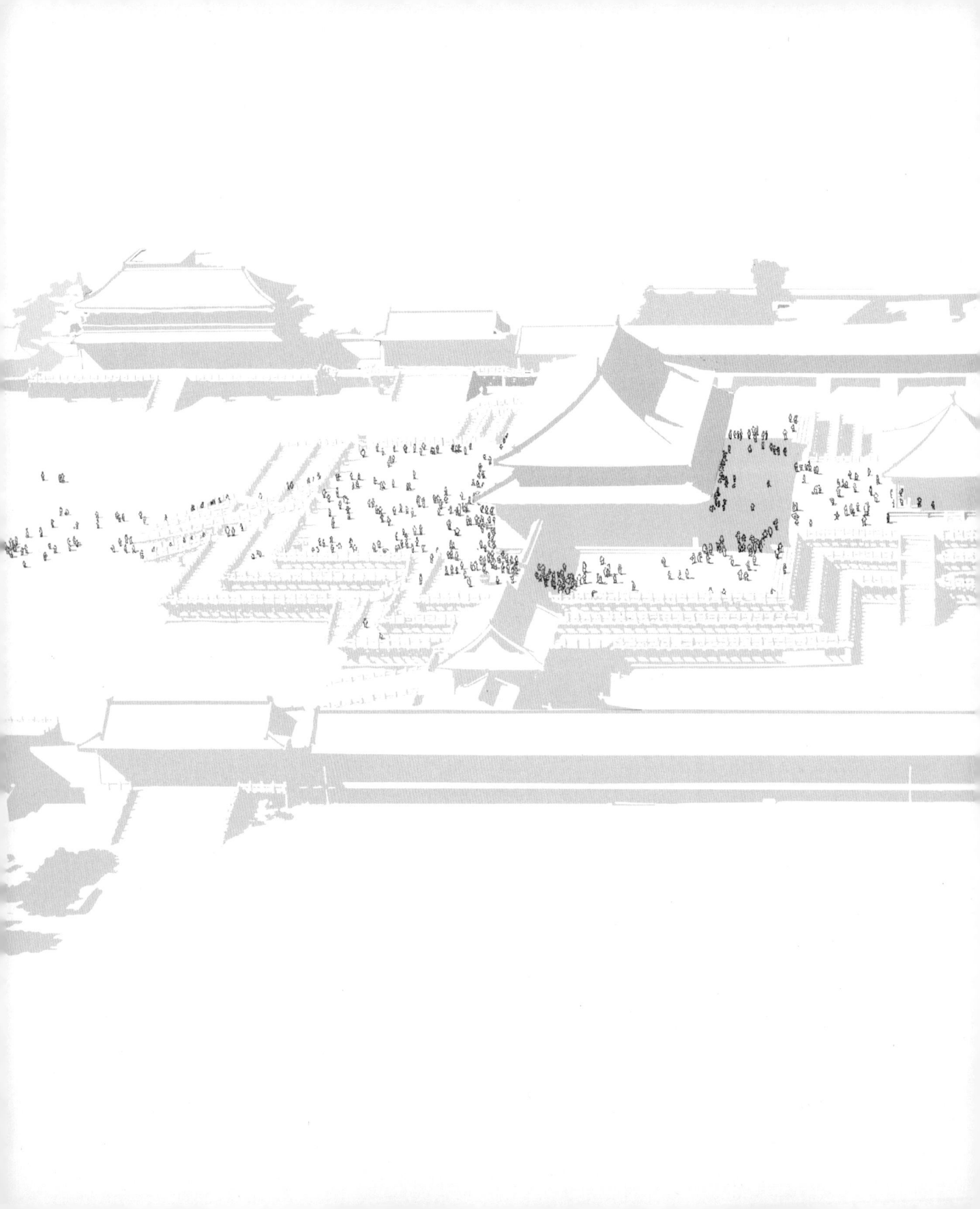

References:

1. *Zhong Guo Da Bai Ke Cong Shu*, mei shu juan yi, juan er, xiu ding ben, Zhong guo da bai ke quan shu chu ban she, 2003.
2. *Luo Zhewen Gu Jian Zhu Wen Ji*, Luo Zhewen, Wen wu chu ban she, 1998.
3. *Fu Xinian Jian Zhu Shi Lun Wen Ji*, Fu Xi Nian, Wen wu chu ban she, 1998.
4. *Zhong Guo Gong Dian Jian Zhu Lun Wen Ji*, Gu gong bo wu guan xue shu wen ku, Yu Zhuoyun, Zi jin cheng chu ban she, 2002.
5. *Zi Jin Cheng Gong Dian*, Yu Zhuoyun, Xiang gang shang wu yin shu guan, 1982.
6. *Zhong Guo Zi Jin Cheng Xue Hui Lun Wen Ji Di Yi Ji*, Shan Shiyuan, Yu Zhuoyun, Zi jin cheng chu ban she, 1997.
7. *Zhong Guo Zi Jin Cheng Xue Hui Lun Wen Ji Di Er Ji*, Yu Zhuoyun, Zhu Chengra, Zi jin cheng chu ban she, 2002.
8. *Zhong Guo Zi Jin Cheng Xue Hui Lun Wen Ji Di San Ji*, Yu Zhuoyun, Zhu Chengra, Zi jin cheng chu ban she, 2004.
9. *Zhong Guo Gong Dian Jian Zhu*, Lou Qingxi, Yi shu jia chu ban she, 1994.
10. *Jiu Du Wen Wu Lue*, Tai wan guo li gu gong bo wu guan, 1974.
11. *Qing Bai Lei Chao*, Xu ke (Qing), Bei jing zhong hua shu ju, 1984.
12. *Wo Zai Gu Gong Qi Shi Nian*, Shan Shiyuan, Bei jing shi fan da xue chu ban she, 1997.
13. *Bu Zhi Zhong Guo Mu Jian Zhu*, Chiu Kwong Chiu, Xiang gang san lian shu dian, 2000.
14. *Zhou Yi Xi Ci Shang*.
15. *Fu Xinian Jian Zhu Shi Lun Wen Ji : Guan Yu Ming Dai Gong Dian Tan Miao Deng Da Jian Zhu Qun Zong Ti Gui Hua Shou Fa De Chu Bu Tan Tao*, Fu Xinian, Wen wu chu ban she.
16. *Zhong Hua Wen Ming Chuan Zhen : Ming, Xing Yu Shuai De Qi Ji*, Liu Wei, Wang Li, Xiang Gang Shang Wu Yin Shu Guan.
17. *Gong Nv Tang Wang Lu*, Jin Yi, Shen Yiling.
18. *Nan Shi Qi Dong Hun Hou Ji*.
19. *Zhi Ci Nv Tong Zhuan*.
20. *Zi Jin Cheng Gong Dian : Jian Zhu He Sheng Huo De Yi Shu*, Yu Zhuoyun, Xiang Gang Shang Wu Yin Shu Guan.

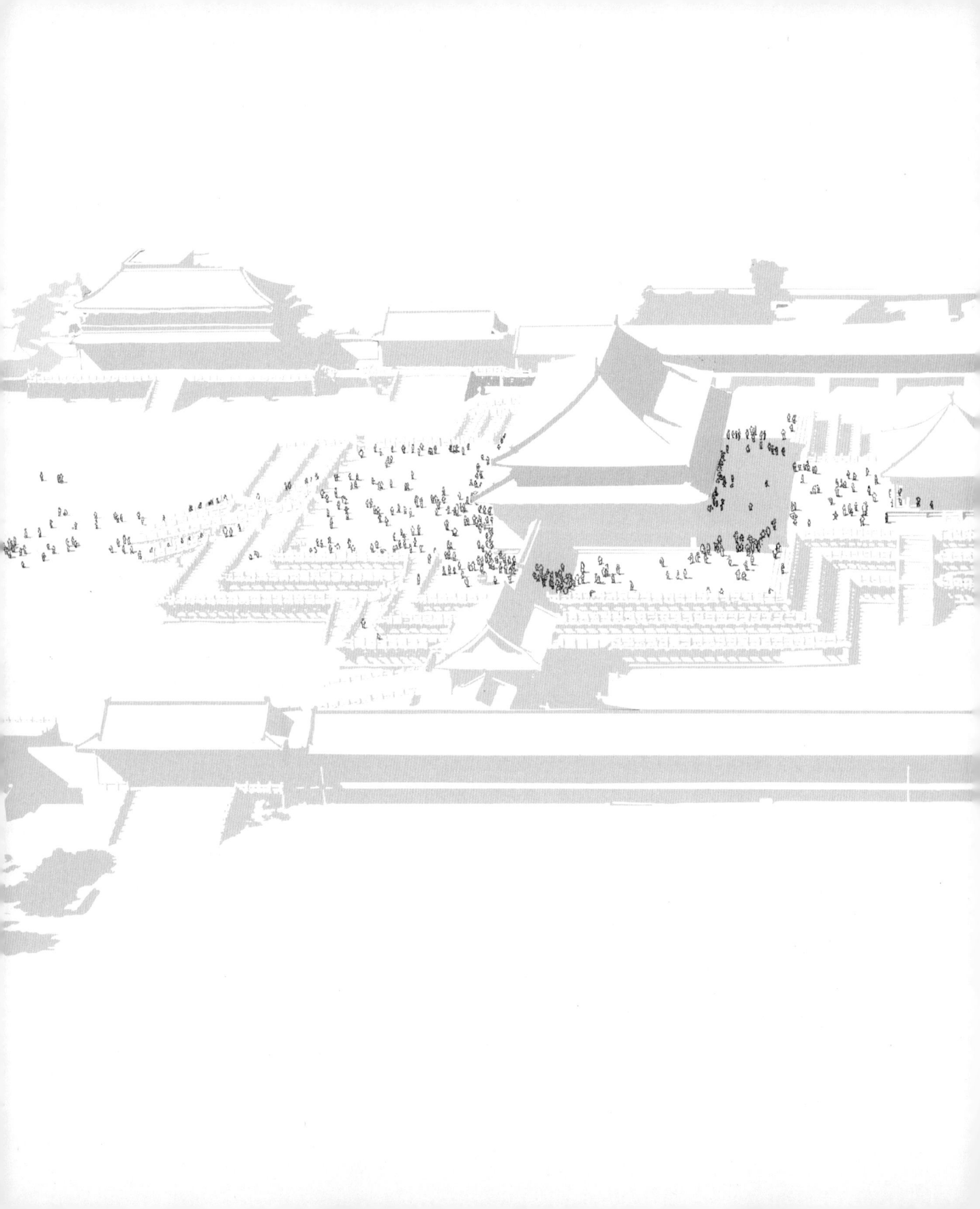

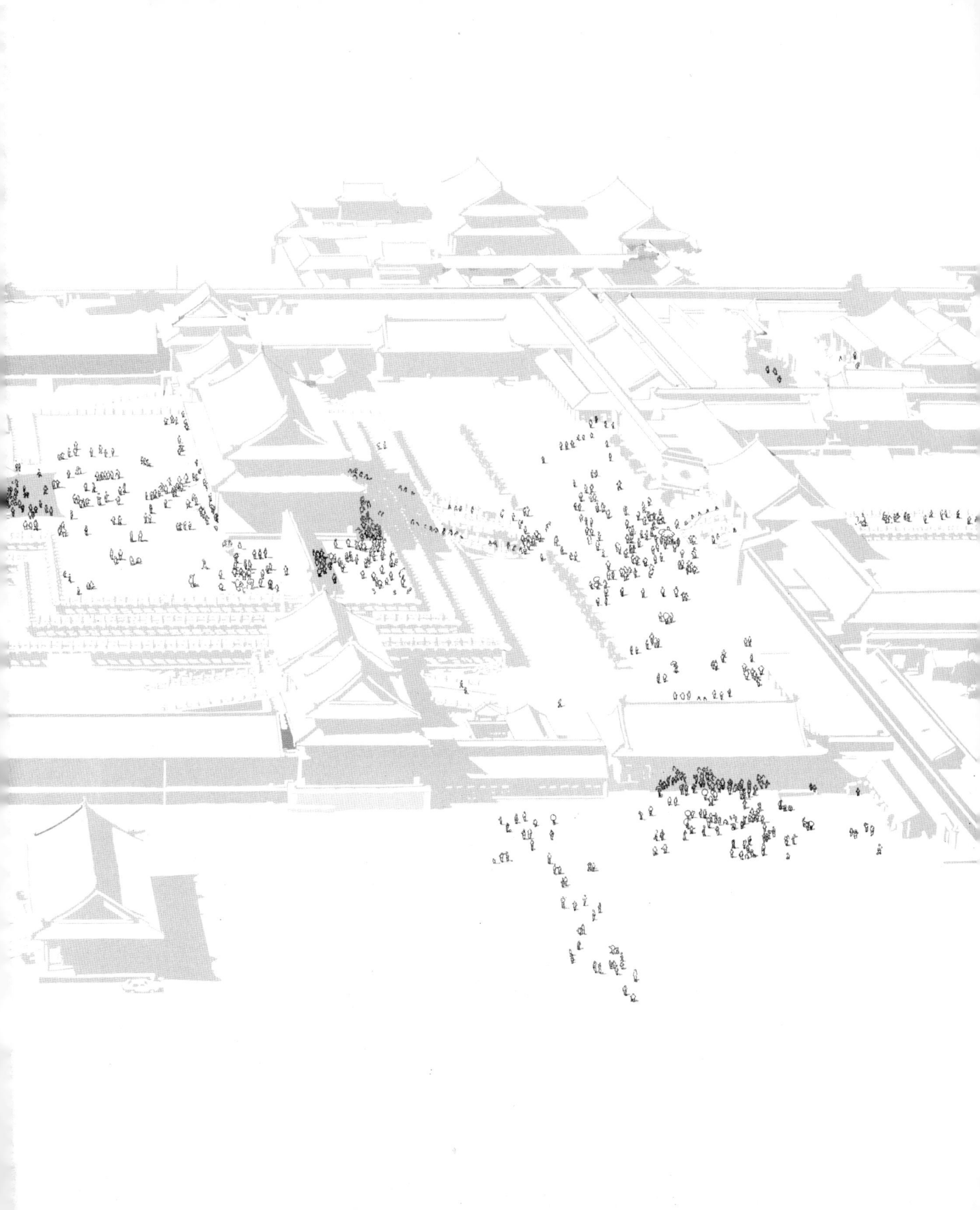

About the author

Born in Hong Kong. Chiu Kwong Chiu had studied in France in his early years. At the moment, he is working on art, design commentaries and education. He is a respected consultant who is involved in research and development of traditional Chinese furniture, at Wood Workshop. Also, he is the head of Design and Cultural Studies Workshop.
Translation Project: *Ten Days in the Mountains* by Dr. Eric Wear, published by Hanyaxuan.
Author of: *Beyond Chinese Wooden Architecture*
Beyond Chinese Wooden Artchitecture,
Ink and Paper of Chinese Painting,
Running Notes on Qingming Shanghe Tu

All published by Joint Publishing (Hong Kong) Company Limited